Computer Communications and Networks

T0189324

The **Computer Communications and Networks** series is a range of textbooks, monographs and handbooks. It sets out to provide students, researchers and non-specialists alike with a sure grounding in current knowledge, together with comprehensible access to the latest developments in computer communications and networking.

Emphasis is placed on clear and explanatory styles that support a tutorial approach, so that even the most complex of topics is presented in a lucid and intelligible manner.

Also in this series:

An Information Security Handbook
John M.D. Hunter
1-85233-180-1

Multimedia Internet Broadcasting: Quality, Technology and Interface
Andy Sloane and Dave Lawrence (Eds)
1-85233-283-2

Information Assurance: Surviving in the Information Environment
Andrew Blyth and Gerald L. Kovacich
1-85233-326-X

UMTS: Origins, Architecture and the Standard
Pierre Lescuyer (Translation Editor: Frank Bott)
1-85233-676-5

Designing Software for the Mobile Context: A Practitioner's Guide
Roman Longoria
1-85233-785-0

OSS for Telecom Networks
Kundan Misra
1-85233-808-3

The Quintessential PIC® Microcontroller 2nd edition
Sid Katzen
1-85233-942-X

From P2P to Web Services and Grids: Peers in a Client/Server World
Ian J. Taylor
1-85233-869-5

Intelligent Spaces: The Application of Pervasive ICT
Alan Steventon and Steve Wright (Eds)
1-84628-002-8

Ubiquitous and Pervasive Commerce
George Roussos (Ed.)
1-84628-035-4

Andrew Blyth and Gerald L. Kovacich

Information Assurance

Security in the Information Environment

Second Edition

 Springer

Andrew Blyth, BSc, MSc, PhD
School of Computing, University of Glamorgan, UK

Gerald L. Kovacich, MA, MSc, D.Crim
ShockwaveWriters.com, Whidbey Island, WA, USA

Series Editor
Professor A.J. Sammes, BSc, MPhil, PhD, FBCS, CEng
CISM Group, Cranfield University, RMCS, Shrivenham, Swindon SN6 8LA, UK

British Library Cataloguing in Publication Data
A catalogue record for this book is available from the British Library

Library of Congress Control Number: 2005935460

Computer Communications and Networks ISSN 1617-7975
ISBN-10: 1-84628-266-7   Printed on acid-free paper
ISBN-13: 978-1-84628-266-9

Printed in the United States of America   (SPI/EB)

9 8 7 6 5 4 3 2 1

Springer Science+Business Media

springer.com

Second Edition Dedications

This book is dedicated to my family without whose love and support this book would not have been possible.

Dr Andrew J. C. Blyth, Ph.D.
University of Glamorgan
United Kingdom

This book is dedicated to all those who dedicate their lives to ridding the world of high-technology crime miscreants and bringing cyberspace freedom to those who want it.

Dr Gerald L. Kovacich
Whidbey Island, Washington
United States of America

Quotations

"Any community's arm of force – military, police, security – needs people in it who can do necessary evil, and yet not be made evil by it. To do only the necessary and no more. To constantly question the assumptions, to stop the slide into atrocity." – Lois McMaster Bujold, *Barrayar*, 1991

"The superior man, when resting in safety, does not forget that danger may come. When in a state of security he does not forget the possibility of ruin. When all is orderly, he does not forget that disorder may come. Thus his person is not endangered, and his States and all their clans are preserved." – Confucius (551 BC–479 BC)

Foreword

When you first hear the term information assurance you tend to conjure up an image of a balanced set of reasonable measures that have been taken to protect the information after an assessment has been made of risks that are posed to it. In truth, this is the Holy Grail that all organisations that value their information should strive to achieve, but which few even understand.

Information assurance is a term that has recently come into common use. When talking with old timers in IT (or at least those that are over 35-year old), you will hear them talking about information security, a term that has survived since the birth of the computer. In the recent past, the term information warfare was coined to describe the measures that need to be taken to defend and attack information. This term, however, has military connotations – after all, warfare is normally their domain. Shortly after the term came into regular use, it was applied to a variety of situations encapsulated by Winn Schwartau as the following three classes of information warfare:

Class 1: Personal information warfare
Class 2: Corporate information warfare
Class 3: Global information warfare

Political sensitivities lead to "warfare" being replaced by the "operations", a much more "politically correct" word. Unfortunately, "operations" also has an offensive connotation and is still the terminology of the military and governments. A term was needed that described the measures needed to safeguard the most precious asset in this modern, connected world – information. The measures are much more than just security, encompassing the concepts of risk assessment, management and the protection of your information from compromise, theft, modification and lack of availability.

Information assurance is ensuring that your information is where you want it, when you want it, in the condition that you need it and available to those that you want to have access to it – but only to them. In the past, information was recorded, stored and transported on paper; the methods of achieving security were developed over more than 3000 years and had the distinct advantage that any action taken on the information could be easily observed. Now and increasingly in the future, information exists digitally and digital technology has only been in common use for less than 30 years. Add this shortage of time in which to gain experience in the best methods of protecting digital information to the fact that it can be moved from one place to another in a fraction of a second. Then add the facts that it can be stolen and yet remain unaffected in its original location; vast quantities of it can be stored on increasingly small storage mediums and you can no longer easily view, even with equipment to assist you, what is contained on the storage medium; and you begin to comprehend the problems of information assurance.

Modern day security specialists have an increasingly difficult problem to solve. In addition to the aforementioned factors, the technologies (both in hardware and software) are changing with increasing rapidity, making it even more difficult for even the most dedicated of professionals to gain and maintain the knowledge needed to allow them to effectively carry out their tasks.

The problem is compounded by the way in which we as a society organise ourselves. People involved in information assurance are mostly employed in the business of security and use the skills and knowledge that they have obtained to stop unauthorised users from gaining access to the information. As a result, they will tend not to share the information and knowledge that they have collected in order to protect the methods that have been used to acquire it. They will also tend not to advertise that they have suffered an attack to avoid embarrassment to their organisation and limit the damage that such an attack has caused. Those who attack information systems gain their knowledge by sharing and communicating with others of a similar persuasion in a culture of peer recognition and a shared goal.

We are all striving for a globally connected society where everyone is encouraged to make use of the information systems that are available, and those who cannot are considered to be disadvantaged. It is not surprising in this environment that we are seeing a growth in the level of a whole range of crimes that were previously seen in the paper-based society migrating to this new medium. We have made it possible for a person who would wish to harm our interests to gain the three elements that they seek most – access to our valuables, the opportunity to remain anonymous and the potential to carry out the attack without having to physically visit the site of the attack – indeed, it is not even necessary to visit the country in which the attack is mounted.

Given that the problem is, in historical terms, very new and also global, it is not surprising that national legal systems are having difficulty in addressing the problem and the international community, not renowned for its speed, is talking about the problem but not acting in response to it.

In the coming months and years, we will witness technological solutions to information assurance needs and comparisons to be seen with the way in which we handle the physical valuables of today. Strong-rooms that protect the physical environment will be matched by secured data warehouses and protected servers, couriers by encryption and digital signatures, locks on the doors by firewalls and security alarms and burglar alarms by intruder detection systems in the virtual world. What of keys, oh yes, biometric devices and smart cards – whatever next?

Dr Andy Jones, Ph.D. MBE BSc MBCS
Research Group Leader Security Research Centre
BT Group Chief Technology Office (UK)

Second Edition Preface

In the first edition of this book, we provided an introduction to the "world of information assurance (IA)". Due to the popularity of the first edition (for which we thank all our readers), and after a gap of approximately 4 years, which is a lifetime in high technology, we were asked to update this book in order to provide the readers with more current information than is available in the First Edition.

In preparation for that update, we found that much of what we had written has remained current. There is a good reason for that. We wrote this as a basic introduction to an IA and the basic principles are grounded in a solid foundation built over many years – in fact decades! Therefore, it continues to be the baseline for building a solid IA program.

We have, however, found areas in almost every chapter that required updating. So, hopefully this Second Edition adds new information that will help you to maintain a current and dynamic IA program for your business or government agency.

We have maintained the basic format of the First Edition's four sections, added new information throughout the Second Edition, which includes three new chapters:

- Chapter 7: The Role of Policy in Information Assurance
- Chapter 13: Incident Management and Response
- Chapter 17: Security Standards

The titles of these new chapters speak for themselves as to their content. We decided to add these chapters to further provide the reader with as much of a holistic view of the topic of IA as possible.

As we stated in the First Edition, in the late 1970s and early 1980s, information systems security began to gain importance as more and more government agencies and businesses began to integrate computers into their processes. The 1990s was the decade of the massive integration of computers into corporate, national and international networks. The Internet became the backbone for the global networking of networks.

The information systems security profession was born and began to mature during this time. The concept of protecting computer systems and thereby the information they processed, stored and transmitted was the norm. However, gradually another concept began to take hold, and that is the concept of IAs. An IA is more than just information systems security or information security. The development of the concept of IAs is another step in the maturation of concepts, practices and processes needed to protect information, the vital asset of today's information-based, information-dependent nation-states and corporations.

As the threats, internal, national and global, to information grow, so is the need to develop new and more sophisticated holistic IA processes. However, before that can successfully be accomplished, one must understand the concept of IAs and surviving in the information environment. It is hoped that this book will assist in meeting those challenges.

This book aims to perform two very important functions:

- To bridge the gap between IA as a technical concept and as a business concept. Thus, allowing information system managers to effectively manage information systems' security in a manner so as to facilitate the business process and contribute to the competitive advantage of the organisation.
- To provide information systems managers and students with a core text on assuring accurate information is available when needed to only those that need it. As the Internet continues to expand and more companies start conducting business on the Internet, e-business, there is going to be a need for people who understand not only the IA concepts and best practices, but also the business, legal and technical aspects of conducting business online. It is hoped that this book provides some assistance in that endeavour.

As stated earlier, this Second Edition is divided into four sections with a total of 18 chapters as follows:

Section 1 – An Introduction to Information Assurance

This section sets the context of the book and talks about the need for all organisations to take the IA seriously. It also provides an introduction to the IA and related topics. It provides the reader with a baseline on which to build an understanding of the theories, philosophies, models, processes, management and technical aspects of the IA.

Chapter 1.   What Is Information Assurance?

This chapter defines basic terms such as IA, information operations, information security, information systems security and information warfare. It also provides a short history of these concepts. This chapter explores what is meant by the terms of CND, CNA and CNO.

Chapter 2.   The World of Information

This chapter discusses the global and national economic and political environment, as it relates to conducting business and the increasing need for an IA in this new global marketplace.

Chapter 3.   The Theory of Risks

This chapter defines and discusses threats, vulnerabilities and risks. It also addresses the concepts of qualitative and quantitative risk analysis and risk management vis-à-vis the IA.

Chapter 4.   The Information World of Crime

The IA is required because of human error and because there are people in business and throughout the world who may use any legal and illegal means in order to obtain information for resale or to give others a competitive advantage. These issues are discussed in this chapter.

Chapter 5.   IA Trust and Supply Chains
This chapter discusses the idea of trust within organisations, processes and systems along with the idea of supply chains.

Chapter 6.   Basic IA Concepts and Models
Building on the above, this chapter addresses the various IA-related models such as the CIA model, the PDRD model, the need-to-know model and the information value model.

Chapter 7.   The Role of Policy in Information Assurance
This new chapter examines what is meant by the term "security policy" in terms of IA. In particular, it examines various types of security policy and provides a template for an AUP.

Section 2 – IA in the World of Corporations
This section begins with a discussion of the corporate security officer, to include a description and discussion of the duties and responsibilities and their IA role. This is followed by a discussion of the corporate IA officer and the functions of an IA organisation within a corporation.

Chapter 8.   The Corporate Security Officer
This chapter identifies and discusses the duties and responsibilities of a corporate security officer, as it relates to the IA and the protection of the corporate assets to include the protection of information and information systems.

Chapter 9.   Corporate Security Functions
This chapter identifies and describes security functions of a corporation to include those functions that are an integral part of any corporation's IA program.

Chapter 10.   IA in the Interest of National Security
This chapter describes and discusses the IA requirements in the national security environment of government agencies and defence-related businesses since many of the philosophies and processes can be adapted to meet the IA needs of corporations.

Chapter 11.   The Corporate IA Officer
This chapter addresses the position of the corporate IA officer. It describes the basic qualifications, duties and responsibilities required to lead an IA effort for a corporation into the 21st century.

Chapter 12.   IA Organisational Functions

This chapter identifies and discusses a corporation's IA organisational structure and its IA functions.

Chapter 13.   Incident Management and Response

This new chapter defines what is meant by the term incident response and how you construct a CSIRT. It also defines the process and tools associated with incident triage.

Section 3 – Technical Aspects of IA

This section discusses the technical aspects of IA as it relates to the storing, processing and transmitting of information.

Chapter 14.   IA and Software

This chapter discusses the problems and possible solutions to the IA questions in the software and firmware environment of operating systems, databases and applications software. It also includes a discussion of malicious codes.

Chapter 15.   Applying Cryptography to IA

This chapter describes and discusses cryptography to include when to use it, when not to use it, and the related political ramifications of cryptography in the global marketplace. Topics discussed include algorithms, public and private key, key management, digital signatures, and the world of PKI and IPSEC.

Chapter 16.   IA Technology Security

This chapter discusses the technical equipment available and in use to protect or attack the IA processes to include ADT, CCTV, biometrics, EMP weapons, HERF guns, TEMPEST, line filtering, etc.

Chapter 17.   Security Standards

This new chapter discusses various security standards that are available to the IA professional. In particular, attention will be paid to BS7799/ISO17799, ISO13335 and Common Criteria.

Section 4 – The Future and Final Comments

This section provides the authors' final comments, predictions and conclusions.

Chapter 18.   The Future, Conclusions and Comments

This chapter summarises the main points of the book, draws some conclusions and looks into the future of IA as we enter the 21st century.

Acknowledgements

For their assistance and support over the years, we again thank all our friends and colleagues.

Regardless of how much good advice we received from our friends and colleagues, this book could never have been successfully written and published if it were not for Catherine Brett and Helen Callaghan of Springer-Verlag, our publisher, who were willing to once again risk signing a couple of "crazy doctors" to a book contract. Thanks to them for not only their continued support and confidence in us but also more importantly, this time, for their "patience of saints" in dealing with us! So, to St Catherine and St Helen, we say thank you, thank you and thank you!

Writing and publishing this book was truly a team effort. Other members of this book's project team who made this all possible deserve a note of appreciation. They are Joanne Cooling and Jeff Taub.

Contents

Section 1

An Introduction to Information Assurance

This section sets the context of the book and discusses the need for all organisations to take information assurance (IA) seriously. It also provides an introduction to the IA and related topics. It provides the reader with a baseline on which to build an understanding of the theories, philosophies, models, processes, management, policies and technical aspects of the IA.

When introducing the topic of an IA, it is important that the reader understands the basic terminology to avoid possible confusion later. Therefore, Chapter 1 defines the basic terms, beginning of course with the term IA. It also provides a short history of basic IA related concepts. Chapter 2 discusses the basic global economic, political, and business environment in which information is a vital asset and the IA a vital necessity. With that understanding, Chapter 3 discusses risk theories, as well as risk assessment, risk management and the threats and vulnerabilities associated with risk.

Building on the first three chapters, Chapter 4 explains why there is a need for an IA. Chapters 5 and 6 describe the basic philosophies that should be applied while developing the IA processes and programs. Chapter 7 focuses on the role of policy in the IA. It ends with a focus on the role and function of an acceptable usage policy within an organisation.

1

What is Information Assurance?

When one hears the term, information assurance (IA), what does one think of? What exactly is an IA? Is it information systems security by another name? Is an IA a subset of information security, or is information security a subset of an IA? These terms and other basic terms, such as information operations and information warfare, will be defined and discussed.

1.1 Information Assurance and Its Subset: Information Security

Information assurance (IA) is about protecting your information assets from **destruction, degradation, manipulation and exploitation** by an opponent. The difficulty with achieving this is that one day a party may be collaborating on a project and therefore needs access to confidential information, and the next day that party may be an opponent. In 1996, the US Department of Defence (DoD) defined the IA as:

"Actions taken that protect and defend information and information systems by ensuring their availability, integrity, authentication, confidentiality and non-repudiation. This includes providing for restoration of information systems by incorporating protection, detection and reaction capabilities."

The HMG Strategy for IAdefines it as:

"Information assurance is the confidence that the information assets will protect the information they handle and will function as they need to, when they need to, under the control of legitimate users."

Information security can be defined as:

"The protection of information against unauthorised disclosure, transfer, modification, or destruction, whether accidental or intentional."

BS7799/ISO17799 defines information security as:

"Information Security is the preservation of confidentiality, integrity and availability of information."

Information security and IA are concerned with both intentional and unintentional attacks. Information assurance covers those areas that are not covered by the information security such as perception management. Information assurance can be considered at three levels: physical, information infrastructure and perceptual. These three levels are considered in Table 1.1.

In information security, an exposure is a form of possible loss or harm against an information asset. That information asset may be either logically based (i.e. 1's and 0's inside a computer) or physically based (i.e. paper, nuts and bolts or hardware). Examples of exposure include unauthorised disclosure of data, modification of data or denial of legitimate access to the information asset. This type of exposure is often referred to as risk. ISO13335 defines risk and threat as:

"Risk is the potential that a given threat will exploit vulnerabilities of an asset or group of assets and thereby cause harm to the organisation. The threat is the potential cause of an incident that may result in harm to a system or organisation."

1.1.1   Interruption, Interception, Modification and Fabrication

The following factors adversely impact the IA:

* ***Interruption***: In an interruption, an information asset of the system becomes unusable, unavailable or lost. For example, the physical theft or physical destruction of a computer system would be viewed as an interruption. The removal of information or software from an information system would also be viewed as an interruption.
* ***Interception***: An interception means that some unauthorised party has gained access to an information asset. The party can be a program, computer system or person. For example, recording a telephone conversation or monitoring a computer network can be viewed as interception (see Figure 1.1).
* ***Modification***: Modification of an asset means that some unauthorised party tampers with the asset. For example, the unauthorised installation of monitoring software or hardware, or the unauthorised insertion, manipulation or deletion of information can be viewed as modification.
* ***Fabrication***: Fabrication of an asset means the counterfeiting of an asset. For example, an intruder may insert spurious transactions into a computer network.

TABLE 1.1. Characteristics of Information Assurance

Characteristics and Components	Security Measure
Knowledge and understanding in human decision space	Physical and technical measures to maintain accurate, objective perception of the security state of the system and the information contained in the system
	Personnel measures to maintain personnel security to protect from insider attacks and to provide protection from psychological operations
Information and data manipulation ability maintained in cyberspace.	Make use of cyber defensive techniques such as encryption, intrusion detection, integrity analysis, etc.
Data and data processing activities that are managed and performed in the physical space	Physical access controls and facility protection
	Personnel management and security
	Contingency planning and disaster recovery

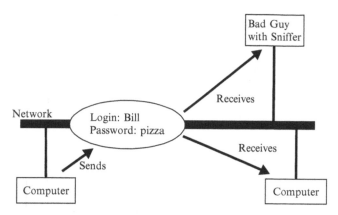

FIGURE 1.1. Sniffing

1.1.2   Information Assurance in Context

Financial losses attributed to malicious hacking, online corporate espionage and other computer crimes probably doubled in 2002, according to a survey by the Computer Security Institute (CSI). The survey covered 503 major corporations and public agencies that estimated their computer crime losses at $455 million in 2002. Based on that number, the CSI estimates that total losses attributable to computer crime are around $10 billion annually, mostly from financial fraud and proprietary information theft. Based on the survey responses, 74% of the companies said the computer attacks initiated from the Internet, while 33% said these initiated from internal company computers.

Information assurance is sometimes referred to as information operations (IOs) that protect and defend information systems by ensuring their availability, integrity, authentication, confidentiality and non-repudiation. This includes providing for restoration of information systems by incorporating protection, detection and reaction capabilities. Information assurance is concerned with the containment of, and recovery from, an attack. It also defines how attacks are to be detected through the use of a set of indicators and warnings, and how once an attack has occurred we should respond to the attack. In addition, the IA deals with deterring attacks and the application of legislation designed to address issues of privacy, computer-related crime, computer forensics and the like. The term "IO" is used to refer to actions taken to affect an opponent's information and information systems while defending one's own information and information systems.

Figure 1.2 depicts the various components and their relationships that function to set the concept of IA in context. The *owner* of the system is the organisation, group-of-individuals or an individual, which functions as the stakeholder of the security requirements. Stakeholders are defined as all those claimants within and without an organisation who have a vested interest in

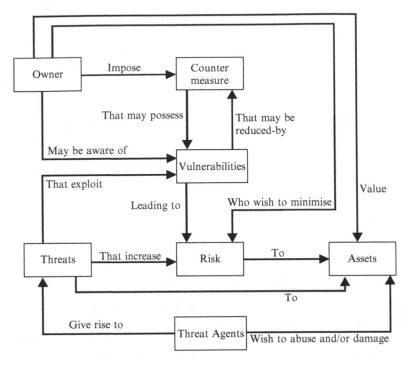

FIGURE 1.2. Information Security in Context

decisions faced by the organisation in adopting and utilising information technology (IT). The *owner* possesses a set of *assets* that have *value* to the *owner*. The *owner* may be *aware* of a set of *vulnerabilities* that could lead to the loss of an *asset*. In order to protect the *asset*, the owner *imposes* a set of protection and defensive *countermeasures* on the *asset* in the belief that by doing so that *owner* is protecting the *asset* from possible *loss, exploitation, abuse* or *damage* by a *threat-agent*. The *threat-agents* are the parties that *give rise to* the *threats* to the *assets* of the system. An *asset* can be a physical component of a system, such as a hard disk, or it can be a logical component of a system such as a file stored on a hard disk.

The objective of a countermeasure is to reduce the vulnerabilities contained in a system. However, no countermeasure is perfect, and a countermeasure may have the effect of possessing a vulnerability of its own. A threat may wish to exploit vulnerability in order to gain access to the assets of a system. Thus, a threat has the effect of increasing the risk posed to an asset, and vulnerabilities have the effect of leading to a potential risk. The owner will wish to minimise the level of risk posed to the assets, which the owner values. In order to minimise the risk, and thus reduce the level of threat posed to the assets by a threat-agent, the owner of the assets may impose a set of security countermeasures.

Information Warfare

Action Taken

OFFENSIVE
To deny, corrupt, destroy, or exploit another's
information or influence another's perception

DEFENSIVE
To safeguard your information or systems from
similar action

EXPLOITATIVE
To exploit available information in a timely fashion

PURPOSE
In order to enhance the decision/action cycle and
disrupt another's cycle

FIGURE 1.3. Information Warfare

1.2   Information Warfare

"In the practical art of war, the best thing of all is to take the enemy's country whole and intact; to shatter and destroy it is not so good. So, too, it is better to recapture an army entire than to destroy it, to capture a regiment, a detachment or a company entire than to destroy them. Hence to fight and conquer in all your battles is not supreme excellence; supreme excellence consists in breaking the enemy's resistance without fighting."

Sun Tzu

Information warfare (IW) is not new; in fact, it has been around for centuries. The IW is also not unique to the human species. Within nature, many types of plants and animals rely on some forms of IW in order to ensure survival via the acquisition of key resources. In today's terminology, an IW is about information dominance (see Figure 1.3).

The offensive part of IW is referred to as IOs, and the defensive part of IW is referred to as an IA.[1]

---

[1] As with any "new" concepts, such as IA, IW, IO, there is some disagreement as to their definitions and their order. For example, some believe InfoSec is a subset of the IA while others believe it is just the opposite. When it comes to protecting information assets, does it really matter, except to the "information protection bureaucrats"? It is not the intention of the authors to get into a "what came first, the chicken or the egg" debate. We are presenting it one way while others may disagree. The real issue is information asset protection; however, you want to view it.

Most countries today are making heavy use of IT for the purpose of meeting commerce and government objectives. This heavy dependency on IT creates the ability for one country to cripple another without the use of deadly force. For example:

In the Gulf War (1990–1991), the allied forces used modern IW techniques to cripple the ability of the Iraqi government to communicate with its armed forces. In addition, the US armed forces allegedly also became the victim of IW when a group of five Dutch hackers allegedly broke into the US military computers. They allegedly stole information relating to the exact locations of the US troops, the types of weapons they had, the capabilities of the Patriot missile and the movement of warships in the Gulf region. According to Jim Christy, a program manager with the computer crime investigations and an IW unit of the Air Force Office of Special Investigations, "They didn't, but they could have; instead of sending bullets to the Gulf, they could have sent toothbrushes".

This example illustrates the complex web of dependencies that are created when any organisation uses the IT and that if you disrupt one element in that complex web of dependencies, then you can stop or delay an organisation achieving its objectives.

The IW is defined in terms of three types of warfare, and these are:

Type I involves the managing of the opponent's perception through deception operations and psychological operations. Within military circles this type of the IW is often called Truth Projection.

Type II involves denying, destroying, degrading or distorting the opponent's information flows in order to break down their organisation and their ability to co-ordinate operations.

Type III gathers intelligence by exploiting the opponent's use of information systems.

In addition, the IW can be decomposed down into three classes,[2] and these are:

- *Class 1*: Personal IW is waged against an individual's privacy.
- *Class 2*: Corporate IW is waged against a business or a corporation.
- *Class 3*: Global IW is waged against industries, political spheres of influence, global economic forces and all countries.

The art of IW can be summed up as using an information infrastructure to break the opponent's resistance without fighting. Consequently, the IW offers the ability for a smaller country to neutralise the offensive and defensive potential of a much larger country. In more detailed terms, one can define the IW as follows:

"*The implementation of Information Warfare (IW) is the sequence of actions undertaken by all sides in a conflict to destroy, degrade, manipulate and exploit the information assets of their adversaries. Conversely, information warfare implementation also comprises all the actions aimed at protecting information assets against hostile attempts at destruction, degradation, manipulation and exploitation. It is*

---

[2] See Winn Schwartau's IW Website at infowar.com and Dr Kovacich's site at shockwavewriters.com for additional information.

very easy for any country, group, or individual to develop and deploy information warfare techniques. The term conflict is used to refer to fight or struggle between opposing forces. These forces could be national, corporate, or individual in nature."

1.2.1   Perspectives on Information Warfare

Over the past few years various people have tried to define what IW means. These definitions tend to characterise it rather than define it. A definition of IW by Col. D. Hotard, Director of Information Warfare, US Office of the Assistant Secretary of Defence, January 1996 is:

"Actions taken to achieve information superiority by affecting adversary information, information-based processes, information systems and computer-based networks, while defending our own information, information-based processes, information systems and computer-based networks."

In addition, the DoD in USA has also defined the military element of IW as:

"Actions taken to achieve information superiority in support of national military strategy by affecting adversary information and information systems while leveraging and defending our information systems."

Both of the above definitions talk about IW in terms of achieving information superiority with regard to the information-based activities of an adversary. In addition, these explicitly mention computer-based networks. Note that the US view of IW does not directly mention psychological warfare and does not define IW in terms of a nation-state. The view taken by USA is wider and attempts to encompass some of the commercial considerations. The Russian view of IW is:

"Information Warfare is a way of resolving a conflict between opposing sides. The goal is for one side to gain and hold information advantage over the other. This is achieved by exerting a specific information/psychological and information/technical influence on a nation's decision-making systems, on the nation's populace and on its information resource structures, as well as by defeating the enemy's control systems and his information resource structures with the help of additional means."

The Russian view of IW makes an explicit reference to psychological warfare and defines IW in terms of the nation-state. It defines IW with regard to a nation's decision-making systems and the nation's population. Thus, any IW attack against any part of Russia would be seen as an attack on the Russian nation-state. The Chinese view of IW is:

"Information Warfare is a transformation from mechanised warfare of the industrial age to a war of decision and control, a war of knowledge and a war of intellect."

The interesting point to observe about the Chinese definition of IW is that they explicitly view IW about control and controlling the decisions and actions of an opponent. It refers to the IW as a war of intellect and not a mechanised war. This is logical based on the Chinese view of warfare starting with Sun Tzu, Wei Liao and others. In addition, the Chinese definition makes no direct reference to the systems that may be targeted or the methods that may be used in order to achieve the control of an opponent.

1.2.2   Nature of the Threat

All a person needs to enter the world of IW is motive, means and opportunity. A motive is a function of the players' concerns, commitments and beliefs. Means are determined capabilities and availability of technical and information-based resources. An opportunity is a function of access and also includes other factors such as perception and belief. For example, many individuals may believe in their cause so much that they are prepared to go to prison for it. However, most do not believe they will be caught.

Although anyone can engage in offensive IW, in general offensive players in the world of IW come in six types: insiders, hackers, criminals, corporations, governments and terrorists.[3]

- *The insider*: Insiders consist of employees and may also include former employees and contractors. If a company outsources its IT functions, then the employees of the outsource company may also be considered as insiders. Studies have shown that this group is the biggest threat that any organisation faces. They act as information brokers, selling information that belongs to the organisation to foreign governments, competitors and organised crime. In addition, insiders can also intentionally or unintentionally damage or destroy information and equipment. For example, Volkswagen lost almost $260 million as the result of an insider scam that created phony currency-exchange transactions and then covered them with real transactions a few days later, pocketing the float as the exchange rate was changing. Four insiders and one outsider were subsequently convicted with the maximum jail sentence being 6 years.
- *The hacker*: A hacker was once thought of as a "computer enthusiast". However, thanks to the news media, the hacker has become one who gains unauthorised access to or breaks into computer-based information systems. Often for this group-of-individuals the motives include thrills, challenges and power. There are, however, a growing number of hackers who are breaking into systems for financial reward.
- *The criminal*: Criminals target information that is of value to them, such as bank accounts, credit cards or intellectual property that can be converted into money. For example, the Pennsylvania State lottery was presented with a winning lottery ticket worth $15.2 million that was printed after the drawing by someone who browsed through the online file of still-valid, unclaimed winning combinations. The scam was detected because the ticket was printed on card stock that was different from that of the legitimate ticket. The main motivation in this case was money. Criminals will often make use of insiders to help them. They may be in collusion with the insiders or use such tactics as threats, blackmail and the like.

---

[3] Although hackers, terrorists and other criminals can also be insiders, for our purposes we have distinguished between insiders and the others since they generally operate outside the business or government agency.

- *The corporation*: Corporations engage in offensive IW when they actively seek intelligence about their competitors or steal their sensitive information, e.g. trade secrets. Money, market position and competitive stance are examples of some of the corporate motivations for using the IW tactics. In addition, corporations have always engaged in a form of IW even before the term was first used. This type of IW is called advertising and marketing.
- *Governments and government agencies*: Most governments now recognise the need to protect the information assets that their country has created. These assets have a financial value for business and can have a value in terms of national security. Intelligence agencies seek the military, diplomatic and economic secrets of foreign governments, foreign corporations and foreign adversaries. They always have; however, they can now do it remotely and with less risk due to information systems vulnerabilities. In addition, intelligence and law enforcement agencies seek to protect the information assets of the nation by targeting the activities of criminals and foreign intelligence operatives. In times of war, a government may target the national infrastructure of another country in order to help it achieve its objectives. For example, in the Gulf War, the allied forces targeted and partially destroyed the national infrastructure (physical and information) of Iraq. In fact, in probably every war fought in the last 100 years, examples can be found of targeting the adversaries' infrastructures.
- *Terrorists*: Terrorists are of particular interest because of the damage that they can cause against the information infrastructure, such as emergency services, utilities, such as water and electricity and financial services. Terrorists are politically motivated and have their own political agenda that they use to select targets. However, terrorists have been slow to use offensive IW tactics. Why? No one really knows for sure, but most agree that it is just a matter of time. For example, alleged terrorist, Usama bin Laden, has access to massive telecommunications systems, money and other resources; however, it appears that most terrorists are still concerned with destroying people than destroying nation-state economies. Destroyed buildings and "blood in the streets" still seem to have more of a major propaganda value on the six o'clock news than showing a burned out computer.

1.3   Information Operations

Information operations (IOs) are about manipulating the Global Information Environment (GIE) to achieve an advantage over one's competitors. It can include legal activities, such as marketing and advertising, and illegal activities such as espionage and hacking. Information operations are performed in the context of a strategy that has a desired objective (or end state) that may be achieved by influencing a target (the object of influence). The following is a definition of IOs and derived from the US Army military definition:

"*Continuous operations within the Global Information Environment (GIE) that enable, enhance and protect friendly organisations' ability to collect, process and act on information to achieve a competitive advantage across the full range of organisational operations; information operations include interacting with the Global Information Environment (GIE) and exploiting or denying an adversary's information and decision capabilities."*

The term "organisation" is used to refer to commercial, government and/or military organisations. The definition is intended to include the wide range of activities of both commercial and military perspectives. As more organisations (both commercial and military) integrate their supply chains, more organisations want to share information across supply chains. One of the consequences of this is that information security is much harder to achieve and maintain. The definition recognises that IOs function at three distinct levels, and these are: (1) physical space, (2) cyberspace and (3) the minds of humans (perception level).

1.3.1   The Physical Level

The lowest level is the physical level. This level includes computers, physical networks, telecommunications and supporting systems such as power, facilities and environmental controls. Also at this level are the people who manage the systems. Many organisations have a single system administrator who understands how the system functions. If this person is removed from the organisation, then the organisation will lose its ability to manage information systems and to recover from any potential disaster. The characteristics of the physical level are summarised in Table 1.2. For example:

> In 2005, a study of 105 second-hand computer hard disks purchased on eBay found that (a) 60% contained commercially sensitive information, (b) 18% contained financial information and (c) 7% contained network information.

This example illustrates the critical dependencies that can exist between the people who create and manage the system and the services offered by the system.

TABLE 1.2. Characteristics of the Physical Level

Characteristics and Components	Attacker's Operations	Defender's Operations	Desired Effects
Data and data processing activities that are managed and performed in the physical space, including:	Physical attack and destruction, including: Electro-magnetic (EMP) attack.	Physical security (OPSEC), including: TEMPEST	Technical To affect the technical performance and capacity of the
Data gathering equipment	Visual spying Intrusion		physical systems, so as to disrupt the capabilities of the
Computers and data processing equipment	Physical scavenging and physical removal		defender to function at the
Storage	Wiretapping, including:		physical level
Networks	Covert channel analysis		
Electrical power	Interference Eavesdropping		

1.3.2   The Information Structure Level

The next layer is the information infrastructure layer, which includes the abstract information that accepts, processes, manages and stores the information. This layer is most commonly considered to be the cyberspace level, at which malicious software and infrastructure exploitation (hacking) occur. The effect of disrupting this level is to disrupt the functional behaviour of the system. The function of this level is to deliver meaningful information to humans so that they can make informed decisions and control the objects at the physical level. Attacks at this level can have effects at both the perception and the physical levels. For example:

- In 1994, Vladimir Levin broke into the computers at Citibank and stole $10 million. Using a mis-configured modem, he was able to gain access to the electronic fund transfer system, and he simply transferred money from a series of bank accounts to his own. This attack is limited to the information structure level as only information in the digital sense was manipulated.
- In 1998, two crackers broke into a bank computer network and allegedly stole 260,000 yuan (US$31,400). The two crackers were Hao Jing-Long, formerly an accountant at the Zhenjiang branch of the Industrial and Commercial Bank of China, and his brother Hao Jing-Wen. The two opened 16 accounts under various names in a branch of the bank in September 1998 and later broke into the branch to install a controlling device in a bank computer terminal. They used the device to electronically wire 720,000 yuan in non-existent deposits into the bank accounts. Afterwards, they successfully withdrew 260,000 yuan from eight different branches of the bank. The two crackers were captured by the Chinese police in 1998 and found guilty and sentenced to death. This example illustrates how attacks at two levels can be combined. The two crackers attacked both the physical level and the information structure level.
- In 2000, Yahoo, Excite and USA.net all implemented new security measures in an attempt to combat Phishing attacks that are being targeted against home user. In 2003, it was estimated that 30 million people have been subjected to Phishing attacks and that the cost to the US backs along is more than $1.2 billion.
- In 2005, the Police in London foiled a plot to steal £220 million from the London offices of the Japanese bank Sumitomo Mitsu. Computer experts are believed to have tried to transfer the money electronically after hacking into the bank's systems.

The characteristics of the information structure level are summarised in Table 1.3.

1.3.3   Perceptual Level

The next layer is the perception layer. This layer is abstract in nature and concerned with the management of perceptions of a target. In particular, this layer is about influencing the perceptions of the people who are making the decisions. The goal is to get your opponent to make the decisions and implement the actions that you want. This is achieved by controlling the information that your

TABLE 1.3. Characteristics of the Information Structure Level

Characteristics and Components	Attacker's Operations	Defender's Operations	Desired Effects
Information and data manipulation ability maintained in cyber-space, including: Data structures Process and programs Protocols Data content and databases	Cyber-based attack including: Impersonation Piggybacking Spoofing Network weaving Network sniffing Trojan horse Logic bomb Malevolent worms Virus attacks Trapdoors Authorisation Basic active misuse Incremental attacks Denial of service	Information security technical measures such as: encryption and key management Intrusion detection systems and computer misuse detection systems Anti-virus software Systems auditing Use of redundancy Security assessment tools The use of security Standards, such as: ITSEC BS7799	Functional Influence the effectiveness and performance of information functions supporting perception, decision making and control of physical processes

opponent accesses and knowing how the opponent will react after receiving that information – in a way favourable to you. The abstract components of this layer include objectives, plans, perceptions, beliefs and decisions. The golden rule at the perception layer is that information is power, and whoever controls the flow of information within a given environment will control the behaviour of various parties in that environment. For example:

- In 1992, during the Gulf War it was reported in the press that the US government had released a virus into the Iraqi computer systems via a chip in dot-matrix printers that the Iraqis had purchased. The virus was said to have been developed by the NSA and installed by the CIA. It was designed to disable Windows and mainframe computers. This was a hoax and designed to misinform the Iraqi government, an example of the psychological warfare aspects of IW, or possibly an urban legend (a tale or rumour that is spread through the Internet).
- In 2003, it was reported that about 3.3 million American consumers discovered within the last year that their personal information was used to open fraudulent bank, credit card or utility accounts, or to commit other crimes. These cases had collectively cost businesses $32.9 billion and consumers $3.8 billion. The net effect of such losses is to create the perception that business on the Internet is insecure.
- In 2004, a report commissioned by the OST in the UK concluded that Cyber Trust and the perception of security on the Internet would play a major role in the development of online business-to-business (B2B), consumer-to-business (C2B) and citizen-to-government (C2G), communication in the next 10 years.

The characteristics of the perception level are summarised in Table 1.4.

TABLE 1.4. Characteristics of the Information Structure Level

Characteristics and Components	Attacker's Operations	Defender's Operations	Desired Effects
Knowledge and understanding in human decision space: Perception Beliefs Reasoning	Psychological operations, such as: Deception Blackmail Bribery and corruption Social engineering Trademark and copyright infringement Distortion and fabrication Defamation Diplomacy Civil and public affairs Creating distrust Identity theft	Personnel security, including: Psychological security Profiling Training and education of staff Fake detection, including: Biometrics Watermarks Public/Private Key Passwords	Cognitive influence decisions and behaviour

1.4   Summary

This chapter introduced the concepts of IA, information security and IW. These concepts are all interrelated and play major roles in the protection and defence of information systems and the information that the systems process, store and transmit. The definitions of these terms may vary somewhat; as well as which concept is a subset of the other. This "what came first, the chicken or the egg" issue is not important. What is important is that protection professionals focus on the threats, vulnerabilities and risks associated with the protection and defence of information and information systems and then develop a holistic program to protect and defend these valuable assets.

2

The World of Information

We live in an information-dependent and information-driven world. A world where information and information systems are used to drive the rapid changes in the global marketplace, which is having a major effect on the economic and political aspects of every modern nation. This chapter discusses this phenomenon as it relates to information assurance.

2.1 What is Information?

For our purposes we will adopt the following definition:

"Information is data endowed with relevance and purpose. Converting data into information thus requires knowledge. Knowledge by definition is specialised."

2.2 Properties of Information

If an organisation is to be successful, then there is a need for the data to be relevant and the processing to be meaningful in order for the information to be of value. The value of information itself cannot be guaranteed, but there are certain characteristics of information that must be present if the information is to be useful. Information should be *accurate, timely, complete, verifiable* and *consistent*.

- *Accurate*: Naturally, if decision-makers go to the trouble of identifying some information that will help reduce the uncertainty in the decision environment, they will have to be confident of the accuracy of that information. Misinformation can be used to direct an opponent to make the decision that you want. For example, the Internet has been used to leak false information about stock and shares, thus adversely affecting a company and allowing a fraudster to purchase cheap stock and then sell them when the share price bounces back.
- *Timely*: For an information to be effective, it must be timely. For example, a woman from Vancouver, British Columbia, visiting Honolulu, Hawaii, attempted to withdraw $1100 (Canadian) from her home bank using an

ATM, which was controlled by a computer in the state of New Jersey, USA. The satellite delays combined with a flaw in the supposedly atomic transaction protocol resulted in her account debited without her getting the money. On seeing her monthly statement, she accused her fiancé of theft and had him apprehended. It took a month to sort it all out.

- **Complete**: For an information to be effective, it must be as complete as possible. For example, on 5 July 1988, the USS *Vincennes*, a US ship of war, shot down an Iranian passenger airliner, killing every person onboard. An inquiry concluded that the decision to fire at the passenger airliner was in part based upon information that did not paint a complete picture of the situation.
- **Verifiable**: Increasingly, managers are asked to justify the decision they have made. For example, Jean Paul Barrett, a convicted forger serving a 33-year term, was released from a Tucson, Arizona, jail, after a forged fax was received, ordering his release. A legitimate fax was altered to bear his name.
- **Consistent**: For an information to be effective, it must be consistent. For example, in November 1998, a man in North Carolina attempted to open a checking account at a BB&T branch by presenting relevant information, including birth date and social security number. One of the bank's tellers examined the paperwork, and she called the police after she realised that the information described her husband, who had died 3 weeks earlier. Police charged the suspect with two charges of obtaining property under false pretences.

2.3   Information and Competitive Advantage

"Information is power and they who control information and its flow control the world."

Information is a national and corporate resource and has a real financial cost associated with it. It is through the correct application of information that value is added and wealth is created (see Figure 2.1). Consequently, any restrictions on the flow of information between departments will adversely affect the organisation. In essence, there are four strategies that an organisation can adopt to achieve a competitive advantage. The term value-added can be used to mean the following:

- Reducing costs through the optimisation of the business process
- Creating new business opportunities
- Improving the competitive position of the organisation
- Modifying the structure of the industry

What are the strategies that an organisation could utilise in order to achieve success and what are the security implications? These are:

- Proprietary advantage
- One-step ahead
- Discontinuity
- Implementation

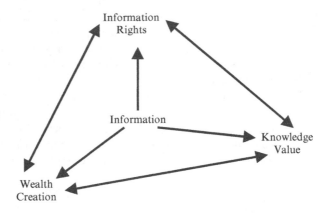

FIGURE 2.1. The Power of Information

2.3.1   Proprietary Advantage

Within the proprietary advantage strategy an organisation develops a distinctive technology – one that sets it apart from the rest of the industry. It then protects this lead, which is based, of course, on such things as barriers, e.g. patents, extraordinary investment, long lead times or rare skill base. The key factor to the success of this strategy is intellectual property. Many organisations invest large sums of money into research and development, which in turn creates new products and thus commercial success for the organisation. Because of the important role that research and development play within this strategy, organisations go to extreme lengths both to protect and acquire it from a competitor.

2.3.2   One-Step Ahead

The one-step ahead strategy demands that an organisation continually releases new and improved technology. This ongoing innovation keeps it just ahead of the competition, despite the ability of rivals to duplicate particular aspects of the techno-logy. Within this strategy, an organisation needs to protect the new features that it will embed within its technology. If a competitor could release a piece of technology first that possesses these new features, then that company could increase its market share at the expense of the developing company, and the development costs could be lost. For example, in the pharmaceutical industry all new developments have a lifetime of about six months, which means that about six months after their release a competitor will create a similar drug. Thus, the majority of the research and development costs should be recovered within 6 months of the release of a new product.

2.3.3   Discontinuity

Within the discontinuity strategy an organisation applies technology to produce a quick, decisive shift in the market it serves. For example, Citibank was the first bank in USA to install ATMs. Its widespread installation of ATMs, reportedly, almost tripled its market share.

2.3.4   Implementation

Within the implementation strategy an organisation applies commonly available technology uncommonly well. This strategy can offer a double pay-off, both delivering a competitive advantage in itself and improving the performance of other strategies. For example, the Society for Worldwide Interbank Financial Telecommunications (SWIFT, see swift.com) network is an e-mail system owned by over 1000 banks, which use it to send payment instructions and other messages from one bank's computer to another through a network of encrypted-leased lines. The technology that the banks are using is standard commercial encryption and networking systems. They have applied the technology uncommonly well to create a single robust and secure system that now supports most of the world's banks and commerce. The creation and deployment of this system has allowed banks to maintain a competitive advantage over their rivals in the commercial finance sector.

2.4   Birth of the Internet and Cyber-Crime

In 1965, the US Advanced Research Project Agency (ARPA) sponsored a study on networking technologies, and from this initial study the Internet was born. By January 1996, 20,000 dot-com domains were registered, and there was an estimated 9.5 million hosts connected to the Internet. In January 2000, 29.1 million dot-com domains were registered, and there was an estimated 72.4 million hosts connected to the Internet. The World Wide Web (WWW) was created by Tim Berners-Lee in 1991 and now accounts for most of the traffic on the Internet. In November 1996, Version 3.0 of the secure socket layer (SSL) was released. The SSL provides the WWW clients and browsers with encryption and thus the ability to have a secure conversation via the Internet.

It seems that fraud has been perpetrated against every commerce system ever invented, from gold coins to stock certificates to paper cheques to credit cards. Information systems are not different; if that is where the money is and that is where the crime will be. The growth of the Internet has also allowed criminals to communicate and more effectively share information.

Commercial organisations have not been slow to embrace the ability of the Internet to communicate with users and engage users in business transactions. In 1990, the World-Comes-On-Line (world.std.com) became the first commercial provider of Internet dial-up access. In 1992, the World Bank (www.worldbank.org) was among the first banks to go online, and shopping malls appeared on the Internet in 1994. In 1994, a pizza company called Hut-Online allowed to order a pizza on the Internet, First Virtual opened for business and became the first Cyber-Bank. On 22 February 1999, the First Internet Bank of Indiana, USA (firstib.com) became the first full-service bank available only on the Internet.

In what may be the first instance of government-supported information warfare (IW), an Irish Internet service provider (ISP) recently accused Indonesia of attacking its computer servers. The Indonesian government denied the allegations. Connect-Ireland hosts the *.tp* country code domain for the disputed territory of East Timor, which has been under Indonesian occupation for almost 25 years. On 28 January 1998, the domain of East Timor (*.tp*) was removed from the Internet when hackers broke into the Dublin, Ireland-based ISP that was hosting the domain. The attacks against the ISP came from computer servers in Canada, the United States, Australia and Japan, and thus it was impossible to identify the individual(s) who perpetrated the attack. *"I believe the attack was sponsored by the Indonesian government"*, said Martin Maguire, Connect-Ireland's founder and managing director. *"I have lodged a complaint with the Indonesian Embassy in London."*

A study conducted by Deloitte & Touche on behalf of the European Commission estimates that international fraud has cost the European Union anywhere from 6 to 60 billion European currency units, with much of that fraud perpetrated over the Internet. "At its simplest, the Internet allows a fraudster to set up a site on the WWW, which claims to be the site of a reputable company or organisation. Victims are then induced to part with funds via credit card payments or induced to reveal valuable information. At least one major international bank is known to have suffered from this although details of losses are not available", says the study. And while encryption can help ameliorate some of the problems, it is a "double-edged sword" says the study, because it can also shield the nefarious doings of crooks on the Net. The study calls for international co-operation among governments in apprehending electronic fraudsters and says the issue poses "huge" challenges to law enforcement and civil agencies: "The traditional sources of forensic and other evidence will become rarer, and a range of new types of evidence will need to be acceptable to the courts" (BNA Daily Report for Executives, 5 May 1997).

The Internet and the sites on it, which engage in electronic commerce, are now targeted for extortion.

On Monday, 10 January 2000, the US newspaper, the *New York Times*, reported an extortion attempt, involving credit card numbers stolen from online merchant CD Universe. Someone who called himself "Maxim" and claimed to be Russian said that he had copied 300,000 credit card numbers from their system and that he would post them on the Internet unless he was paid $100,000. The article quoted the chairman of eUniverse, the company that operates the site, as confirming that Maxim did have their data. eUniverse declined to pay the $100,000; Maxim posted 25,000 card numbers to a Website. Several thousand people downloaded the file before it was removed.

According to an article by Jon Ungoed-Thomas and Stan Arnaud in *The Sunday Times of London* for 16 January 2000, British hackers have compromised the source code for the Visa card system and sought ransom for it.

Excerpts from the story, which were found online under the headline, "Hacker gang blackmails firms with stolen files", follow: Visa confirmed last week that it had received a ransom demand last month, believed to have been for £10 million. "We were hacked into in mid-July last year" (despite layers of firewalls), said Russ Yarrow, a company spokesman. It is understood that the hackers stole critical source code and threatened to crash the entire system. Visa's system handles nearly £1 trillion of business in a year from customers holding 800 million Visa cards.

During 2003–2004 there was a dramatic increase in the number of frauds attempted that made use of online payment systems such as paypal and eBay. In addition, online backs, such as Natwest and Lloyds, have been targeted for phishings attacks. A phishings attack is when a hacker creates a face Website that looks like the real Website and then tries to trick users in divulging personal and confidential information.

A UK Foresight report, published in April 2004, concluded that organisations did not fully understand cyber-crime or the trades-offs between security and trust necessary for an organisation to implement security policies and procedures that allow an organisation to function. It has been estimated that the loss of intellectual property relating to software costs the global software industry $11.2 billion. In 2002, the downfall of Enron in USA highlighted the need for organisations to keep accurate records and the accountability of senior management if such records are not kept.

2.5   Power of Information

"It is a matter of life and death, a road either to safety or to ruin. Hence it is a subject of inquiry, which can on no account be neglected." Sun Tzu

In relation to the global nature of information, the meaning of the above-mentioned comment is clear: in business and war, information on an opponent's capabilities and tactics is the key to success. In short, the most important asset an organisation has is its own information capital.

Intellectual property rights deal with copyrights, patents, trademarks and designs. Basically, intellectual property rights are the rights designed to provide remedies against those who steal the fruits of another person's ideas or works. An example of an intellectual property right is the power to execute a computer program. The effect of information, in general, is to create knowledge by allowing one to add value to a resource. That resource may be physical (such as a new cure for an illness), or it may be logical (such as a piece of information). The effect of adding value to a resource is to create wealth for the individuals and organisation that owns it and/or the users who consume it (see Figure 2.1). In 2004, the School of Computing at the University of Glamorgan conducted an analysis of 106 computer hard disks for sale on eBay. They concluded that 60% of the disks contained personal or confidential information that was of commercial value.

For example, the growth of Silicon Valley in California, USA is largely based upon the concentration of expertise in the area of information technology. This expertise has created wealth for the companies that have located themselves in Silicon Valley and used the skilled workforce to create intellectual property and consequently add value. The net effect is that if California were considered as a country, it would have the sixth largest gross domestic product (GDP) of any country in the world.

The growth of the Internet currently allows organisations around the globe to communicate with each other in ways that were not previously heard of. This ability to share information has transformed the marketplace and has become one of the major factors governing business success and competitive advantage. This ability to share information and the market pressures of a competitive world economy has driven many organisations to integrate their supply chain. This integration has allowed many organisations to react faster to the changing demands of the world marketplace and create strategic relationships with its customers.

The ability to integrate a supply chain using technologies, such as the Internet, has created commercial organisations that span the globe. The effect of these global organisations is that they can directly affect the state of a nation's economy. In addition, as governments have sought to achieve cost savings, they have made use of outsourcing certain functions such as information technology management. This has increased the dependency between commercial organisations and their associated government. This dependency has reached such a state that in terms of the IW, major global corporations face increased risks. If a large multinational organisation's information systems were destroyed, subsequently the loss of critical business information could have disastrous consequences for a government in financial and economic terms, global power and public relations and so on.

Industrial espionage is when a competitor uses illegal means to obtain proprietary information. Typically, this type of activity will have a detrimental effect on the victim and could ultimately lead to bankruptcy. If enough of this activity was targeted against a nation-state, it could have a substantial effect on a nation's economy. A few examples are given below.

In July 2003, Samsung Electronics restricted use of camera phones at key factories and research centres to preclude industrial espionage.

In July 2000, The UK electricity utility Powergen advised all its online customers to change credit card numbers after details of 7000 customers were mistakenly made available to its competitors on the web in early July 2000.

In November 1999, the online bookseller Alibris, admitted to snooping on e-mails intended for Amazon.com, after Amazon accused it of deliberately collecting intelligence on the market. Although Alibris pleaded guilty to the charges, CEO Marty Manley claimed that the e-mails were not used for commercial profit or to breach confidential information.

As one moves into an information economy, the ability to protect information from leakage to third parties and unwanted exploitation will undoubtedly increase. Increasingly, more companies are becoming the victims of industrial espionage, as well as Netspionage and economic espionage, and thus, more and more governments are introducing industrial/economic espionage laws.[1]

2.6   Consumer-Provider Model of Information Usage

Figure 2.2 depicts the cyclic process that exists when parties act as information providers and information consumers. An information consumer can also act as a consumer for many information providers, and an information provider can also act as a provider to many information consumers. Within this model, information security is concerned:

- *From the perspective of the provider*: That the information is flowing to the intended party and that the confidentiality, integrity and availability of the information have not been compromised.
- *From the perspective of the consumer*: That the confidentiality, integrity and availability of the information has not been compromised and that the source of the information can be validated and is known to be reliable.

In terms of the IW, its objective is to achieve information dominance over a rival. One method of achieving this is to control the information providers that the rival has access to. Misinformation, through the pollution of information from an information provider, can be used to control and direct the actions of an opponent.

Misinformation can be used directly to corrupt the information base that an opponent is using to make decisions by calling into question a piece of valid information.

Misinformation can be used to give a false impression of one's intentions.

Within a military context, this can be achieved by eliminating sources of information such as radar and radio installations. Within a commercial context this can be achieved by introducing misinformation into the information provider. In the Gulf War (1991), the Iraqi government was known to be using CNN as an information provider. Thus, the US forces staged several amphibious exercises along the Saudi coast in front of CNN crews in order to trick Saddam into believing that the coalition planned an amphibious assault to flank Iraqi forces along the Kuwaiti border. The deception paid off as several Iraqi divisions were tied down defending the coast.

Within the commercial context the Internet is increasingly used as an information provider, and companies are placing more and more information on the

---

[1] According to the US Federal Bureau of Investigation, industrial espionage is when one company spies on another; and economic espionage is when a nation spies on a company or assists a company on spying on another company, normally a foreign firm. Netspionage, according to Dr Kovacich and William C. Boni, in their popular book, *Netspionage: The Global Threat to Information,* is defined as network-enabled espionage, e.g. using the Internet for espionage purposes.

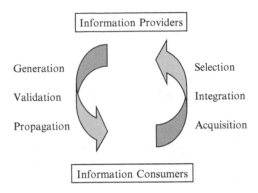

FIGURE 2.2. A Model of Information Provision and Consumption

Internet. For example, the growth of companies, such as www.192.com that make available public information on the names and address of individuals, has allowed criminals to target key people within an organisation by identifying where people live and who they live with.

2.6.1   Generation, Validation and Propagation

An information provider has to create or synthesise the information that an information consumer requires. This is achieved by observing the domain of interest of the information consumer. For example, in the Gulf War in 1991, CNN acted as an information provider for most of the world. In particular, CNN acted as one information provider for the Iraqi government. This allowed the allied forces to feed misinformation to the Iraqi government.

In any organisation, if a person uses only one source of information in its decision-making process, then it is at risk of acting on misinformation. Once an information provider has obtained a piece of information, then it should attempt to validate that information. This validation process can take one of the two forms. It can either be validated through other information providers or through observation and information that is already known to the information provider. Once the information has been validated, it can be propagated to the information consumers that require it.

2.6.2   Acquisition, Integration and Selection

In order for an information consumer to acquire information it has to know:

- What type of information is required
- Where that information can be obtained
- How much the consumer is to pay to obtain that information

Once that information is obtained, then it has to be integrated with the rest of the information that the information consumer possesses. This process of integration also involves an element of validation. An information consumer may draw upon many information providers in an effort to identify the truth. Once the information has been integrated, then the information consumer can select and apply the information required. Once the information consumer has done this, the information provider may, or may not, observe the affect that the information consumer is having on the world. This observation then feeds into the generation, validation and propagation process executed by the information provider.

2.7   Intelligence Model of Information Usage

Intelligence, the information and knowledge about an adversary obtained through observation, investigation or understanding, is the product that provides awareness. There are three major categories of intelligence products – strategic, tactical and operational. The objective of strategic intelligence is to understand the current and future status and behaviour of a domain of interest. A domain of interest is a term that is used to describe the subject of inquiry. It can include the current status of a nation-state or the future state of a business competitor or marketplace. In military terms, tactical intelligence is used to refer to the real-time situation awareness of military units and the active behaviour of the battle-space. In business terms, tactical intelligence is used to refer to the indicators and warnings associated with the status of a business competitor or marketplace. In military terms, operational intelligence is used to refer to the indicators and warnings associated with the order of battle and possible future developments. In business terms, operational intelligence is used to refer to the real-time situation awareness of a business competitor or market.

The process that delivers strategic, tactical and operational intelligence is generally depicted in a cyclic form with six distinct phases (see Figure 2.3).

- **Planning, requirements and direction**: This stage involves determining the decision-makers' requirements. The decision-makers define the information that is required to make: (a) policy and (b) decisions at the strategic, tactical and operation levels. The requirements are then analysed in order to identify the specific information elements that are required in order to create the correct understanding of the problem and thus make the correct decision. Once these information elements are identified, the specific collection methods can be identified and a collection plan constructed.
- **Collection**: Following the collection plan, human and technical sources of data are used to collect information. The following shows the major intelligence categories and collection means (see Table 2.1).
- **Processing**: In general, the processing is the conversion of collected information into a form suitable for analysis. The collected data is indexed and

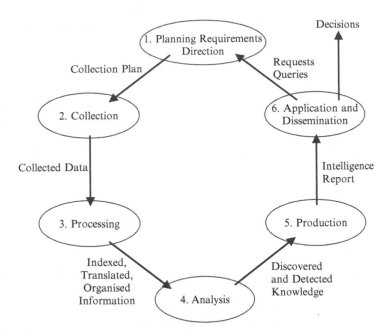

FIGURE 2.3. An Intelligence Model of Information

organised in an information base, and progress on meeting the requirements of the collection plan is monitored.

- *Analysis*: The organised information is processed using deductive inference techniques that fuse all the sources of data in an attempt to answer the

TABLE 2.1. Sources of Intelligence

Source Type	Representative Sources
Open source intelligence (OSINT)	Radio and television news sources Printed material: books, magazines, periodicals, journals and sales literature Internet news and discussion groups Websites
Human intelligence (HUMINT)	Messages from friendly third-party sources Reports from agents located within the adversary Reports from defectors from the adversary
Signal intelligence (SIGINT)	Electromagnetic (EM) signals monitoring such as EM radiation given off by Visual Display Units (VDU) screen Communications traffic monitoring for internal and external traffic such as telephone tapping and electronic surveillance Analysis of discharged media such as computer hard disks.
Network intelligence (NETINT)	Network analysis and monitoring Network message interception and traffic analysis Computer intrusion, penetration and exploitation
Imagery intelligence (IMINT)	Surveillance imagery

requester's questions. At this stage, attempts are made to remove and reduce errors and omissions in the analysed information.

- *Production*: The analysed data is taken, and an intelligence report is produced. This report directly attempts to answer the questions raised by the consumers of the intelligence. In essence, there are three types of intelligence reports.
- Current intelligence reports that are like news reports and describe recent events, indicators and warnings.
- Basic intelligence reports that attempt to provide a complete description of a particular situation or question.
- Intelligence estimates that attempt to predict feasible future outcomes as a result of current situations, constraints and possible influences.
- *Application and dissemination*: The intelligence report is disseminated to the user, providing answers to specific questions. The goal of the application and dissemination of the intelligence report is to allow the user to achieve some form of dominance and/or competitive advantage over a competitor/adversary. In terms of IW, the role of intelligence is to aid the achievement of information dominance.

2.8   Summary

Information, to be useful, must be accurate, timely, complete, verifiable and consistent. One that has useful information *and* knows how to use it can gain an advantage over its competitors – whether they are nation-states or businesses. The Internet is a useful tool to gain an advantage, but it is also the tool of fraudsters and other criminals who prey on businesses and government agencies. In this information age, information is power. To be successful, one must know how to get the information needed. There are information providers who make a business of fulfilling that need for information. Some resort to economic, industrial and/or Netspionage to obtain information.

3

The Theory of Risks

Information assurance (IA) is more of a goal than a reality today. The IA is all about mitigating risks to information and information systems. This chapter will define and discuss the theory of risk – risk assessment, risk management, threats and vulnerabilities and integrating risk concepts into an IA program.

3.1 Threats, Vulnerabilities and Risks

The concept of risk management is often neglected and turned into a manual or automated nightmare. Thus, this basic concept, which is an integral part of information assurance (IA), InfoSec, information operation, and defensive information warfare programs, is often ignored.

The fundamentals of identifying the current threats, the processes' and information systems' vulnerabilities and their associated risks must be conducted if one is to have a cost-effective information protection and defence program.

3.2 Threats and Threat Agents

Within the context of IA, a threat to a system can be defined as:

"A potential cause of an Incident that may result in harm to a system or organisation [ISO13335],"

a vulnerability can be defined as:

"A weakness of an asset or group of assets that can be exploited by one or more threats."

This exploitation implies that there is a threat agent capable of exploiting a vulnerability and by doing so that agent can have an impact on the system. The term threat agent can be defined as:

"Those parties that would knowingly seek to make a threat manifest."

The term impact can be defined as:

"The result of an information security incident, caused by a threat, which affects one or more assets [ISO13335]."

In today's networked environment, organisations are connecting their information infrastructures together in a bid to achieve a competitive advantage over their rivals. Figure 3.1 illustrates the extent of the interdependence that now exists. With the drive for more organisations to engage in e-commerce, the interdependence between systems is further increased. For example, on 28 January 1998, the root level domain-name servers for the East Timor (*.tp*) were attacked, and the entries for East Timor were deleted. As a result, all the sites with a *.tp* suffix were removed from the domain-name lookup system used by the Internet. The overall effect was that one could not connect to sites located in the *.tp* domain by using their domain name. In effect, East Timor had been removed from the Internet. Thus, one could not engage in e-commerce with sites having a *.tp* suffix. In January 2001, the first outage, which began on Tuesday sometime around 11:00 p.m. EST and lasted for approximately 20 hours, occurred when a Microsoft technician incorrectly configured a router on the edge of Microsoft's DNS network, thereby preventing Web traffic from reaching a number of Microsoft sites.

In general, information will flow via some medium from an information source to an information destination. The medium through which information flows can be physical, such as transcribed on a piece of paper, or it can be logical such as 1's and 0's used to encode information into a digital form.

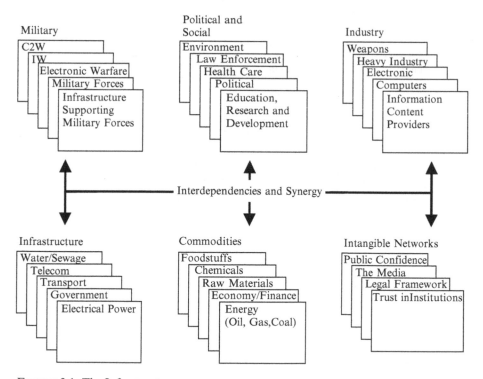

FIGURE 3.1. The Infrastructure

In essence there are four types of events that can manifest themselves with regard to the flow/processing of information, and these are depicted in Figure 3.2.

- *Interruption*: This term refers to an asset of a system that is destroyed or becomes unavailable. This type of threat is a direct attack on the availability of a system.
- *Interception*: This is when an unauthorised party gains access to an asset. This type of threat is a direct attack on the confidentiality of a system.
- *Modification*: This type of threat occurs when an unauthorised party not only gains access to but also modifies the asset. This type of threat is a direct attack on the integrity of a system.
- *Fabrication*: This is when an unauthorised party inserts a counterfeit asset into the system. This type of threat is a direct attack on the authenticity of a system.

Threat agents can take many forms, but in general we can classify threats into three broad categories: Natural, unintentional and intentional (see Figure 3.3).

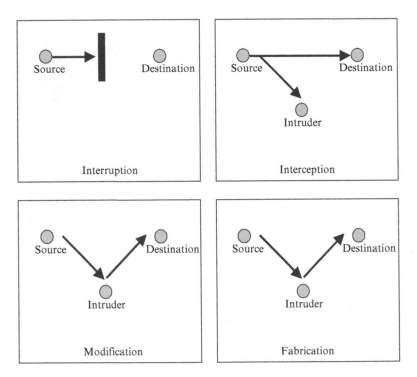

FIGURE 3.2. Types of Events

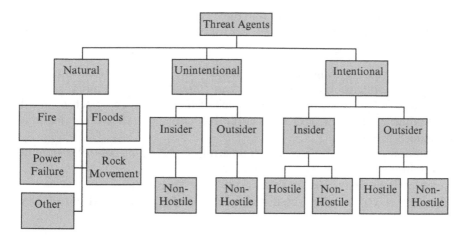

FIGURE 3.3. Types of Threat Agents

3.2.1   The Natural Threat Agents

The natural threat agents include things such as fire, floods, power failures and rock movements (e.g. mudslides). The *other* is a catch-all term used to refer to all of the natural threat agents not covered in the list such as ambient interference and small animals. For example, a squirrel shorted out the power for US-based SRI International. The power remained off for 9 hours, and many computers remained down after that time. Some of the computers had had their monitors burned out by the power surge created when the squirrel stepped in a high voltage isolation point. Needless to say, the squirrel also was the victim of a power surge!

Fire and floods can pose a serious threat to IA. The following are examples of these natural threat agents:

A fire and the ensuing water damage in the US town of Hinsdale, Illinois seriously affected computers and communications throughout the area. Some 300 ATM machines were rendered inoperative. In addition, 35,000 telephone subscribers were out of operation and a new telephone switch had to be brought in to replace the old one.

3.2.2   The Unintentional Threat Agents

The unintentional threat agents are parties that cause damage or loss of service without direct intent. Such threats can be from employees of the organisation or external to it.

For example, a previously unknown software flaw in a widely deployed General Electric (GE) energy management system contributed to the devastating scope of the 14 August 2003 northeastern US blackout. The bug in GE Energy's XA/21 system was discovered in an intensive code audit conducted by GE and a contractor in the weeks following the blackout, according to First Energy Corp., the Ohio utility where investigators say the blackout began.

"It had never evidenced itself until that day", said spokesman Ralph DiNicola. "This fault was so deeply embedded; it took them weeks of pouring through millions of lines of code and data to find it."

- An AT&T crew, removing an old cable in Newark, New Jersey, accidentally severed a fiber-optic cable carrying more than 100,000 calls. Starting at 9:30 a.m. on 4 January 1991 and continuing for much of the next day the effects included:
- Downtime of the New York Mercantile Exchange and several commodities exchanges
- Disruption of Federal Aviation Administration (FAA) air-control communication in the New York metropolitan area
- Lengthy flight delays into and out of the New York area
- Blockage of 60% of the long-distance telephone calls into and out of New York City

The largest component of the unintentional threat agent arises from the use of software. The problem is that software can never be exhaustively tested for bugs, and the larger the piece of software the greater the chance of encountering a bug when using the software. The following are examples of unintentional threats:

The Bank of New York (BoNY) experienced a $32 billion overdraft as a result of the overflow of a 16-bit counter that went unchecked. The BoNY was unable to process the incoming credits from security transfers while the New York Federal Reserve automatically debited BoNY's cash account. The BoNY had to borrow $24 billion to cover itself for 1 day (until the software was fixed); the interest on which was about $5 million. Many customers were also affected by the delayed transfer completions. The net result of this was a loss of business prestige, trust and confidence in the company.

3.2.3   The Intentional Threat Agents

The intentional threat agent is a party that knowingly sets out to cause damage or loss to a system. The hostile component of the intentional threat can cause serious damage or financial loss to a company. The following are examples of the intentional threat:

Volkswagen lost almost $260 million as the result of an insider scam that created phony currency-exchange transactions and then covered them with real transactions a few days later. Four insiders and one outsider were convicted and jailed for 6 years.

The non-hostile component of the intentional threat agent refers to the fact that the actions of an intentional threat agent may have consequences other than those intended by the threat agent. For example, in Clifford Stoll's book called *The Cuckoo's Egg*, he noted that German hackers had broken into a computer that was being used to control radiotherapy for cancer victims. In their search for information, the actions of the hackers could have had dire consequences for the cancer sufferers, but the hackers were unaware of the medical use of the computer. Table 3.1 depicts a refinement of the threat agent category.

TABLE 3.1. Threats

Threat Type	Threat Description
Foreign agents	These are people who professionally gather information and commit sabotage for governments • They are highly trained and highly funded • They are backed by substantial scientific capabilities, directed towards specific goals, and skilful in avoiding detection • They can be very dangerous to life and property. There is limited evidence to support the assertion that this threat agent is real
Industrial or economic espionage	Corporate or Industrial Espionage involves operations conducted by one corporation against another for the purpose of acquiring a competitive advantage in domestic or global markets. There is ample evidence to support the assertion that this threat agent is real and its use is widespread
Terrorists	Terrorists use attacks to inflict fear and achieve either social or political change. • The FBI defines terrorism as "the unlawful use of force or violence against a person or property to intimidate or coerce a government, the civilian population, or any segment thereof, in furtherance of political or social objectives." • They can be very dangerous to life and property. There is limited evidence to support the assertion that this threat agent is real
Organised crime	The threat from organised criminals arises as organised crime has realised that information has a distinct financial value attached to it, and information technology (IT) can be used to hide criminal activities. There is evidence to support the assertion that this threat agent is real
Insiders	The biggest threat that any organisation faces is from its own employees. There are many documented cases where employees have sabotaged, modified, or stolen information belonging to their employing organisation. One of the key aspects to the insider threat is that the insider may have legitimate access to the information. There is ample evidence to support the assertion that this threat agent is real and its use is widespread
Hackers and crackers	This class of threat is often referred to as cyber vandals. The image is generally that of a teenager breaking into a system for the fun of it and the recognition of his peers. However, we are now starting to see hackers selling their services as the cyber warrior equivalent of a soldier-of-fortune. There is ample evidence to support the assertion that this threat agent is real and its use is widespread
Political dissidents	These are people who are attempting to use information and IT to achieve a political objective. • They are using IT to inform the civilian population and other organisations or individuals about the alleged activities of their government. • They are using IT to gather (via legal, or illegal means) information relating to the activities of their government. • They are using IT to disrupt or undermine the activities of their government. There is ample evidence to support the assertion that this threat agent is real and its use is widespread
Vendors and suppliers	Vendors and suppliers are now integrated into the fabric of most organisations. For example, when we outsource IT functions to a third party, the security of the outsourcing organisations become critically dependent on the security of the third party. The same dependency is true when organisations integrate their supply chain using IT. Evidence exists to demonstrate that this type of threat agent already exists and is growing

The problem that we face when dealing with threats and threat agents is the question of measurement. The potential for a threat agent to pose an actual threat to an information infrastructure will be influenced by a number of factors. In reality, for the threat agent to pose a real threat to an information infrastructure, the agent must possess a capability and also be able to gain either physical or electronic access. Its level of capability will influence the impact that such a threat agent will have. The threat agent will be weakened by factors that will inhibit its ability to form a threat and will be strengthened by other factors. In addition, there will be some type of catalyst that will cause the threat agent to act, depending on his or her motivation. The components of "threat" that apply to a malicious threat and their interrelationships are detailed in Figure 3.4.

3.3   Threat Components Applying to Malicious Threats

The components of "threat" that apply to a malicious threat are discussed as follows (see Figure 3.4).

3.3.1   Threat Agent

The "threat agent" element expands into the types of threat agents that may be seen. These, for convenience and because they can be dealt with in a number of very different ways, have been sub-divided into two different groups; the natural threat agents and the malicious threat agents. Natural threats are a relatively well-understood set of threats, and there is actuarial history for the effects of fire, wind, water and earthquake components that are based on long established experience within the insurance industry.

A malicious threat can be divided into the following categories: (a) criminals, (b) terrorists, (c) subversive or secret groups, (d) state sponsored, (e) disaffected employees,

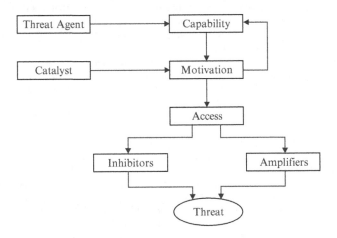

FIGURE 3.4. The Threat Components and Their Relationships

(f) hackers, (g) pressure groups and (f) commercial groups. A malicious threat agent can be generated from any one of the groups or group combinations that are identified previously.

3.3.2   Capability

In order for a malicious threat agent to be effective, he or she must have the capability to conduct and sustain an attack or to totally destroy the system and any replacement. The components of a capability can be divided into the following categories: (a) software, (b) technology, (c) facilities, (d) education and training, (e) methods and (f) books and manuals. For malicious threat agents to be able to carry out an attack, they must have the means and the necessary skills and methods to be successful.

3.3.3   Threat Inhibitors

A threat inhibitor will be any factor that decreases either the likelihood of an attack taking place or the likelihood of an attack being successful. Of the factors that were identified, those that are detailed later were considered to be the most significant. Taking each of these factors in turn:

- *Fear of capture*: If the threat agents have the perception that, if they initiate an attack, they are likely to be identified and captured, this will act as a deterrent and will inhibit the perpetrators.
- *Fear of failure*: If the threat agents believe that they are likely to fail in their attempt to conduct an attack, this may act to deter them from trying. This effect will be further enhanced if they are sensitive to the opinions of others and believe that the failure will be known to them.
- *Level of technical difficulty*: If the defences of a target that has been identified by a threat agent are shown to be difficult to overcome, then this will, in most cases, reduce the likelihood of the threat agent attacking the system as the threat agent will search for a less challenging target. In some cases, this may be inverted as the threat agents will attack the most difficult of targets to prove or demonstrate their skills and abilities.
- *Cost of participation*: If the cost of undertaking the attack is too high, then this will inhibit the threat agent from initiating the attack. The cost may be in terms of finances the appropriate equipment, time or information.
- *Sensitivity to public perception*: If the target that the threat agent has selected is one that would gain the threat agent disfavour in the eyes of the public, this may act as a deterrent. The sensitivity of the threat agent to the public feelings may inhibit the action.

Other issues that may inhibit the threat to a system are:

- *Law enforcement activity*: If the laws within the target country or the country from which the threat agent is operating are strong, relevant laws have been tested in the courts and shown to be effective, and if the law enforcement community is seen to be aggressive in its application of the law, these will act as an inhibiting factor.

- **Target vulnerability**: If the target that the threat agent has identified is perceived to be in a well-protected state or the system is thought to be protected by a variety of devices, this should inhibit the likelihood of the threat agent undertaking the attack.
- **Target profile**: If the profile of the target is such that in comparison to similar organisations, it is less attractive to the threat agent, this will inhibit the likelihood of an attack.
- **Public perception**: If the perception of the public is in favour of the organisation that the target represents, then this will reduce the likelihood of a threat agent carrying out an attack.
- **Peer perception**: If the consensus of opinion of the peers of the threat agent is that the target would be "poor" for reasons of ease of access, resulting in no peer acknowledgement for a successful attack, or because of the business of the target receives the support of the peer, then these decrease the likelihood of an attack.

3.3.4   Threat Amplifiers

A threat amplifier will be any factor that increases either the likelihood of an attack taking place or the attack being successful. Of the factors that were identified, those that are detailed later were considered to be the most significant. Taking each of these factors in turn:

- **Peer pressure**: Threat agents are more likely to carry out an attack if they feel that to do so will advance their prestige or status within their peer group. Particularly within hacking circles, elevated status and regard by other hackers will gain the individual access to information and resources that they did not have before and will also achieve one of their aspirations of increased status within the community.
- **Fame**: In all social groupings, a proportion of the individuals will seek to be recognised for the actions that they have undertaken.
- **Access to information**: If an individual or a group believes that they will gain access to information that is of use to them, either as a direct result of carrying out an attack or as an indirect reward for it, they will, in some cases, be more inclined to carry out the attack.
- **Changing high technology**: As technology develops, there is a recurrent theme that has developed of a release of a new technology, acceptance into common use, discovery of weaknesses in the technology, then exploitation of the weaknesses for illicit purposes.
- **De-skilling through scripting**: As new techniques to subvert the security of systems are understood, the more skilled attackers, most particularly from the hacking community, will write scripts that will automate the attack.
- **Skills and education levels**: As the general level of education with regard to technology increases, the use of technology becomes almost ubiquitous and the skill level with regard to the use of new technologies increases, the

number of people who have the understanding of the technology and ways to carry out attacks will rise.

Other issues that will amplify the threat to a system are:

- **Law enforcement activity**: The following characteristics with regard to law enforcement may influence a threat agent to attempt to carry out an attack:

1. If the laws within the target country or the country from which the threat agent is operating are perceived to be weak or not relevant to the types of activity that the attackers are using.
2. If the laws that are being used have not been tested in the courts or have been tested and shown to be ineffective.
3. If the law enforcement community is seen to be reluctant in its application of the law, this will act as an amplifying factor.

- **Target vulnerability**: If the target that the threat agent has identified is perceived to be in a poorly protected state or it has vulnerabilities that come into effect through no fault of the system management, this may amplify the likelihood of the threat agent undertaking the attack.
- **Target profile**: If the profile of the target is such that in comparison to similar organisations, it is more attractive to the threat agent, this will amplify the likelihood of an attack.
- **Public perception**: If the perception of the public is against the organisation that the target represents, then this will increase the likelihood of a threat agent carrying out an attack.

3.3.5   Threat Catalysts

Threat catalysts are those factors or actions that cause an attack to be initiated at the time and on the target selected. Again, the catalyst may be either real or perceived. The main groupings of threat catalysts have been identified as:

- **Events**: An event may be related to the attacker or the target, either directly or indirectly. An event that influences the threat agent might be a personal experience or exposure to news that triggers pre-determined actions.
- **Technology changes**: A change in technology occurs approximately at 9-month intervals and as a result, new uses for technology become apparent and also shortcomings in the technologies that are in use become understood in the wider community.
- **Personal circumstances**: A change in the personal circumstances of the threat agent may be as a result of exposure to information that affects their values and beliefs.

3.3.6   Threat Agent Motivators

The factors and influences that motivate a threat agent are diverse and may operate singly or in unison. The primary groupings of threat agent motivators are detailed later, together with a general description. The main motivational factors as depicted above are:

- *Political*: If the motivation is for the advancement of a political cause, it may be because the threat agent wishes to further the cause of the political organisation or his or her own position within the political grouping.
- *Secular*: If the motivation of the threat agents is to support their secular beliefs, it is possible that the level of action they will be prepared to take is quite high. A person supporting their secular beliefs will be likely to pursue an attack to a final conclusion.
- *Personal gain*: There are a number of aspects that have been grouped together under this general descriptor, as individuals are motivated by different rewards and gains.
- *Religion*: Religious conflicts are among the most common and as a result it is expected that this will be a major motivational factor for a threat agent.
- *Power*: If individuals seek to gain or demonstrate that they have gained power, they may choose to demonstrate their capability through an attack on an information system.
- *Terrorism*: The use of information systems by terrorists for the purpose of information dissemination and propaganda.
- *Curiosity*: This is a strong and difficult to quantify motive. As it is normally unfocussed and will only be directed at the target in question while the curiosity lasts, it is difficult to predict or determine when the threat agents will have sated their curiosity.

3.4   Vulnerabilities

Within the context of IA, a threat to a system can be defined as:
   "Some weakness of a system that could allow security to be violated."
   Vulnerability assessments are concerned with the identification of the weakness that may be exploited. In general, vulnerabilities exist throughout the information systems processes, software, hardware and information. Software can be vulnerable to interruption of execution, deletion, interception of software in transit and modification. Hardware is vulnerable to theft and interruption of service. Finally, information is vulnerable to interruption (loss), interception, modification and fabrication. In essence, there are seven types of vulnerabilities that can exist in any system, and these are:

- *Physical vulnerabilities*: Intruders can break into computing facilities. Once in, they can sabotage and vandalise computers and steal hardware, diskettes, printouts, etc.
- *Natural vulnerabilities*: Computers may be vulnerable to natural disasters and environmental threats. Disasters, such as fire, flood, earthquakes and power loss, can wreck your computer and destroy information.
- *Hardware/software vulnerabilities*: Certain kinds of hardware and software failures can compromise the IA of a computer system. Software failures of

any kind may cause systems to fail, and may open up systems to penetration, or make systems so unreliable that they cannot be trusted.

- *Media vulnerabilities*: Disk packs and tapes can be stolen or damaged by such mundane perils as dust and ballpoint pens.
- *Emanation vulnerabilities*: All electronic equipment emit radiation that can be intercepted.
- *Communication vulnerabilities*: If your computer is attached to a network then its message can be intercepted and possibly modified or misrouted.
- *Human vulnerabilities*: The people who administer and use your computer facilities represent the greatest vulnerability of all. They may be vulnerable to greed, revenge, blackmail and the like.

These vulnerabilities can manifest themselves via the following types of misuse (Tables 3.2–3.10).

External misuse of an information system is related to the creation, manipulation and destruction of information by a user within the organisation. This type of misuse forces one to examine how, when, where and by whom information is created, manipulated and destroyed. This type of analysis is primarily concerned with the physical environment within which the users execute the business processes.

Generally non-technological and unobserved, external misuse is physically removed from computer and communications facilities. It has no direct observable effects on the systems and is usually undetectable by the computer IA systems. Types of external misuse include:

- *Visual spying*: For example, remote observation of typed keystrokes or screen images.
- *Physical scavenging*: For example, collection of waste paper or other externally accessible computer media – so-called Dumpster Diving.
- *Deception*: Various forms of deception external to computer systems and telecommunications such as social engineering (having one act in a manner conducive to another's needs, e.g. release their password).

TABLE 3.2. External Misuse

Mode of Misuse	Description
Visual spying	Observation of keystrokes or screen
Misrepresentation	Deceiving operators and users
Physical scavenging	Dumpster diving for printouts, floppy disks, etc.

TABLE 3.3. Hardware Misuse

Mode of Misuse	Description
Logical scavenging	Examining discarded/stolen media
Eavesdropping	Intercepting electronic or other information
Interference	Jamming, electronic or otherwise
Physical attack	Damaging or modifying equipment or power
Physical removal	Removing equipment and storage media

Hardware misuse of an information system is primarily concerned with the IA of the physical devices that form the physical infrastructure of the organisation's information system. It is important that this type of misuse also includes theft of removable storage media, such as printout and electromagnetic tapes and other electronic, removable media. In essence, there are two types of hardware misuse: Passive and active.

- *Passive hardware misuse*: This tends to have no immediate side effect on hardware or software behaviour and includes:

  Logical scavenging, such as the examination of discarded computer media

  Electronic or other types of eavesdropping that intercept signals, generally unbeknownst to the victims, for example, picking up emanations, known as TEMPEST

  Planting a spy-tap device in a terminal, workstation or mainframe or other hardware sub-system

- *Active hardware misuse*: This generally has noticeable effects and includes:
- Theft of computing equipment and physical storage media
- Hardware modifications, such as internally planted Trojan horse hardware devices
- Physical attacks on equipment and media, such as interruption of power supplies. This type of attack can also make use of electromagnetic pulse (EMP) weapons
- Masquerading misuse of an information system is primarily concerned with the authentication of information, its source, destination and users. Masquerading attacks include:
- *Impersonation of the identity of some other individual or computer subject*: For example, using a computer identifier and password to gain access to a computer system. The computer identifier and password may belong to a person or a computer demon.

TABLE 3.4. Masquerading

Mode of Misuse	Description
Impersonation	Using false identities external to the computer system
Piggybacking attacks	Usurping communication lines and workstations
Spoofing attacks	Using playback, creating bogus nodes and systems
Network weaving	Masking physical whereabouts or routing

TABLE 3.5. Pest Programs

Mode of Misuse	Description
Trojan horse attacks	Implanting malicious code, sending letter bombs
Logic bombs	Setting up time or event bombs
Malevolent worms	Acquiring distributed resources
Virus attacks	Attaching to programs and replicating

- *Spoofing attacks*: For example, using the identity of another machine on a network to gain unauthorised access. Types of attacks include (a) IP spoofing, (b) machine spoofing and (c) demon spoofing.
- *Piggyback attacks*: For example, an unauthorised user may hijack a communication channel to a computer.
- *Playback attacks*: For example, the playback of network traffic in the attempt to recreate a transaction.
- *Network weaving to hide physical whereabouts*: This is where a person will connect through several machines to a target machine.

Pest programs are primarily concerned with the availability of information system services and the expected behaviour of those services.

- *Trojan horse*: A Trojan horse is an entity (typically a program, but not always) that contains a code or something interpretable as a code which, when executed, will have undesirable effects such as the clandestine copying of information or the disabling of the information system.
- *Logic bomb*: A logic bomb is a Trojan horse in which the attack is detonated by the occurrence of some specified logical event such as the first subsequent login by a particular user.
- *Time bomb*: A time bomb is a logic bomb in which the attack is detonated by the occurrence of some specified time-related logic event, e.g. the next time the date is 18 December.
- *Letter bomb*: A letter bomb is a peculiar type of Trojan horse attack in which the harmful agent is not contained in a program, but rather hidden in a piece of mail or information. The harmful agent usually consists of special characters that are only meaningful to a particular mail agent. This bomb is triggered when it is read as a piece of e-mail.
- *Virus*: Viruses and worms often attack the Internet and other networks. For example, in May 2000, the "*I Love You*" e-mail virus was released. When the worm executes, it will search for certain types of files and make changes to those files depending on the type of file. For files on fixed or network drives, it will take the following steps:

  - Files with the extension *vbs* or *vbe* are overwritten with a copy of the virus.
  - Files with the extension *mp3*, *mp2*, *js*, *jse*, *css*, *wsh*, *sct*, *jpg*, *jpeg* or *hta* are overwritten with a copy of the virus and the extension is changed to *vbs*.

Since the modified files are overwritten by the worm code rather than being deleted, file recovery is difficult and may be impossible. By 10 May 2000, it was

TABLE 3.6. Bypasses

Mode of Misuse	Description
Trapdoor attacks	Utilising existing flaws in the system and mis-configured network programs
Authorisation attacks	Password cracking etc

estimated that the viruses had infected 600,000 machines in the US alone and had cost American business $2.5 billion in damages and lost income.

Bypasses are a type of misuse of an information system primarily concerned with authorisation and configuration management. A *trapdoor* is an entry path that is not normally expected to be used. There are several types of trapdoors:

- Inadequate identification, authentication and authorisation of users, tasks and systems: For example, the sendmail debug option that was used by the Internet Worm.
- *Improper initialisation*: Many bypasses are enabled by systems being incorrectly configured so that when they are initialised the IA features can be bypassed.
- *Improper finalisation*: When a program terminates it must ensure that it disposes of all secure information properly. If not, improper finalisation occurs.
- *Incomplete or inconsistent authentication and validation*: This can be caused by improper argument validation, e.g. the Internet Worm used a bug in the *get* function located in the finger demon to gain root access. The bug was that the *get* function did not do a bounds check on the number of arguments.
- *Improper encapsulation of the internals of a system*: This can allow users to access information or functions that they are not authorised to access.

Active misuse of an information system is primarily concerned with modifying information, or entering false, or misleading information. The following are also examples of active misuse:

- A box-office supervisor cancelled tickets, which had been sold and later resold the tickets, keeping the cash. The box-office supervisor falsified the audit trail, but this was detected after problems with the software were investigated. The employee was prosecuted and given 6-month imprisonment.
- The World Wide Web provides a vehicle through which organisations and people can communicate and disseminate information. Hundreds, if not thousands, of businesses and government agencies have had their Websites attacked. The general effect of unauthorised alteration of a Website is a loss of public confidence in the agency's ability to protect its information systems, and often a public relations nightmare.

In addition, this type of misuse is concerned with the denial of service. For example, a company that specialises in trading on the Internet is exposed to the

TABLE 3.7. Active Misuse

Mode of Misuse	Description
Basic active attack	Creating, modifying, entering false, or misleading information
Incremental attack	Using salami attacks
Denial of service	Perpetrating saturation attacks

TABLE 3.8. Passive Misuse

Mode of Misuse	Description
Browsing	Making random and selective searches
Inference, aggregation	Exploiting database inferences and traffic analysis
Covert channels	Exploiting covert channels or other information leakage

threat that if the Internet connection is lost then the ability for the company to conduct business is lost and the supply chain is broken.

- Passive misuse of an information system is primarily concerned with exploiting the information within the system so as to conduct analysis and make inferences about the existence of sensitive information.
- Inactive misuse of an information system is primarily concerned with wilfully failing to perform expected duties or committing errors of omission.
- Indirect misuse of an information system is primarily concerned with preparing for subsequent misuses, as in off-line pre-encryption matching, factoring large numbers to obtain private keys, autodialer scanning.

3.5 Risk and Risk Management

The term risk can be used in a multitude of ways. For the purposes of this book, we will use the definition of risk provided in the security standard ISO13335.

"Risk is the potential that a given threat will exploit vulnerabilities of an asset or group of assets and thereby cause harm to the organisation."

Risk management is concerned with the assessment of risk and the implementation of procedures and practices designed to control the level of risk. Figure 3.5 depicts the various components that comprise a risk management strategy. ISO17799 defines risk management as:

"Risk Management is the process of identifying, controlling and minimising or eliminating security risks that may affect information systems, for an acceptable cost."

TABLE 3.9. Inactive Misuse

Mode of Misuse	Description
Inactive misuse	Willfully failing to perform expected duties, or committing errors of omission

TABLE 3.10. Indirect Misuse

Mode of Misuse	Description
Indirect misuse	Preparing for subsequent misuses, as in off-line pre-encryption matching, factoring large numbers to obtain private keys, autodialer scanning

The security standard ISO17799 defines risk assessment as:

"Risk Assessment is the assessment of threats to, impacts on and vulnerabilities of information and information processing facilities and the likelihood of their occurrence."

- Risk assessment is concerned with:
- The identification of the risk
- The analysis of the risk in terms of performance, cost and other quality factors
- Risk prioritisation in terms of exposure and leverage

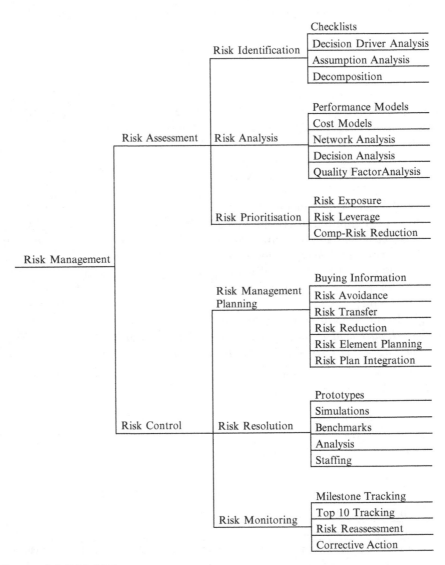

FIGURE 3.5. Risk Management

- Risk control is concerned with:
- Management planning in terms of risk avoidance, transfer and reduction
- Risk resolution, in terms of prototyping and simulation
- Risk monitoring

The process of IA risk management in the context of IA and InfoSec is about identifying the level of risk that is acceptable, and then putting procedures in place to ensure that that level of risk is maintained and managed.

The process of IA risk management is shown in Figure 3.6 as a constant iterative process. The first stage of risk management begins with an assessment of the threats and their associated capabilities. For a vulnerability assessment one would identify all of an organisation's assets and their known vulnerabilities. The process of IA risk management is a constant process because the nature and capability of the threat is always changing, and the list of known vulnerabilities is always growing.

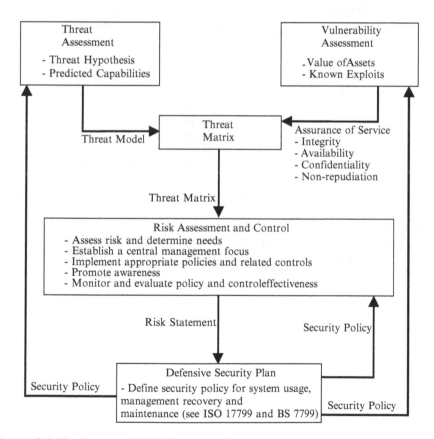

FIGURE 3.6. The Process of Risk Management

The vulnerability and threat assessments are used to create a threat matrix and that matrix is used to define and direct the process of risk assessment and mitigation. This process is concerned with identifying how the risk is to be controlled and then putting methods in place to manage the risk evaluated. The output of risk assessment and control is a risk statement. This statement is used to create an IA plan that defines:

How the system is to be managed/maintained
What methods will be used to recover from an IA incident

Once an IA plan has been created then the whole process of risk management can begin again. In fact, the process of monitoring threats and vulnerabilities and updating policies and procedures, when changes occur in the level of threat or vulnerability, is a constant one.

3.5.1   Threat Matrix

A threat matrix is a matrix in which the IA capabilities of a threat are set against the type of vulnerabilities that can exist for a given asset. The vulnerability assessment defines a set of assurance levels for each asset in terms of confidentiality, integrity, availability and non-repudiation. A cell of a threat matrix is illustrated in Figure 3.7.

The nature of the compromise is used as part of the risk assessment and risk control process. For each asset identified in a threat matrix, one can examine how the nature of the compromise affects the ability of the organisation to conduct business. This analysis is performed by focusing on the role of the asset in the business process from a particular perspective:

- *Performance perspective*: This analysis examines the role of the asset in determining the performance of the business process.
- *Cost perspective*: This analysis examines the cost of recovery from the loss or corruption of the asset.
- *Decision-making perspective*: This analysis examines the role of the asset in the organisation's process of decision making. In particular, it focuses on the cost of the corruption and deletion of the asset.

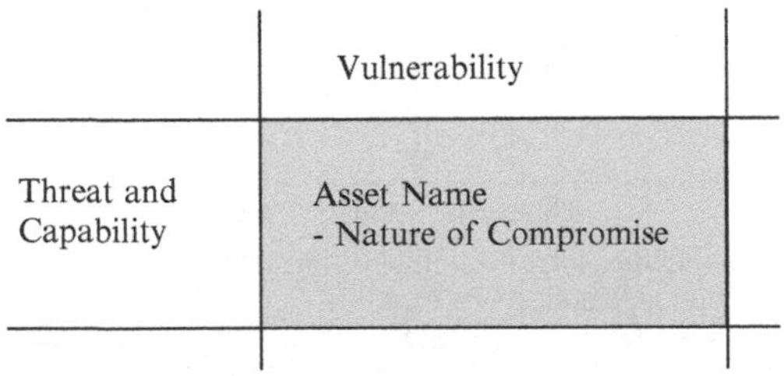

	Vulnerability
Threat and Capability	Asset Name - Nature of Compromise

FIGURE 3.7. A Threat Matrix

3.5.2   Risk Management

Risk management is the process of assessing risk, taking steps to reduce risk to an acceptable level and maintaining that level of risk. Managers analyse risks for many aspects of their business; they consider alternatives and implement plans to maximise returns on their investments. A risk management process for information systems enables managers and their organisations to build an in-depth knowledge about their systems and how they are interrelated. Risk management is a vital element of a comprehensive IA program.

3.5.3   Five Principles of Risk Management

The five principles of risk management are as follows:

- Assess risk and determine needs
- Establish a central management focus
- Implement appropriate policies and related controls
- Promote awareness
- Monitor and evaluate policy and control effectiveness

The successful organisation will apply these principles by linking them into a cycle of activity that enables the organisation to address risks in a continuous process. The success of IA programs depends on the recognition and understanding of the senior executives that their information systems are subject to risks and these risks affect their business operations. After assessing the risks of their business operations, the organisation should:

- Establish policies and selected controls
- Increase awareness of users to the policies and controls
- Monitor the effectiveness of the policies and controls
- Use the results to determine if modifications of policies and controls are needed

All organisations studied said that risk considerations and related cost-benefit tradeoffs were a primary focus of their IA-related programs. The IA is not an end in itself, but integrated into business processes, e.g. set of policies and controls designed to support business operations.

3.5.4   Sixteen Successful Practices

3.5.4.1   Principle: Assess Risk and Determine Needs

- **Practice 1. Recognise information resources as essential organisational assets that must be protected**: The efforts of high-level executives to understand and manage risks help to ensure that the IA is taken seriously at lower levels in the organisation and that the IA programs have adequate resources. The IA specialists should keep managers at all levels informed of developing the IA issues.

- *Practice 2. Develop practical risk assessment procedures that link IA to business needs*: For example, an organisation can make use of automated checklists in risk assessment.
- *Practice 3. Hold program and business managers accountable*: Organisations should hold business managers accountable for managing the IA risks associated with their operations, just as they are held accountable for other business risks. The IA specialists in these organisations can have an advisory role, including keeping management informed about risks.
- *Practice 4. Manage risk on a continuing basis*: Organisations should emphasise a continuous attention to the IA. Continuity of attention can help to ensure that controls are appropriate and effective and the individuals who use and maintain information systems comply with the organisational policies.

3.5.4.2   Principle: Establish a Central Management Focal Point

- *Practice 5. Designate a central group to carry out key activities*: A central IA group can serve as a catalyst for ensuring those IA risks considered in planned and ongoing operations. This group can provide advice and expertise to all organisational levels and keep managers informed about the IA issues. They can develop organisation-wide policies and guidance; educate users about the IA risks; research potential threats, vulnerabilities and control techniques; test controls; assess risks; and identify needed policies.
- *Practice 6. Organisations should provide the central group with ready and independent access to senior executives*: The IA concerns can be at odds with the desires of business managers and system developers. Elevating the IA concerns to higher management levels can help to ensure that the risks are understood and taken into account when decisions are made.
- *Practice 7. Designate dedicated funding and staff*: Organisations should define budgets that will enable them to plan and set goals for the IA programs. The budgets should cover central staff salaries, training and the IA software and hardware. The IA responsibilities should be clearly defined for the groups carrying out the IA programs, and dedicated staff resources should be provided to carry out these responsibilities.
- *Practice 8. Enhance staff professionalism and technical skills*: Organisations should take steps to provide personnel involved in the IA programs with the skills and knowledge that they need. Staff expertise should be updated frequently to keep skills and knowledge current. Staff members should attend technical conferences and specialised courses and review technical literature and bulletins. Special training courses should be provided for system administrators who are the first line of defence against the IA intrusions and often in the best position to notice unusual activities.

3.5.4.3   Principle: Implement Appropriate Policies and Related Controls

- *Practice 9. Link policies to business risks*: Organisations should stress the importance of up-to-date policies that make sense to users and others who are expected to understand them. A current and comprehensive set of policies is a key component in an effective IA program. These policies must be adjusted on a continuing basis to respond to newly identified risks. In today's interconnected network environment, users can accidentally disclose sensitive information to many people through e-mail or introduce damaging viruses that are then transmitted to other computers in the organisation's networks. For example, one of the methods that the Love-Bug uses to propagate itself is through users reading e-mail and executing an attachment.

- *Practice 10. Distinguish between policies and guidelines*: Policies generally outline fundamental requirements that managers consider to be mandatory, while guidelines contain more detailed rules for implementing the policies. By distinguishing between the two, the organisation should emphasise the most important element of IA while providing flexibility to unit managers in implementing policies.
- *Practice 11. Support policies through the central IA group*: Organisations should have a central IA management group who are responsible for writing policies in partnership with other organisational officials. The central group provides explanations, guidance and support to the various units within the organisation. This practice encourages business managers to support centrally developed policies that address organisational requirements and are practical to implement.

3.5.4.4   Principle: Promote Awareness

- *Practice 12. Continually educate users and others on risks and related policies*: The central IA management group should work to improve everyone's understanding of the risks associated with information systems and of the policies and controls in place. They should encourage compliance with policies and awareness on the part of the users of the risks involved in disclosing sensitive information or passwords.
- *Practice 13. Use attention-getting and user-friendly techniques*: The techniques used can include intranet Websites that explain policies, standards, procedures, alerts and special notices; awareness videos with messages from top managers about the IA program; interactive presentations by the IA staff with various user groups; the IA awareness days; and products with the IA-related slogans.

3.5.4.5   Principle: Monitor and Evaluate Policy and Control Effectiveness

- *Practice 14. Monitor factors that affect risk and indicate IA effectiveness*: Organisations should test the effectiveness of their controls. Most organisations rely primarily on auditors to carry out this function. This enables the IA organisations to maintain their role as advisors. A central IA management group should keep track of audit findings and the organisation's progress in implementing corrective actions. In some cases, the central IA management group should conduct their own tests, and some organisations allow designated individuals to try to penetrate systems. The testing of controls enables the organisations to identify unknown vulnerabilities and eliminate or reduce them. Organisations should monitor compliance with policies, mostly through informal feedback to the central IA group from system administrators. Organisations should keep summary records of actual IA incidents to measure the types of violations and the damage suffered from the incidents. The records are valuable input for risk assessments and budget decisions.

- *Practice 15. Use results to direct future efforts and hold managers accountable*: Organisation officials have stated that monitoring encourages compliance with the IA policies, but the full benefits of monitoring are not achieved unless results are used to improve the IA program. Results can be used to hold managers accountable for their IA responsibilities.
- *Practice 16. You should constantly be on the lookout for new monitoring tools and techniques*: If one does not keep up with new versions of the IA-related products and use software patches as soon as they are available, the organisation's information systems will soon be more vulnerable than before.

3.6   Summary

The risk management processes are an integral part of any IA program. One should begin by identifying the current threats to information systems and match those threats to the corporation's information systems' vulnerabilities. Then through a risk assessment process, one can begin to develop a cost-effective IA program.

4

The Information World of Crime

Information assurance (IA) is not a luxury but a necessity because intentional and unintentional acts are constantly occurring that place information at risk. With the advent of the global information infrastructure based on the Internet, more people have more access to more systems and more information than at any other time in our history. Many of these individuals make human errors that adversely impact information. There are also a small but growing group of people who have taken advantage of the vulnerabilities of these systems to steal, modify, destroy or deny their use and the information that they store, process and transmit. This chapter will address this world of crime; as well as the conduct of inquiries, investigations and forensic examinations.

4.1 Introduction

The term "information systems crime" is used to denote a crime or crimes that takes place "on" an information system such as theft of software or data, or unauthorised access-of/modification- to information. For example, the following would be classed as an information system's crime:

In June 2005, a British man arrested for allegedly carrying out the "biggest military computer hack of all time" has been released on bail by magistrates. Gary McKinnon is accused of hacking into computer networks operated by NASA, the US Army, the US Navy, Department of Defence, and the US Air Force. The US estimates of the costs of tracking and correcting the problems he allegedly caused were around $1million (£570,000).

In 2005, the UK hackers were convicted of software piracy. Alex Bell, 29, and three others ran the UK end of DrinkorDie – an international code-cracking group – and thought of themselves as modern-day Robin Hoods. Alex Bell was jailed for two and a half years. The sentences were exacerbated by the distribution of illegally obtained credit card numbers that the gang used to buy original copies of the software.

Early in 2005, news broke of a hack that had attempted to relieve the computer systems of the Sumitomo Mitsui Bank of £220 million. Hackers had slipped through the Sumitomo's hi-tech defences, placed key logging software on the bank's workstations and tried to suck the cash away to bank accounts all over the world.

The term "cyber-crime" is used to denote any crime that involves information systems and networks, including crimes that do not heavily rely on information systems or networks. For example, the following would be classified as a cyber-crime:

In July 2004, several members of a Russian gang involved in extortion and money laundering were arrested in a joint operation with police in St Petersburg. The gang had threatened online bookmakers with denial-of-service (DoS) attacks on their Websites.

In February, 2005, John Harrison from Denton, Greater Manchester, was jailed for two and a half years for distributing thousands of child abuse images. He was arrested in October 2003 as part of Operation Twins, a global investigation of a paedophile group called The Shadowz Brotherhood.

In May, 2004, computers, passports, chequebooks, bank cards and crack cocaine were seized during raids on "phishing" gangs in London. Phishers pose as a bank and then e-mail customers asking for personal details.

In November, 2004, Ian Baldock, a 35-year-old computer consultant from St Leonards, East Sussex, was jailed for 4 years for downloading more than 96,000 child porn images and movies.

4.2   Information Systems and Crime

We can classify how information systems are involved in crime in the following ways:

An information system can be the *object* of a crime. When the criminal act has an affect on an information system, then the information system is the object of crime (e.g. when an information system is stolen or destroyed).

An information system can be the *subject* of a crime. When an information system is the enviroment in which the crime is committed, it is the subject of the crime (e.g. when an information system is infected with a virus, or the functioning of the information system is impaired in some manner such as a Trojan horse or logic bomb).

An information system can be used as the tool for conducting or planning a crime. For example, when an information system is used to forge documents, create/manipulate illegal images or to break into other information systems, then it is the *instrument* of the crime.

The *symbol* of the information systems can be used to intimidate or deceive. For example, a stockbroker tells his clients that he was able to make huge profits on rapid stock option trading by using a secret information system program. Although the stockbroker had no such program, hundreds of clients were convinced enough to invest a minimum of $100,000 each.

4.3   Modus Operandi

The term *"modus operandi"* is Latin and it means "a method of operating". A criminal's *modus operandi* (MO) is composed of learned behaviours that can evolve and develop over time. As time passes and the criminal becomes more experienced, sophisticated and confident, the MO of the criminal will change to reflect this. The MO of a criminal will function to serve one or more of the following three purposes:

- To protect the offender's identity
- To ensure the successful completion of the crime
- To facilitate the offender's escape

With regard to the Internet, examples of MO behaviours include:

Amount of planning before a crime, evidenced by behaviour and materials (i.e. notes taken in planning stage regarding location selection and potential victim information found in e-mails or personal journals on a PC)

- Materials used by the offender in the commission of the specific offence (i.e. system type, connection type, software involved, etc.)
- Pre-surveillance on a discussion list, learning about a potential victim's lifestyle or occupation on their personal Website; contacting a potential victim directly using a friendly alias or a pretence, etc
- Offence location selection (i.e. a threatening message sent to a Usenet newsgroup, a conversation in an Internet relay chat (IRC) room to groom a potential victim, a server hosting illicit materials for covert distribution, etc.)
- Use as a weapon during a crime (i.e. harmful virus or Trojan program sent to a victim's PC as an e-mail attachment, etc.)
- Offender precautionary acts (i.e. the use of an alias, stealing time on a private system for use as a base of operations, IP spoofing, etc.)

In the following example, the MO consists of manufacturing and marketing child pornography to other distributors using enhanced digital imaging technology and the Internet. Contact with the buyers was first made through the use of IRC rooms. The materials were then distributed on CD-ROM.

In August 1997, a Swiss couple, John (52-year old) and Buntham (26-year old) Grabenstetter, were arrested at the Hilton in Buffalo, New York, and accused of smuggling into USA thousands of information systemised pictures of children having sex. The couple were alleged by authorities to have sold wholesale amounts of child pornography through the Internet, and carried with them thousands of electronic files of child pornography to USA from their Swiss home. They were alleged to have agreed over the Internet to sell child pornography to the US custom agents posing as local US porn shop owners. They were alleged to have agreed to sell 250 CD-ROMs to the US investigators for $10,000. According to reports, one CD-ROM had over 7000 images. It is further alleged that their 2-year-old daughter, who was travelling with them at the time of their arrest, was also a victim. Authorities claim that photographs of their daughter are on the CD-ROMs her parents were distributing.

4.4   Information Systems Crime Adversarial Matrix

This matrix (Table 4.1) was first developed by the US Federal Bureau of Investigation (FBI), and describes a number of different information systems criminals and their characteristics. The matrix categorises offenders into three types:

- *Crackers*: Many of this type of adversaries are teenagers. Despite their tender years, they have broken into banks, companies that manufacture games, traditional corporate machines and military systems. In one reported case, a 14-year-old boy broke into the information systems that position the US Air Force satellites. Despite their intelligence, many teenagers do poorly at school and have few friends. Their major form of human interaction is via bulletin board system (BBS), IRC and e-mail, where they share information and stories with their other cracker friends. Typically this type of adversary break into systems for the intellectual challenge, however, some see themselves as a Robin Hood-type character fighting for truth, justice and freedom. In recent years, many crackers have become a good deal more professional.
- *Information systems' criminals*: This type of adversary can be subdivided into espionage and fraud/abuse. A nation-state or an industrial competitor typically backs the espionage adversary. The drive for this crime is for a nation-state or industrial competitor to gain a competitive edge over its rivals. The fraud and abuse adversary is typically either an individual or a criminal organisation. Major criminal organisations are now moving into information systems crime as a direct source of illegal income generation and intelligence gathering.
- *Vandals*: This type of adversary can be subdivided into users and strangers. Typically, this type of adversary does not commit crimes for profit or the intellectual challenge. In general they are motivated by anger directed at an individual, organisation, or life in general. The user group is the category of individuals who have authorised access to the system, but perform unauthorised actions. Typically, a user is a person who feels wronged in some way and wants to retaliate. The stranger group is the category of individuals who do not have authorised access to the system at all and break into a system in order to do damage. Outside vandals are rare, most often the stranger who breaks into a system is a cracker or a true criminal.

The aim of the matrix is to create a profile of the adversary from four perspectives:

- Organisational
- Operational

TABLE 4.1. Organisational Characteristics

Categories of offenders	Organisation	Recruitment and Attraction	International Connections
Crackers			
Group	Unstructured organisation with counterculture orientation	Peer group attraction	Interacts and corresponds with other groups around the world using tools such as IRC and e-mail
Individual	None. These people are true loners	Attracted by intellectual challenge	Subscribes to cracker journals and may interact with other group and/or individuals around the world using tools such as IRC and e-mail
Criminals			
Espionage	Supported by hostile organisation	In most cases, money; some cases of ideological attraction; attention	Uses information systems' networks to break into target information systems around the world
Fraud/abuse	May operate as small organised crime group or as a loner	Money; power.	Uses wire service to transfer money internationally
Vandals			
Strangers	Loner or small group. May be quite young	Revenge; intellectual challenge; money	Use of information systems' networks and phone systems to break into target information systems
Users	Often employee or former employee	Revenge; power; intellectual challenge; disgruntled	None

- Behavioural
- Resource

4.4.1   Organisational Characteristics

Organisational characteristics describe the ways in which some information systems' criminals group themselves. It describes the group structure and social hierarchy, and motivational factors that govern the group.

4.4.2   Operational Characteristics

Operational characteristics describe the ways in which information systems' criminals actually carry out their crimes (Table 4.2). This characteristic describes how much care they take while planning their crimes, their skill level and the typical techniques they use while performing the crime.

TABLE 4.2. Operational Characteristics

Categories of Offender	Planning	Level of Expertise	Tactics and Methods Used
Crackers			
Groups	May involve detailed planning	High	Enter target information systems via information systems' networks. Exchange information with other crackers and groups
Individuals	Study networks before attempts are made	Medium to high. Experience gained through social networks	Enter target information systems via information systems' networks. If skill level is low, then more likely to use trial and error online than to do careful research and planning
Criminals			
Espionage	May involve detailed planning	High	May make use of crackers to perform information operation
Fraud/abuse	Careful planning prior to crime	Medium to high, although is typically more experienced at fraud than at information system's programming	May use more traditional intrusion methods such as wiretapping and trapdoors. Will break into systems using basic methods
Vandals			
Strangers	Not much planning, more a crime of opportunity	Varies	Looks around until able to gain access to system
Users	May involve detailed planning and execution	Varies. May have high level of expertise	Trapdoor and Trojan horse programs. Data modification

4.4.3 Behavioural Characteristics

Behavioural characteristics describe the information systems' criminals themselves (Table 4.3). They define what motivates them and what their personal characteristics are. In addition, they define any potential weaknesses the information systems' criminal may possess, which may be exploited by those who investigate their crimes.

4.4.4 Resource Characteristics

Resource characteristics describe what resources the information systems' criminal requires (Table 4.4). In particular, it focuses on the training required, the equipment required, and the support structure required in order to perform the crime.

TABLE 4.3. Behavioural Characteristics

Categories of Offenders	Motivation	Personal Characteristics	Potential Weaknesses
Crackers			
Groups	Intellectual challenge; peer group fun; in support of a cause	Highly intelligent individuals Counterculture oriented	Do not consider offences crimes Talk freely about actions
Individuals	Intellectual challenge; problem solving; power; money; in support of a cause	Moderate to high intelligence	May keep notes and other documentation on actions. Those of high intelligence will typically encrypt these notes
Criminals			
Espionage	Money and a chance to attack the system	May be cracker operating in a group or as an individual	Becomes greedy for more information and may then become careless
Fraud/abuse	Money or other personal gain; power	Same characteristics as other fraud offenders	Becomes greedy and then makes mistakes
Vandals			
Strangers	Intellectual challenge; money; power	Same characteristics as crackers	May become too brazen and make mistakes
Users	Revenge against an organisation; problem solving; money	Usually has some information systems' expertise	May leave audit trail in information systems' logs

4.5 Motives of the Cyber Criminal

"What does he do, the man you want?"
"He kills–"
"Ah–" he said sharply, "That's incidental. What is the first and principal thing he does, what need does he serve by killing?"

Hannibal Lector to Agent Starling (Silence of the Lambs, 1989)

The term "motive" refers to the emotional, psychological or material need that impels and is satisfied by behaviour. In general terms there are five types of behaviours that an intruder will engage in, and these are:

- Power assurance
- Power assertive
- Anger retaliatory
- Sadistic
- Profit oriented

4.5.1 Power Assurance (aka Compensatory)

There are criminal behaviours that are intended to restore the criminal's self-confidence or self-worth through the use of low-aggression means. This type of

TABLE 4.4. Resource Characteristics

Categories of Offenders	Training Skills	Minimum Equipment Required	Support Structure
Crackers			
Groups	High level of informal training	Basic information systems' equipment with modem	Peer group support
Individuals	Expertise gained through experience	Basic information systems' equipment with modem	Information exchange mechanisms such as BBS, IRC, e-mail, etc.
Criminals			
Espionage	Various levels of expertise	Basic information systems' equipment with modem. In some cases may use more sophisticated equipment	Support may come from sponsoring organisation
Fraud/abuse	Some programming experience	Information systems with modem or access to target information systems	Peer group; possible organised crime enterprise
Vandals			
Strangers	Range from basic to highly skilled	Basic information systems' equipment with modem	Peer group support
Users	Some information systems' expertise. Knowledge of programming ranges from basic to advanced	Access to target information systems	None

behaviour suggests that the criminal has an underlying lack of self-confidence and personal inadequacy. This type of criminal will often engage in cyber-stalking. In 1996, Neal Rockind, Oakland County Assistant Prosecutor said that times have changed and people no longer have to leave the confines and comfort of their homes to harass somebody. In 1996, Mr Archambeau, 32, was charged with a misdemeanour for cyber-stalking a woman from Farmington Hills. He met her through an information system dating agency. After they had met in person a couple of times, she dumped him by e-mail. He continued to leave phone messages and e-mail messages even after a police warning. He was arrested and charged under the state's stalking laws in May 1994.

4.5.1.1   MO Behaviour

- Targets an individual who typically lives alone or with a small child
- Selects victims who live in the same general area, often near offender's home, work or other places where they feel comfortable

- They will engage in surveillance of the target in advance of the crime in both the physical world and cyberspace

4.5.1.2   Signature Behaviour

- They will keep records/journals of the attack
- Engage in voyeuristic behaviour of the victim before and after the attack

4.5.2   Power Assertive (aka Entitlement)

These include offender behaviours that are intended to restore the offender's self-confidence or self-worth through the use of moderate- to high-aggression means. These behaviours suggest an underlying lack of confidence and a sense of personal inadequacy that are expressed through control, mastery and humiliation of the victim, while demonstrating the offender's sense of authority. Offenders evidencing this type of behaviour may grow more confident over time, as their egocentricity may be very high. They may begin to do things that can lead to their identification. Law enforcement may interpret this as a desire by the offender to be caught. In fact, this is not true as the offender has no respect for law enforcement. This type of behaviour does not indicate a desire to harm the victim, but rather to possess the victim. Demonstrating power over their victims is their means of expressing mastery, strength, control, authority and identity to themselves. The attacks are therefore intended to reinforce the offender's inflated sense of self-worth, self-value and self-confidence. In the perception of the intruder, they are entitled to the fruits of their attack by virtue of being superior. For example, on 23 March 2000, police in Wales arrested Curador, a hacker suspected of stealing thousands of credit cards from nine e-commerce sites and posting many of them on the Web. On 8 March 2000, he took part in an interview for Internet-Radio News. During the interview Curador taunted the police, saying he didn not think they would ever be able to catch him, and even if they did there was no prison in the world that could hold him.

4.5.2.1   MO Behaviour

- The victim is pre-selected or opportunistic (too good an opportunity to pass up).
- The victim is chosen by availability, accessibility and vulnerability.
- The intruder will engage in surveillance and intelligence gathering against the victim.
- The attacker will take a trophy to prove superiority; however, the attacker will usually not keep a detailed journal of the attack.

4.5.2.2   Signature Behaviour

- Demeans and humiliates the victim demonstrating the offender's power of control over the victim.
- Offender's pleasure is primary as it reinforces the offender's belief in his invulnerability.

- Offender may demonstrate a lack of care with regard to covering of his tracks/evidence.
- The victim is a prop only to support the offender's belief in his invulnerability.

4.5.3   Anger Retaliatory

These include criminal behaviours that suggest a great deal of rage, either towards a specific person, group, institution or a symbol of either. These types of behaviours are commonly evidenced in stranger-to-stranger sexual assaults, domestic homicides, work-related homicides, harassment and cases involving political or religious terrorism. Anger retaliation is just what the name suggests – the offender is acting on the basis of cumulative real or imagined wrongs from those that are in their world. The victim may symbolise that person to the offender in occupation, or other characteristics. The main goal of the behaviour is to serve their cumulative aggression. They are retaliating against the victim for wrongs or perceived wrongs. The offender may believe that they are correcting some injustice.

On 11 February 1997, a hacker by the name of Toxyn broke into the Web server of the East Timor Government and defaced it with anti-Indonesian government pictures and text messages.

During December 1996, a hacker group called Portuguese Hackers Against Indonesian Tyranny (PHAIT) broke into various Indonesian Websites and defaced them with political anti-government messages. In addition, they also erased data on a variety of government servers such as the Directorate for the Human Settlement and Environmental Technology server (huset.pt.bppt.go.id).

4.5.3.1   MO Behaviour

- Attack is unplanned; a result of an emotional reaction on the part of the offender.
- Attack is skilfully planned and focused on a particular victim or victim population.
- Offences appear sporadic over time, occurring at any location, at any time of day or night (whenever the offender gets irritated or whenever a particular victim type is accessible).
- If planned, the offender will make excessive preparation.
- Offender knows the victim, or the victim symbolises something specific to the offender.

4.5.3.2   Signature Behaviour

- There is a lot of anger directed towards the victim.
- Collateral victims in the crime scene are a result of anger and lack of planning. Collateral victims are guilty by association.
- The attack is directed towards a particular person, group, institution or organisation.

4.5.4 Sadistic

These include criminal behaviours that evidence offender gratification from the pain and suffering of others. The primary motivation for this behaviour is sexual; however, sexual expression for the offender is manifested in physical aggression, or torture, towards the victim. The offender wants the victim to suffer and see him suffering. The goal of this behaviour is total victim fear and submission for the purposes of feeding the offender's sexual desires. The result is that the victim must be physically or psychologically abused and humiliated for the offender to become sexually excited and subsequently gratified. Any example of sadistic behaviour must include evidence of sexual gratification that an offender achieves as a result of directly experiencing the suffering of their conscious victim.

4.5.4.1 MO Behaviour

The offender chooses or impersonates an occupation that allows them to act as an authority figure, placing them in a position to identify and acquire victims.

* Offences planned in exacting detail.
* Offences executed methodically.

4.5.4.2 Signature Behaviour

The attacks can last for an extended period of time.
Offender is good at presenting the image of a loving and sincere individual.
Victims are strangers to the offender.

4.5.5 Profit Oriented

These include criminal behaviours that evidence an offender motivation oriented towards material or personal gain. These can be found in all types of homicides, robberies, burglaries, mugging, arson, bombing, kidnapping and fraud to name just a few. This type of behaviour will not necessarily satisfy psychological and emotional needs. In terms of information systems' crime and cyber-crime this type of profile is one of the most common.

In 2005, organised crime attempted to blackmail the online gambling company bluesq.com. The company was targeted by a criminal group and threatened with a DoS unless protection money was paid.

In 1994, Vladimir Levin broke into Citibank information systems and stole $10.6 million. This crime was committed by the Russian Mafia and Vladimir Levin was only a small part of the operation. They gained access to the Citibank network via a mis-configured modem, and from there broke into the VAX information systems that controlled the transfer of money on the banking network. From there Levin transferred money from Citibank customers to accounts controlled by the Russian Mafia in Finland, the Netherlands, Germany, Israel and USA. He is now serving time in a US prison.

In mid-July 1999, a British group of hackers broke into the information systems of Visa and stole confidential files. The group then issued a ransom demand for £10 million and is also suspected of hiring out its services. In addition, in January 2000 a company called CD Universe confirmed that it had called in the FBI after being blackmailed by a hacker who had copied more than 300,000 of its customer credit card files.

4.5.5.1 MO Behaviour

- Shows interest in completing an offence as quickly as possible, and disinterested in activities that may prolong the offence.
- Depending on the skill and ability of the offender, they may attempt to gather intelligence on the victim in the belief that this will aid them in the successful execution of the crime.
- Depending on the skill and ability of the offender, they may attempt to cover their tracks by corrupting/destroying evidence.

4.5.5.2 Signature Behaviour

- This type of offender usually does not keep trophies or journals associated with the crime.
- Special materials are brought to the scene of the crime to aid in the execution of the crime.
- The offender will attempt to minimise their length of exposure to the victim in order to minimise the chance of being caught.

4.6   A Model of Information Systems' Intrusions

Hackers operate in a characteristic fashion, performing a set of analytic, probing and exploiting behaviour with information systems or networks. This behaviour is identifiable and, to an extent, predictable. Within this element of the work package, the authors have constructed a general-purpose model of hackers' activity – a model that can be applied not only to the recreational, low-skill "Kiddie Script" hacker aimlessly exploring information systems' networks, but also to the more determined "professional" criminal.

Central to this model is the recognition of a sequence of activities, but it crucially incorporates a sense of *expenditure* on the part of the intruder in terms of time, equipment, finance and commitment. Using this model, we can address the most fundamental of our questions for consideration: *"How do hackers penetrate information systems' networks and systems?"* The diagram (Figure 4.1) provides one example of a flowcharted model for the individual decision points and activities that are common to intrusion attempts. The model is a simple, general-purpose one, in which hackers of any persuasion perform a series of increasingly refined actions against an increasingly focused set of target information systems.

Figure 4.1 shows the basic process that an intruder would go through when penetrating a system. This process is divided into three distinct phases:

- The first phase is concerned with the processes by which an intruder identifies and selects the machine(s) and network(s) to be penetrated.
- The second phase is concerned with the processes by which an intruder would gather intelligence about the machine(s) and network(s) to be penetrated.
- Phase three is concerned with the processes by which an information systems' system is penetrated. This phase involves the selection and deployment of a vulnerability against a set of target machine(s) and network(s).

4.6.1   Target Identification

The world contains untold millions of information systems, each of which might be a potential target for a hacker, depending on the criteria that the hacker applies in selecting information systems for attention. For some hackers, every one of these millions of systems is indeed a potential target. They are as likely to attack any one as any other, with a selection criterion that is essentially

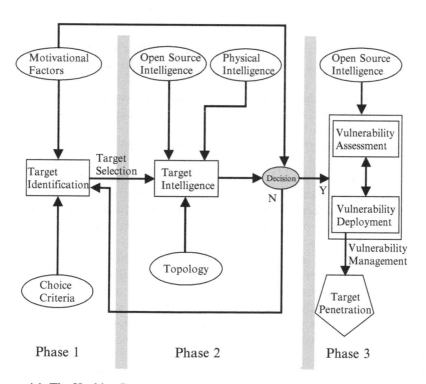

FIGURE 4.1. The Hacking Process

opportunistic. For others, the total set of systems can be more finely subdivided into systems that do not interest them and systems in which they have a very specific interest and a determination to perform a more focused sequence of activities.

In the target identification section of the model, we uncover the decisions and activities that have been applied by the hacker in uncovering the specific types of information systems of interest to them. All government information systems belonging to animal testing organisations, Irish Republican newspaper sites, all banking information systems networks, etc. This represents a subdivision of the universal set of information systems, with decisions made by the hacker based on two important elements:

- Their determination to penetrate the information systems
- The specific criteria to be applied
- These are the two important aspects in constructing a profile of the hackers' activity – the footprint.

4.6.2   Motivational Factors

The motivational factors are the specific real-world elements that drive a hacker to consider penetrating an information systems' system. Analysis of information systems' criminals suggests that the primary motivations include the following, sometimes in combination:

- The need to resolve intense personal problems such as job-related difficulties, mental instability, debt, drug addiction, loneliness, jealousy and the desire for revenge
- Peer pressure and other challenges, for example, among malevolent hackers
- Idealism and extreme advocacy, for example, by espionage agents and terrorists
- Financial gain
- There are a variety of features that are worth considering in the question of motivation.

First, motivation provides the *impetus* for the hacking attempts. It determines how persistent the hacker will be in his attempts. It determines how much effort (time, money) the hacker is prepared to expend on the attempt. It determines, in short, just how much one should be concerned about the hacker. This aspect is examined further below.

A second feature of importance in motivation is the *continuity* that it implies. A strong and focused motivation – say in pursuit of animal rights or Irish liberation – will suffuse much of the individual's offensive activity. A recreational motivation will lead predominantly to a recreational approach to hacking attempts – though it is of course important to understand that recreational motivations can easily translate under certain circumstances, such as duress, into more sinister activities.

This indeed leads to the third important feature of the motivation, which we can classify as its *flavour*. For example: Is the hacker motivated by the opportunity for financial gain? Is the motivation ideological, personal or even trivial in nature? Is the hacker perhaps motivated by external coercion? This flavour of motivation is important because it has a bearing not only on persistence, but also on the selection criteria that the individual will apply.

Motivational factors in and of themselves cannot be *detected* by intrusion detection system (IDS) technology – at least, not with the current state of the art. However, important motivational elements can be observed in the records that are collected and maintained by a variety of network IA systems, which represent important information that can and should be analysed. Abstracting such profiles is part and parcel of the objective of this new-generation IDS technology, allowing confident identification of individuals to be supported.

4.6.3   Choice Criteria

Driven by the motivation factors, hackers will apply their individual choice criteria to the universal set of information systems, abstracting the (possibly still large) set of targets in which they have an interest.

The choice criteria have several aspects to them:

- First of all, there is the question of criteria *freedom*: Does the hacker in fact have any say in the specific criteria applied, or is the choice pre-determined by an external agency? Again, this element of target selection can be observed as a feature that we can think of as *persistence*: How determined does the intruder seem to be in the face of real or perceived IA measures?
- Second, there is the question of criteria *flexibility*: Will the selected set of targets evolve over time, perhaps compromising choice as the difficulty of hitting specific targets becomes obvious? Or are the criteria immutable?
- Third, what is the criteria breadth? How many systems are considered? Where are they located? How is the choice criteria effectively articulated?

Self-evidently, there is an interaction between motivational and choice aspects, leading to the determination, the persistence, the precision, etc., with which the hacker approaches the subsequent stages of his activity. The target identification stage provides the hacker with a set of potential victims to be considered: a set from which the specific targets are then selected.

4.6.4   Target Selection and Intelligence

The selection of specific targets from the broad set of potential victims is driven by a variety of elements. First and foremost, obviously there is an opportunistic element to even the most highly focused attacks: a range of systems might be scanned in a particular order; or a more intelligent set of choices might be made, based on what intelligence can be gathered about the system on the part of the hacker. Some of this intelligence is also available to the *defender* of the system, although it is unlikely that more than a subset of this will be feasibly obtained by the IDS itself.

4.6.5 Open Source Intelligence

Hackers will attempt to perform a review of an open source material in an attempt to gather intelligence on the network topology for a target organisation or network. This can include such diverse elements as newsgroup postings referring to problems operating a particular type of information system, evidence showing with whom the employees of the target normally communicate, and computer emergency response team (CERT) notices.[2]

For example, a hacker could:

- Perform web searches on related names and terms using web search engines such as:
  - http://www.lycos.com
  - http://www.yahoo.com
  - http://www.google.com
- Analyse postings by users of target systems and target organisations on Usenet such as:
  - http://www.altavista.digital.com
  - http://www.dejanews.com
- Analyse various open source exploit databases such as:
  - http://www.securityfocus.com
  - http://packetstorm.security.com
  - http://www.osvdb.org
- Analyse various other open source material such as:
  - http://www.opensource.org
  - http://www.phrack.com
  - http://www.ripe.net/db
  - http://catless.ncl.ac.uk/Risks
  - Use remote DNS mining tools such as
  - http://www.netsys.com/nslookup.html

Connect to various information systems underground servers and acquire the password file for the target system

It should be noted that from the perspective of an outsider penetrating an information system's network, a review of open source literature is an activity that an IDS is unlikely to detect. However, from the perspective of an employee within an organisation, it is possible that by logging all out-bound traffic one will be able to identify an insider accessing various types of open source intelligence (OSI). This type of analysis of traffic generated by employees within a system can be used as an early-warning system.

---

[2] The CERT announcements are an excellent source of information about systems' vulnerabilities, however, the system defenders are usually very slow to learn about the new vulnerabilities and make the needed IA changes. However, hackers are not!

4.6.6   Topology

The topology of the target information system's network includes a variety of elements:

- The type and distribution of information systems
- The nature of the network
- The geographic coverage of the network
- The personnel responsibilities within each office, etc.

In a classic sense, network topology is uncovered by hackers using a variety of easily obtained scanner tools, or through the OSI available to them, etc. In more determined attacks, though, topology can be readily determined through subversion of personnel, physical intelligence gathering or access to trusted third parties. Once the topology of the network is understood, a realistic assessment of the target's potential to the hacker can be produced, and based on that, a decision point is reached.

4.6.7   The Deployment Decision

The decision whether or not to engage in an attack will be based on the motivation factors of the intruder. The decision is based on the following factors:

- How much it will cost to penetrate the machine and achieve the objective?
- What are the risks of penetrating the machine?
- How much profit would be made if the intruder were successful?

The cost and risks associated with penetrating a machine will then be set against how much benefit the intruder will derive if successful. The intruder will then simply make a decision based on cost-benefit analysis. If the intruder is motivated by greed, then the decision will be based on financial factors such as how much money it will cost to achieve the objectives, and how money will be made when the objective is achieved. If on the other hand, an intruder is motivated by political or ideological factors, then the decision is based on the ideological beliefs and experiences of the intruder; and the peer recognition and acceptance of a group.

4.6.8   Vulnerability Management

This is the phase of activity when the intruder identifies a vulnerability on a target machine and then attempts to exploit that vulnerability to gain unauthorised access. An intruder may have to use several vulnerabilities in order to penetrate a system, and once that is achieved an intruder may have to use several exploits to achieve their objective. Thus, the assessment and deployment of a vulnerability in order to achieve an objective will form a time-line that will form part of the intruder's footprint.

The time-line associated with an attack, and activity on that time-line that is created by the process of an intruder attacking a system, will be virtually unique to every intruder. The reason for this is that the time-line will represent the decision process that an intruder executed when penetrating a system. It will also present the knowledge, in terms of vulnerabilities known, that an intruder possesses. The status of an intruder's knowledge will give us the ability to access the level of threat posed by that intruder.

The decision process that an intruder executes when penetrating a system will also be influenced by the motivational factors that drive a person's behaviour. For example, a criminal who is driven by financial reward will make decisions based upon how much an object is worth versus how much it will cost to obtain. In addition, a political activist may have little in the way of technical skill, but may be prepared to spend a lot of time and money in order to achieve an objective. For both of the examples, the objectives could be the same, but the set of IA countermeasures one would deploy against each threat may be different.

The reason for this is that each incident will have its own time-line that is dependent on the decisions that the intruder has made in order to penetrate a system. One of the contributing factors to the decision process of any individual is the political and social belief system of that individual. Consequently the footprint of an intruder will provide us with the ability to suggest the motivational factors governing his actions; and recommend a set of countermeasures to counter the activity of the intruder.

4.7   Summary

Information systems-related crimes or computer crimes can be classified according to the impact on the computer, e.g. object of the crime, subject of the crime, tool of the crime, and/or symbol of the crime. The offender's MO may vary but functions to protect the offender, support a successful crime and facilitate an escape. An offender's profile can be viewed by organisational, operational, behavioural and resource characteristics.

Motives include power assurance, power assertive, anger retaliatory, sadistic and profit oriented. A model for information system's intrusion includes target identification, motivational factors, choice criteria, target selection and intelligence, topology, deployment decision and vulnerability management.

5

IA Trust and Supply Chains

In today's information-driven and information-dependent organisations, trust and supply chains are key elements. In this chapter, the concept of trust will be explored, in particular, within organisations, processes and systems. In addition, the critical dependencies that now exist for most organisations using information systems to manage and coordinate a supply chain will be analysed and discussed.

5.1 Introduction

Over the past two decades, communications technology has developed to a point where new methods of working and approaches to commerce are exponentially changing. While such technology has the potential to revolutionise the way people do business, both individuals and organisations remain sceptical about their applicability, use and ability to protect information. If the technology is to realise its potential, then ways need to be identified that will help to facilitate its uptake and use. It has been suggested that:

"Participants in collaborative work relationships are likely to vary in the knowledge they possess, and must therefore engage each other in dialogues that allow them to pool resources and knowledge, and negotiate their differences to accomplish their tasks."

Organisations function because people cooperate with each other. A successful organisation is one with constantly evolving trust relationships. If two people were to communicate to solve a problem, then there has to be an element of trust. In fact, virtually all transactions in every domain of human endeavour are built upon the concept of trust to such an extent that without it society and organisation could not function. Ron Chernow summarised this nicely in his book *The House of Morgan*:

"Utermyer: Is not commercial credit based primarily upon money and property?
Morgan: No, sir, the first thing is character.
Utermyer: Before money and property?
Morgan: Before money or anything else. Money cannot buy it. Because a man I do not trust could not get money on all the bonds in Christendom."

Organisations are networks of people who cooperate in order to achieve a variety of goals, and the social networks within them are built upon trusting relationships. Evidence shows that when people have too little or too much trust within an organisation then that organisation can fail to function. Modern management now recognises the importance that trust plays in the governing and managing of people's behaviour. In short, trust properly developed is the glue that binds organisations together and allows them to function.

Within organisations that make extensive use of an information technology (IT) infrastructure, an information assurance (IA) plays a vital role in the creation and mediation of trust and consequently of doing business. For example, if two organisations are using e-mail to engage in contract negotiations then it is vital that the confidentiality, integrity and availability of the e-mail messages are guaranteed. If any of these were to breakdown, then it would adversely affect the relationship and could ultimately result in loss of a business relationship.

Where IA and trust really come together is in the area of e-commerce. When people are engaging in commercial transactions across the Internet, it is vital that a trustworthy image be created and maintained. For example:

In July 1995, Amazon.com opened its virtual doors with a mission to use the Internet to transform book buying into the fastest, easiest, and most enjoyable shopping experience possible. Amazon.com knew that in order to succeed, it would need to create an image so that its customers could trust it to deliver what was ordered and keep their information in a private and secure manner. To this end, Amazon.com created a privacy policy that explicitly told its customers what information they would gather and how they would treat this information. It also spelt out exactly what Amazon would accept responsibility for and what its customers are responsible for.

On Friday, 26 November 1999, a security hole forced the Halifax Building Society to shut its online share shop after a breach of security allowed customers to view other people's accounts. The effect of this incident along with other incidents such as security breaches at Visa (January 2000), and Powergen (July 2000), is to undermine the trust that people place in doing business online.

In short, an IA is the oil that lubricates the working of trust in an IT environment. Without IA it is impossible to create trust and consequently impossible to do business.

5.2   Developing a Conceptual Model of Trust

Over the past decade, various researchers have attempted to define and model trust. Each of them has drawn upon a particular area of concern such as sociological, business, organisational and technological. Each of these attempts to define trust within a particular domain, and thus the lessons learnt from applying each of the models is not transferable.

What is required is a general model of trust that is transferable across multiple application domains and has the ability to make use of benchmarks. The conceptual model of trust presented is a meta-model of trust that attempts to draw together the various strands of research, and to create a model of trust that has a general scope of application. In short, it aims to provide people with a tool that can be used to understand and measure trust within and between organisations and people.

5.2.1   NICE Model of Trust

This conceptual model of trust has four distinct components that are defined as follows.

5.2.1.1   Need

The concept of "need" is one of the four distinct components. For example, I can trust you because I know you need the deal to take place, you are aware of serious penalty clauses, a time limit on your side is close, or you could trust me since I am the one in trouble. I may also need to trust someone as an article of faith, perhaps because I cannot accept a situation without it (e.g. trust in a doctor or a priest, irrespective of whether they can do anything or not). This is a predominantly tactical and calculating approach. Patients may trust a health care provider because they need to feel that they will get better and are not prepared to consider the alternatives.

The need to trust can also be based on the motivation factors governing the behaviour of a person. Note that motivation factors for trusting will always relate to people and never to an information system. The motivation factors can include the following set of needs: (a) physiological, (b) safety, (c) love, (d) esteem and (e) self-actualisation.

5.2.1.2   Identification

The concept of "identification" is another of the four distinct components. This parameter is more strategic than the previous one and more openly subjective. For example, I trust you because I believe we share a common set of values, mission, vision, roles, culture, etc.

The common set of values can be derived from the following:

- Membership in a social club or a society such as supporting the same football team
- Membership in a political party
- Membership in a religious organisation
- Membership in a particular division within an organisation
- Performance in a particular role or activity

One example of this type of trust could be that a patient is only willing to talk to or accept-treatment-from the patient's own doctor. The justification that a patient could give for this behaviour is that the doctor understands the social environment that the patient lives in, as the doctor lives in the same social environment and is a member of the community.

5.2.1.3   Competence

Competence is the third component. For example, I trust you because your processes are visibly good and your skills are accredited. A person wishing to instil trust in another may say, "Trust me because I am an expert".

In particular, competence-based trust can be established through:

Qualification from recognised bodies or agencies
Supervision by a recognised body or agency
Knowledge of the business process and value chains that are at work within the organisation

Medical doctors can be seen to possess competence-based trust because of the Royal College of Physicians (RCP) that accredits their qualifications in the UK. Thus, one can have competence-based trust because of the qualification. In addition, the General Medical Council (GMC) in the UK monitors the behaviour of doctors, and there is a process by which one can complain about a doctor. If a person was to complain about the behaviour of a doctor, and that complain was upheld, then the doctor could be stopped from practising medicine. Consequently, one can have competence-based trust in a doctor because one knows the business process and value chains that govern the evaluation of the behaviour.

5.2.1.4   Evidence

Evidential-based trust is based on an individual having evidence, the fourth component, to support the assertion that he/she or another individual is trustworthy. Evidence-based trust comes in various forms. These include:

- *First-hand evidence*: You have direct experience of how another party behaves and so can decide how they will behave in a given situation.
- *Second-hand evidence*: You have indirect experience of how another party behaves. A person that you know and have contact with has the direct experience of how the other party behaves. The question with second-hand evidence is:
- How trustworthy is the person who has the direct experience of the behaviour of the other party?
- *Third-hand evidence*: You have indirect experience of how another party behaves. In conversational terms, we may say "a friend of a friend" has the direct experience of how another party behaves. The questions with third-hand evidence are:
- How trustworthy is the person who has the direct experience of the behaviour of the other party?
- How trustworthy are the people in the social network that leads from the first-hand knowledge to you?

This progression from first-hand to third-hand evidence leads on to nth-hand evidence, where with nth-hand evidence there are $n - 1$ people in the social network from one to the other party performing the trusted action.

5.2.2 Trust Footprint

The four components of the trust model can be used to create a footprint of a trusted relationship, and this footprint can be used to benchmark the current and future status of the trust relationship. The purpose of the footprint is to allow us to analyse the trusted relationship and to identify the factors that facilitate the creation of trust, and the factors that destroy trust. The footprint model provides a visual mechanism for analysing and benchmarking the trust relationship.

In Figure 5.1, the scales that are used on the axes are as follows: (a) +1 denotes complete trust, (b) −1 denotes complete mistrust and (c) 0 denotes no-trust. The term no-trust is used to indicate that an individual is neutral about trusting another individual. Some factors in the environment will act to reduce the area of the footprint, by reducing the values on the axes. For example, if a doctor misdiagnoses a patient and the patient finds out, then this will have the effect of reducing the competence component of the trust model. If a doctor makes an early diagnosis of an illness for a patient and the diagnosis is correct and saves the patient's life, then that is going to increase the competence component of the trust model. Consequently, the trust footprint allows us to examine the possible effect that a breakdown in the IA will have upon a relationship.

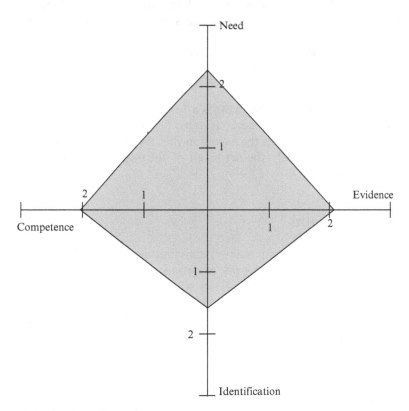

FIGURE 5.1. The Trust Footprint

The footprint model is a graphical representation of how much trust the maker of the footprint feels towards the target of the footprint. Figure 5.1 tells us that:

- The owner of the footprint has an element of mistrust towards the individual who is the target of the footprint because there is a negative element of identification between the individuals (the value of identification axis is negative).
- The owner of the footprint trusts the target to be a competent individual (the value of competence axis is positive).
- The owner of the footprint has an element of limited trust towards the target because the owner believes that the target needs the transaction to take place (the value of need axis is a small positive).
- The owner of the footprint has an element of no-trust towards the target as there is no, or limited, historical data to support the assertion that the target is trustworthy (the value of evidence axis is zero).

This visual representation gives the ability to analyse the component of trust that is the weakest, and to identify the actions required to improve that value which would have the greatest reward on the overall value of the trust between the owner and the target of the footprint. For example:

- In May 1999, UK Internet savings bank, Egg, owned by Prudential, rushed to close a security flaw that allowed some users to see other potential savers' confidential financial information.
- In July 2000, the UK electricity and gas supplier, Powergen, confirmed a security breach in which thousands of customers may have had their banking details revealed.

The result of both of these incidents is a loss of competence in the ability of organisations to manage e-commerce systems in a secure manner; and the creation of evidence that supports the assertion that the Internet is not a safe place to do business. Consequently, the net result of the incidents is a loss in area of the trust footprint.

5.3   Supply Chains

The term supply chain encompasses all activities associated with the flow and transformation of goods from the raw materials stage, through to the end user, as well as the associated information flows. Materials and information flow both up and down the supply chain. A supply chain includes the management of information systems, sourcing and procurement, production scheduling, order processing, inventory management, warehouse, customer service, after sales support, etc. Supply networks consist of all the organisations that provide inputs, either directly or indirectly to the organisation. If we consider an individual firm that makes hard disks for computers, then while examining the supply chain for that company, we must examine both its upstream supplier network and its downstream distribution channel. The company has to order parts/services from its suppliers and manage that process, and supply parts/services to its customers and manage that process. In essence, a supply chain is a series of linked suppliers and customers; every customer is in turn a supplier to the next downstream organisation until the finished product/service reaches the ultimate end user. Figure 5.2 illustrates a supply chain.

The second tier supplier supplies goods/services to the first tier suppliers who then in turn supply goods and services to a manufacturing organisation. The term manufacturing organisation is used to denote any organisation that creates or makes a product or service. For example, the news provider Cable Network News (CNN) can be seen as a manufacturing organisation with the news agency Reuters acting as a first tier supplier. The manufacturing organisation distributes its products/services via a distribution centre to a retailer. The retailer then sells the products/services to the ultimate end user known as the customer. On the Internet, an Internet service provider (ISP) functions as the distributor.

In modern world, many organisations have adopted the just-in-time (JiT) supply chain management philosophy. This means that they only hold the stock that they require for a few days; thus, organisations minimise the amount of storage space required and have more deliveries of stock on a regular basis. This supply philosophy, however, assumes that the supply chain is functioning. If a supplier runs out of stock, then this can have severe consequences for organisations further down the supply chain. For example, in September 2000, a group of people blockaded a fuel depot and distribution points within the UK. Within 2–3 days,

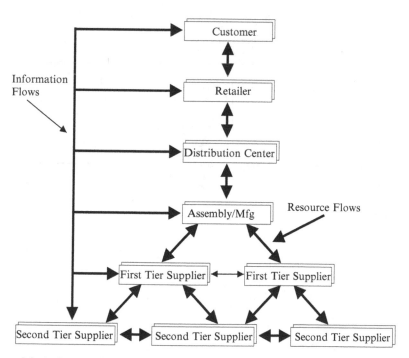

FIGURE 5.2. A General Supply Chain

people were running out of fuel. The consequences were that people could not get to work, and distributors could not distribute goods to the retailers. Thus, shops started to run out of commodities such as bread, milk and toilet roll. Had the fuel blockade not been lifted when it was, it may not have been long before companies were forced into liquidation due to the lack of supplies. The other interesting point about the fuel blockade was that as a result of the blockade and the inability of the government to deal with the people manning the blockades; many people lost their trust in the government and its ability to govern fairly and respond to the needs of the people.

Supply chains are made even more complex when one considers the complex interrelationships that exist between organisations. Figure 5.3 illustrates the many-faceted relationships and dependencies that exist with the modern commercial environment. For example, most organisations make use of water, electricity and telecommunications, and there are numerous examples of what can happen to computer systems when the power fails.

The following illustrate the complex relationships that exist between many different services in a supply chain:

- On 9 October 2004, near Milwaukee, Wisconsin, an 80-foot-tall high-voltage electrical tower collapsed onto a second transmission tower, causing a 4-hour power outage for 17,000 customers. Apparently, someone had removed

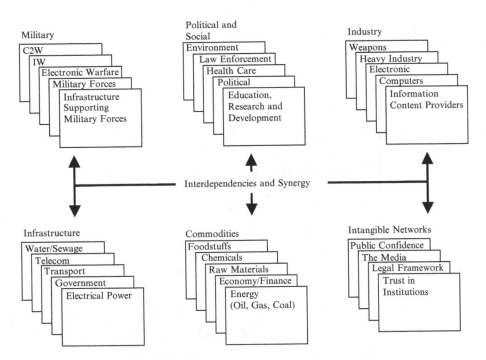

FIGURE 5.3. Complex Relationships

enough bolts from the base of the tower. Wires were still across railroad tracks the next day, delaying Amtrak and Canadian Pacific trains.

- An AT&T crew removing an old cable in Newark, New Jersey accidentally severed a fiber-optic cable carrying more than 100,000 calls. Starting at 9.30 a.m. on 4 January 1991 and continuing for much of the next day, the effects included:

  - Downtime of the New York Mercantile Exchange and several commodities exchanges
  - Disruption of Federal Aviation Administration (FAA) air-control communication in the New York metropolitan area
  - Lengthy flight delays into and out of the New York area
  - Blockage of 60% of the long-distance telephone calls into and out of New York City

The manipulation of supply chains is not new and was used to devastating effect in 1943. In the summer of 1943, the British Navy and Coastal Command managed to sink seven out of eight supply boats sent to resupply the German U-boats. In essence, what they did was to disrupt the supply chain for the German U-boats. This disruption allowed the British and Americans to win the war of the Atlantic and, thus, establish and supply a second front in World War II.

Modern information technology can introduce extremely complex dependencies. During the Gulf War, computer vandals cracked into the US government computers at 34 military sites to steal information about troop movements, missile capabilities and other secret information. They then offered it to the Iraqis, but the Iraqis rejected it because they considered the information a hoax. Dr Eugene Schultz, former head of computer security at the US Department of Energy, has told the British Broadcasting Company, "We realised that these files should not have been stored on Internet-capable machines. This was a huge mistake".

The lessons that we learn from this are that in terms of IA, an organisation is extremely dependent on its supply chain, and physical security is an important part of IA. In terms of IA, the dependencies that govern the flow of information around an organisation are crucial to business success.

These dependencies can become critical when one examines the extent to which a lot of organisations are now outsourcing the provision and support of an information system and information systems infrastructure. Let us consider a fictitious organisation called Blyths Books. This company is located in Cardiff, Wales and sells rare books on the Internet via online auctions. It is considered to be one of the best online bookshops on the Internet and has one of the largest databases of rare books, rare booksellers and customers in the world. It has a large WEB presence (www.blythsbooks.com) and makes use of a single local ISP called Welsh ISP Ltd. (www.wisp.com).

In addition, Blyths Books has also outsourced its information services provision to another local company called Welsh-Net Inc., which also manages and supports the Blyths Books Website. Blyths Books has also outsourced its responsibility for physical security and cleaning of its offices to another local company called Group-101. The objectives of Blyths Books when making use of outsourcing/facilitates-management companies are to minimise costs and maximise profits. The consequence of this is that any of the outsourcing companies has potential access to some/all of Blyths Books corporate information. The loss of any corporate information for Blyths Books could have devastating consequences for the company.

When using a supply chain to control/support a critical organisation function one is only secure as the weakest link in the chain. Consequently, many organisations are now demanding that the organisations in their supply chains take the IA seriously and meet certain minimum standards.

On 16 June 2005, *the Financial Times* published an article stating that hackers were bombarding financial networks in the UK. Rogers Cumming, the Director of the UK National Infrastructure Security Co-ordination Centre (NISCC) said "We have never seen anything like this in terms of the industrial scale of this series of attacks". This is the first official ordered attack against a country's Critical National Information Infrastructure, with most of the attacks originating in Asia.

5.4   Analysis of Supply Chains

Analysis of supply chains can be conducted using the Porter Value Chain model. This model describes the various components that make up an organisation and its supply chain.

Value chain analysis has been widely used as a means for describing the activities within and around an organisation, and relating them to an assessment of the competitive strength of an organisation. Value chain analysis was originally introduced as an analysis tool that was designed to shed light on the "*value added*" of separate steps in complex manufacturing processes, in order to determine where cost improvements could be made and/or value creation improved.

One of the key aspects of value chain analysis is the recognition that organisations are much more than a random collection of machines, money and people. These resources are of no value unless deployed into activities and organised into routines and systems, which ensure that products or services are produced which are valued by the final customer/user. In other words, it is these competencies to perform particular activities and the ability to manage linkages between activities, which are the source of competitive advantage for organisations. It is also these manage linkages that create the potential for the activities of one organisation to affect the performance of another. Thus, when sharing information across a supply, the rule is that one only is as secure as the weakest link in the supply chain. Consequently, some organisations with large and complex supply chains are starting to mandate that suppliers, distributors and resellers comply with security standards such as BS7799.

An understanding of critical dependencies within a supply chain must start with an identification of the value activities that an organisation performs. Figure 5.4 is a schematic representation of a value chain within an organisation. Value chains are a way of modelling the organisation in order to answer questions activity by activity. In order to answer these questions, the organisation must study the primary activities that get the product or service to the customer and the support activities that facilitate these. In addition, there are linkages between these activity processes. It is with improvements to these linkages that information systems can offer the most support and help an organisation achieve a competitive advantage.

The *primary activities* of the organisation are grouped into five main areas: Inbound logistics

- Operations
- Outbound logistics
- Marketing and sales
- Service

Each of the primary activities is linked to *support activities*. The *support activities* can be divided into the following four areas:

- Procurement
- Technology
- Development
- Human resources
- Management
- Infrastructure

5.4.1   Primary Activities

There are five basic activities that apply to supply chains. They are:

- **Inbound logistics** are the activities concerned with receiving, storing and distributing the inputs to the product/service. These include materials handling, stock control, transport, etc.

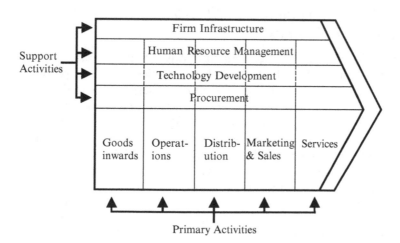

FIGURE 5.4. The Value Chain

- *Operations* transform these various inputs into the final product or service, for example, matching, packaging, assembly, testing, etc.
- *Outbound logistics* collect, store and distribute the product to the customers. For tangible products, this would involve warehousing, materials handling, transport, etc. In the case of services, it may be more concerned with bringing customers to the service if it is at a fixed location.
- *Marketing and sales* provide the means whereby consumers/users are made aware of a product/service and are able to purchase it. This would include sales administration, advertising, selling, etc.
- *Service* covers all those activities that enhance or maintain the value of a product/service such as installation, repair, training, spares, etc.

5.4.2   Support Activities

There are four basic activities that apply to support activities. They are:

- *Infrastructure*: The systems of planning, finance, quality control, etc. are crucially important to an organisation's strategic capabilities in all primary activities. Infrastructure also consists of the structures and routines of the organisation, which sustain its culture.
- *Human resource management*: This is a particularly important area that transcends all primary activities. It is concerned with those activities involved in recruiting, training, developing and rewarding people within the organisation.
- *Technology development*: All value activities have a technology, even if it is simply "know-how". The key technologies may be concerned directly with the product, a process or with a particular resource.
- *Procurement*: This refers to the process of acquiring the various resource inputs to the primary activities.

5.4.3   Industry Value Chain Showing Strategic Alliances Between Organisations

One of the key features of most organisations is that very rarely does a single organisation undertake all of the value activities from the product design through to the delivery of the final product or service to the final consumer. There is usually a specialisation of the role and any one organisation is a part of the wider value system, which creates a product or a service. Figure 5.5 illustrates just how easily a complex web of interdependencies can be created.

In understanding the basis of an organisation's capability, it is not sufficient to look at the organisation's internal position alone. Much of the value creation will occur in the supply and distribution chains, and this *whole process* needs to be analysed and understood. For example, the quality of an automobile when it reaches the final purchaser is not only influenced by the activities, which are undertaken within the manufacturing company itself, but also by the quality of components and the performance of the distributors. The ability of an organisation to

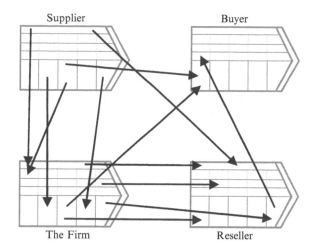

FIGURE 5.5. Strategic Alliances Between Organisations

influence the performance of other organisations in the supply chain may be crucially important in competence and, of course, in competitive advantage.

Some organisations have integrated their supply chains to such an extent that it is very difficult to tell the difference between the suppliers, distributors and resellers. For example:

The Analytical Systems Automotive Purchasing (ASAP) system helped customers of the American Hospital Supply Corporation (AHSC) automate the ordering part of their stock control by placing order entry terminals in their hospitals. This elimination of effort for the customer was, inevitably, popular with all of the AHSC customers. This system grew out of a supply system that was installed between the AHSC and the Stanford Medical Center. In order to maintain AHSC's market share, the ASAP has been continually enhanced and supported.

Federal Express was started up in 1973 as an overnight delivery service. From the very beginning, the company invested in IT and integrated it into its supply chain. Through the use of technology to automate and control the business, the company has been able to reduce operating costs. The low cost and high efficiency of the business are supported by systems such as the "cradle to grave" tracking of packages system. The IT dependency envisioned by the founders of Federal Express has been well managed, and the worldwide market share that Federal Express now has is testimony to this.

The above examples show how supply chains have been managed and integrated to achieve a competitive advantage for the organisation. However, they also show the extent to which such companies now rely on IT to do business. Take away the IA, and the technology cannot be trusted or stops functioning. Take away the technology or not trust it, and the company would simply stop functioning.

5.5 Summary

Information assurance processes are used to assist in providing "trust" of information systems and information. The NICE model of trust incorporates need, identification, competence and evidence. Supply chains and JiT inventories rely on IA to succeed. If any part of the IA is weak, then there is an increased risk to information and information systems, and thus to the corporation.

6

Basic IA Concepts and Models

Information assurance (IA) is based on concepts and models that have migrated from the field of information systems security. This chapter discusses these basic concepts, as well as some models adapted for the IA use. Although many of these models have been around for some time, they are sometimes controversial. For example, some believe they are inaccurate, others believe they are no longer useful. However, the models are valid and useful when properly implemented and integrated into an IA program. These basic IA concepts and models are of little use if applied in an isolated, stovepipe approach. None on their own is the answer to information protection and defence. They are just part of a totally integrated IA program.

6.1   Introduction

The various information assurance (IA) models that will subsequently be addressed may all seem different; however, there are some similarities. They all do have one common theme. They are the building blocks, the sub-systems, sub-processes of a basic IA system and/or program. So what do we mean when we say IA and Information Security?

"Information Assurance is the confidence that information assets will protect the information they handle and will function as they need to, when they need to, under the control of legitimate users."

"Information Security is the preservation of confidentiality, integrity and availability of information."

It is important to have a common definition and understanding of terms in order to understand the concepts and ideas behind the models. For those who believe that they understand the terms, re-reading them will help reinforce that understanding or ensure a better understanding. After all, miscommunications are at the heart of many misunderstandings. If you are responsible for establishing an IA's program and relying on some aspects of this book to help you, the last thing you need is to misinterpret what is being discussed because of different definitions for the same terms.

6.2   IA Goals and Objectives

Like information systems security and information security, the models discussed later are based on simple, yet often misunderstood basic concepts of the IA's goals and objectives:

- *Minimise the probability of IA vulnerability*: In other words, you want to minimise the risks that your information systems and the information that they store, process and transmit are vulnerable to any threats, whether they are deliberate or accidental.
- *Minimise the damage if vulnerability is exploited*: If you are attacked because of some vulnerability you were not aware of or you decided to take a chance, a risk, that the vulnerability would not be exploited, you want to be sure that the damages caused by the attacker are minimal. Also, one must be prepared to defend against human errors.
- *Provide a method to recover efficiently and effectively from the damage*: Since no one can be assured that it is impossible to successfully attack them, there must always be a "back-up plan", a process in place to get back to normal operations as quickly as possible. Remember that in today's fast-paced environment, the old saying "time is money" is truer now than ever before. By the way, watch out for human errors. They will occur more often than attacks and can cause as much, if not more damage.

6.3   Three Basic Concepts

There are three basic concepts that should be established in order to assist in the above-stated goals. These baseline concepts are as follows:

- Access controls
- Individual accountability
- Audit trails

Let us look at each of this triad in order to understand why they are so important to the protection and defence of information and information systems.

6.3.1   Access Controls

The basic defence to support IAs is the concept of access control. The two basic forms of access controls are physical access controls and logical access controls.

6.3.1.1   Physical Access Controls

In today's modern corporations, the information systems are located on almost every desktop and in every department of the corporation. Thus, access to the facility is the first line of defence in protecting the information maintained, processed and stored by those systems.

Physical access controls consist of human and mechanical access controls. Human access controls are the people who have responsibility for ensuring that only authorised personnel enter a building, specific office or area. When one thinks of such human access controllers, one quickly thinks of security guards. However, access control responsibility may also rest with each employee and others, such as the receptionists, and other administrative personnel who work in a specific area or office, where access must be controlled due to the sensitive information and information systems contained therein.

6.3.1.2   Logical Access Controls

Once one has obtained physical access to the facility or information system, logical access controls are used to provide the next filtering system to assist in ensuring that only authorised users have access to information systems and information. Because of the need for telecommuting and mobile access to information systems and their automated information, the use of physical barriers have decreased in importance while the need for good logical access controls have increased. One cannot provide the same degree of information protection through physical access controls as before since more and more information systems' users are mobile. One must understand that are never a 100% proposition. There are many trade-offs with the priority established by executive management — and that priority is, business operations have priority over assurances.

Logical access controls consist of the software programs on an information system that controls access to that system.[1] Just as physical access controls are vulnerable to penetration, so are the software programs used to control logical access to information. Generally, the access control software requires that a user enter some sort of identification. That identification may be a group identification name or number, or one specific to that user. Once entered, a password is generally required. That password may be a shared password or one specific to that individual.

In this day and age, it is surprising that not all systems control access through a unique, individual user access control identification number or name and password. If such a process were in place, it violates another basic concept of IAs through access and that is individual accountability.

6.3.2   Individual Accountability

Individual accountability simply means that each individual who has access to an information system has a unique identification number or name and also a password known only to that individual – or some other way of determining the specific individual taking action, e.g. biometric devices. This assists in identifying

---

[1] The term "system" includes standalone (non-networked systems), networks to include intranets and any Internet or other global network interfaces.

system users in the event when there is a violation of the IA policies, procedures or processes.

It is true that such a system is vulnerable as someone's identification and password can be compromised. Thus, another individual would be in a position to "masquerade" as the authorised user. Remember that the computer through its access control software allows access to information by *assuming* that the individual entering a correct user name or other identification and a correct password, assumed to be known only by the authorised user, is in fact that authorised user.

There are numerous, free, software programs available from various sources, e.g. Internet Websites, which can be implemented to do a mass attack against a system to determine the identification and password used by particular users. So, this process is far from secure. However, it is not only one of the first lines of defences in an IA program, but also it is often the mainstay and only line of defence. This is a true but sad commentary on the state of IA efforts in this modern, information-dependent and information-based world.

One must understand that each of these methods act as a "filter" which allows the presumed authorised users' access to systems and information. Thus, it helps assure such things as the confidentiality, integrity and availability of information, while at the same time filtering out and providing physical and logical barriers to the less sophisticated unauthorised users' access attempts.

6.3.3   Audit Trails

The last basic concept to discuss is the use of audit trails. The audit trails are nothing more than historical records of events that have already occurred. They do not help assure any information or information systems protection or defences. Their sole purpose from an IA standpoint is to provide a historical record of events that can be re-enacted or tracked to assist in identifying events that had occurred which compromised in some way sensitive information or the information systems.

Audit trail records consist of such things as manual logs of individuals who entered a facility or area, video recordings from closed circuit television cameras and automated logs maintained by the systems themselves. In addition, there are many software products on the market that assist in maintaining audit trails of events on the systems that track both programs (e.g. batch programs implemented and running) and users' activities.

Often automated audit trail records are kept to a minimum as many information technology (IT) staffs say that it impedes efficient processing of information. It is not surprising to find that the automated audit trail records keeping have been completely turned off by some IT staffs.

As a minimum, most automated audit trail records track individual users through their identification name or number. The use of the individual and unique password by a user, as noted earlier, is considered the unique identifier that ties the user to the activities on the systems as noted by the audit trail records or logs. Often, the logs only identify a user as accessing a specific system at a specific time and date. Many access control programs have audit trail records that can record a user's activities to different degrees of granularity, including monitoring each keystroke made by a user.

6.4   The Information Value Model

Information has value and to determine that value, various models have been developed. They have not been a resounding success; however, the basic philosophy of information value (IV), as it relates to time, must be discussed as a premise to IAs. This is because an IA is only required when information has some value. Information without value need not be protected or defended as it is of little importance to the holder of the information.

6.4.1   Valuing Information

The basic premise is that certain information and information systems have value. The value of information systems varies over time and is depreciated on the accounting books of the corporation. However, from an IA viewpoint, the value of information systems does not depreciate since it is obviously vital to storing, processing and transmitting the corporation's or government agency's information. However, the main emphasis here is on the value of the information processed, stored or transmitted by the corporate information systems.

All information, regardless of its value, is time-sensitive and time-dependent. In other words, information has value for only a certain period. For example, information relative to a new, unique corporate widget must be highly protected, and that includes its related electronic drawings, diagrams, processes, etc. However, once the new widget is announced to the public, complete with photographs of the widget, selling price, etc., much of the protected information no longer needs protection.

That information which once required protection to maintain the secrecy of the corporation's new widget can now be eliminated. This will obviously save money for the corporation because information protection is expensive when correctly done. Those costs must be reduced or eliminated as soon as possible. It is the constant task of those responsible for the corporation's IA program to continuously look for methods to accomplish this objective.

6.4.2   How to Determine the Value of Corporate Information

Determining the value of a corporation's information is a very important task but is very seldom done with any systematic, logical approach by any corporation. However, in order to provide a cost-effective IA program, this task should be undertaken. The sophistication of such a process must be weighed against the costs and benefits to the corporation.

The consequences of not properly establishing a value and then classifying the information accordingly could lead to over-protection that is costly, or under-protection that could lead to the loss of that information, thus profits and/or the competitive edge.

To determine the value of information, the IA professionals must first understand what is meant by information and what is meant by value. The IA professionals must also know how to properly categorise and classify the information; and what guidelines are set forth by the corporation for determining the value and subsequently the protection requirements for that information. In addition, how the corporation perceives the information and its value is crucial to classifying it.[2]

Remember that if the information has value, it must be protected; protection is expensive. One should only protect that information which:

- Requires protection
- Only in the manner necessary based on the value of that information
- Only for the period required

6.4.3   The Value of Information

One might ask, "Does all the information of a corporation or government agency have value?" If you were asked that question, what would be your response? The follow-on question would be, "What information does *not* have value?" Is it that information which the receiver of the information determines has no value? When does the originator of the information say so? Who determines if information has value?

These are questions that the IA professionals must ask – and answer – before trying to establish a process to set a value to any information. As you read through this material, think about the information where you work, how it is protected, why it is protected in the manner it is being protected, etc.

The originator of the information should determine its value based on a standard corporate criterion. People who rely on access to specific information place a value on that information. This value may be different from the one stated by the originator of that information. That is understandable since not only is the value of information time-dependent, but it is also dependent on the perceptions and needs of its holder. The following example is provided:

It may be the task of an engineer to design a specific part. After the part is designed for a highly advanced widget, it is given a high protection value due to the need to keep it away from the corporate competitors. However, once that part is designed, classified as "corporate proprietary" and transmitted to a corporate database, it is no longer of importance to the engineer who then goes on to the next assigned task. However, that part design now being accessed by a person responsible for making the mould for that part is of utmost importance.

---

[2] In the context used here, the term "classify" has nothing to do with classification as it relates to national security information such as Confidential, Secret, and Top Secret, but only as a way of categorising information based on its value.

For without that information, that person could not accomplish the task of making the mould. In addition, its protection from an overall corporate viewpoint is still required at the highest level to assist in protecting it from the corporation's competitors. However, once the widget is produced, marketed and sold, the part design is not important, as reverse engineering the product is a very simple process. So the drawing for that part is no longer information worth protecting. Furthermore, those involved in the initial development of the part also no longer consider that information worthy of protection. However, the corporation may still provide some level of protection so that the corporation's competitors must expend at least some effort in making the same part for their competitive product.

Ordinarily, the originator should determine the value of the information, and that person categorises or classifies that information, usually in accordance with the established corporate guidelines. This may be a function of an IA organisation or a function of the corporation's executive management who, based on legal guidance, may establish guidelines since any compromise of that information may result in legal action by the corporation.

Generally, the types of information which have value to the corporation and which require protection include all forms and types of the following:

* Financial
* Scientific
* Technical
* Economic
* Engineering

The information includes but is not limited to data, plans, tools, mechanisms, compounds, formulas, designs, prototypes, processes, procedures, programs, codes or commercial strategies, whether tangible or intangible, and whether stored, compiled or memorialised physically, electronically, graphically, photographically or in writing.

6.5   Three Basic Categories of Information

Although there are no global or national business standards that are used to categorise the sensitivity and value of information, information can logically be categorised into three types:

* Personal, private information
* National security (both classified and unclassified) information[3]
* Business information.

6.5.1   Personal, Private Information

Personal, private information is not only an individual matter, but also a matter for the government agencies and corporations. A person may want to keep private

---

[3] National security classified information will be addressed in Chapter 9.

information about themselves such as their age, weight, address, cellular phone number, salary and their likes and dislikes.

While at the same time many countries have laws that protect information under some type of "privacy act", in businesses and government agencies it is a matter of policy to safeguard certain information about an employee such as their age, address, salary, etc. Failure to do so may have serious consequences since the corporation may be liable for failing to safeguard that private, personal information. Such liabilities can result in a poor public relations image for the corporation as well as significant monetary losses as established by the fines directed against the corporation by the courts.

Although the information is personal to the individual, others may require that information, but at the same time, they have an obligation to protect that information because it is considered to have value. As more and more information is being stored in massive databases and accessed from every part of the globe, this issue will take on increased significance and will play a major role in the arena of IA.

6.5.2 Business Information

Business information also requires protection based on its value. This information is sometimes identified in one or more of the following categories:

* Company confidential
* Company internal use only
* Company private
* Company sensitive
* Company proprietary
* Company trade secret

The number of categories used will vary within each corporation, however, the less the categories, the lesser will be the problems in classifying information and also, possibly, less problems in the granularity of protection required. Again, something that must always be considered – the cost versus the benefits of protection. The corporation's information must be protected because it has value to the corporation.

The key point to remember is that *the degree of protection required is dependent on the value of the information to the holder of that information during a specific period of time.*

The following are examples of various types of valuable information:
Types of company internal use only information:

* Not generally known outside the corporation
* Not generally known through product inspection
* Possibly useful to a competitor
* Provide some business advantage to competitors

Examples are corporation telephone books, corporation policies and procedures and corporation organisational charts.

Types of company private information:

- Technical or financial aspects of the corporation
- Indicates corporation's future direction
- Describes portions of the corporate business not known by the public
- Provides a competitive edge
- Identifies personal information of employees

Examples are personnel medical records, salary information, cost data, short-term marketing plans and dates for unannounced events.

- Types of company sensitive information:
- Provides significant competitive advantage
- Could cause serious damage to the corporation if released to the public or competitors
- Reveals long-term corporate direction

Examples are critical corporate technologies; critical engineering processes and critical cost data.

6.6   Determining Information Value Considerations

Based on an understanding of information, its value and some practical and philosophical thoughts on the topic as stated earlier, the IA professionals must have some sense of what must be considered when determining the value of information.

When determining the value of information, the IA professionals must determine what it costs to produce that information. Also, to be considered is the cost in terms of damages caused to the corporation if it were to be released outside protected channels, e.g. to the competitors. Additional consideration must be given to the cost of maintaining and protecting that information. How these factors are combined determine the value of the information. One must also remember to factor-in the time element.

There are two basic assumptions to consider in determining the value of information:

All information costs some type of resource(s) to produce, e.g. money, hours and use of equipment.
Not all information can cause damage if released outside protected channels.

If the information costs resources of any kind to produce (and all information does) and no damage is done if released, you must consider, "Does it still have sufficient value to require that it be protected?"

Since the time factor is a key element in determining the value of information and cannot be over-emphasised, let us look at a simple example where information is not time dependent, or is it? There is a corporate picnic to take place on

22 August 2001. What is the value of the information before, on, or after that date? Does the information have value? To whom? When?

If you are looking forward to the corporation's annual picnic, as was your family, the information as to when and where it was to take place had some value to you. Supposing you found out about it the day after it happened. Your family was disappointed, they were mad at you for not knowing, you felt bad, etc. However, to the corporation that information had no value vis-à-vis competitive advantage. However, you are not receiving that information caused you to be disgruntled and you blamed the corporation for your latest family fights. Based on that, you decided to slow down productivity for a week.

This is a simple illustration but indicates the value of information depending on who has and who does not have that information as well as the time element. It also shows that what appears to be information not worth a second thought may have repercussions costing more than the value of the information.

The following is another example: a new, secret, revolutionary widget built to compete in a very competitive marketplace is to enter the market on 1 January 2001. What is the value of that information on 2 January 2001?

Again, to stress the point, one must consider the cost to produce the information and the damage done if that information were released. If it costs to produce and can cause damage if released, it must be protected. If it costs to produce but cannot cause damage if released, then why should one protect it?

The IA professional must always be sensitive to the dissemination process. Information, to have value, to be useful, must get to the right people at the right time. An IA program can impede that process with adverse impact on the competitive edge of a corporation.

6.6.1   Questions to Ask When Considering Information Value

While determining the value of corporate information, the IA professional should, as a minimum, ask the following questions:

- How much does it cost to produce?
- How much does it cost to replace?
- What would happen if I no longer had that information?
- What would happen if my closest competitor had that information?
- Is protection of the information required by law and if so, what would happen if I did not protect it?

The value of information is one of the most important aspects of IA. The late US Admiral Grace Murray Hopper once said, "*Some day on the corporate balance sheet there will be an entry which reads 'Information'; for in most cases the information is more valuable than the hardware which processes it.*" Yes, we all know that we need information, automated information stored, processed and transmitted by information systems in order to function in our information environment. Thus, it stands to reason that information has value, but how much value? When is it valuable? To whom? That is what an IA program should determine when establishing information protection and defence processes.

6.7   Another View of Information Valuation

The following discussion centres on another's perspective of IV:[4] Headlines and titles tell us that we are in the Information Age, using the Information Highway and part of a knowledge-based economy. Information must be important. The number one issue facing corporations and government agencies is how to value information beyond subjective estimates, changing it from an intangible to a tangible asset. This leads directly to an approach for protecting information because certain types of information are worth more than others. Value or per-ceived value drives resource allocation. But if information is important, why there are no national accounting standards for it? How should a corporation value information? Can there be more than one value? What information is critical enough to require deadly force by law-enforcement or the military? Articles have been published on the value of information by accountants, econ-omists, psychologists, artificial intelligence researchers, knowledge manage-ment experts and others. However, quantitative approaches still elude us. Unless a national standard is established, information will have simultaneous multiple values.

6.7.1   The Information Environment

The information environment is composed of several interrelated areas. Information moves across information infrastructures to support information-based processes. Information as used here means data, information, knowledge and wisdom – the classic hierarchy. No doubt horrific to purists, there is no one good word to describe all four concepts together. All four exist within the cor-poration. Rather than argue about definitions and which is more important, the issue is how to value the intangibility of information, be it data, information, knowledge or wisdom. At any given time, one could be of greater value than the others. The tacit knowledge of employees is the most difficult resource to quan-tify and value.

Information infrastructure is the media within which we store, process and transmit information. Examples are people, computers, fibre optic cable, lasers, telephones and satellites. Examples of information-based processes are the established ways to obtain and exchange information. This includes people to people (e.g. telephone conversations and office meetings), e-commerce/e-data interchange (EC/EDI), data mining, batch processing and surfing the Web.

---

[4] The authors are grateful to Perry Luzwick, Logicon, who provided his views of IV.

6.7.2   *Value of Information*

The corporation must take proactive measures to protect business operations and the bottom line. The corporation could self-insure – in other words eat a loss. Such a decision needs to be made in the presence of hard facts, not a gut feeling. Does the corporation and its individual business units know how much profit they make per year? Per quarter? Per month? Per day? Per hour? Per minute? Is the information protected? How do you know the information has not been stolen or altered? If transactions at Citibank cannot be accomplished, business worth tens of millions of dollars can be lost, and that does not count the ill will of customers and permanent loss of future business to competitors.

How does a corporation know what information to acquire, retain, protect and discard? Laws and practices cover some and product line and consumer base others. What information is more valuable? It depends on the time and context sensitivities of the situation. The corporation's business units produce information elements. At any given time, it is possible to determine the importance of specific information. In the absence of national accounting standards for information as a tangible asset, qualitative approaches are necessary.

From a contextual perspective, the information is of either tactical, operational or strategic nature. From a time perspective, the information is either routine, important or critical. Keeping the categories to a small number is essential, otherwise subjectivity will creep in and result in a rating that is either under- or over-inflated. At any given time, selecting an information element, its contextual perspective and its time perspective will result in the perceived value of that information element. The way to differentiate between identical ratings is to add weighting to the information elements. That unique information in time and context will then be rated relative to other information elements. Does this produce a tangible pound figure? No. Does it help to value intangibles? Absolutely. Can there be more than one perceived values at the same time? Possibly, when two or more people view the contextual and time perspectives differently. A policy can be written to achieve common understanding.

A valuation of information would help prosecutors in computer crime cases. The jury must be convinced there was a loss. What is information in a database worth? A simple approach is that it took people (their compensation) and IT assets to acquire, process, store and maintain.

6.8   The Need-To-Know Model

The need-to-know (NTK) model has been in use long before the invention of computers and probably as long as information itself has been around. The military establishments and governments of nation-states have used the NTK philosophy for hundreds of years in order to protect national security.

This model is based on the philosophy that no information is provided to anyone in any form unless there is a need to have that information in order to complete some assigned task. In order to determine if someone meets the criteria for access to a certain NTK information, a process based on policies and procedures should be formerly established to determine who requires access to what information, and when, in order to accomplish his assigned tasks.

Let us look at an example of how this model is used in a corporation. A corporation has a policy in place, which states that information designated as sensitive must be accessed and used only by those personnel who have an NTK for that information in order for them to do their assigned jobs. Furthermore, the corporation delegated down to its mid-level managers the task of validating that NTK for employees in their respective organisations. The managers have done so by evaluating what specific, corporate sensitive information each employee required access to in order to accomplish their assigned tasks. This was done by evaluating what each person did; validating their job descriptions; and then designating those positions as sensitive. Thus, anyone in a position designated as sensitive would require access to some sensitive information.

However, that was just the beginning. Once the sensitive positions were identified, the specific type of sensitive information for which they required access was also identified. Obviously, no such process is foolproof, however, it is another IA filter used to assist in protecting sensitive information.

So, for example, a person in the accounts payable department would require access to the sensitive information contained in a database listing all the suppliers, their charges and payments to them. Someone in the human resources department, in a sensitive position, would have access to personnel records showing an individual's private information such as salary, home telephone number and the like. However, neither employee would have an NTK for other's information.

It is then up to the IA professionals in co-operation with the IT staff to develop an IA architecture and install a system to ensure that those individuals in sensitive positions had access to the information they needed. However, they also must ensure that no other sensitive information not needed by them to perform their assigned tasks could be accessed.

The NTK model is not easy to implement by any means. It grows in complexity as the corporation, number of employees, databases and networks grow. For efficiency purposes, sensitive information of all types is generally kept on the same networks and on large databases. Compartmenting that information on an NTK basis is a very complex and dynamic undertaking. One must first, of course, identify the information that is considered sensitive, and how much of it is time-dependent, as discussed earlier. Thus, although a very logical and easy model to discuss, it is a very complex model to implement and with many dependencies. However, implementing at least a broad and somewhat general application of such a model is necessary if one is to provide IAs.

6.9   The Confidentiality-Integrity-Availability Model

The confidentiality-integrity-availability model was developed decades ago. Neither the US Central Intelligence Agency did not develop it nor did it have anything to do with its development. As to whom first thought of the term has not been determined. Suffice it to say, it is an easy term to remember if you remember the acronym. It is also one of the basic models of IA. This model obviously has three components:

Confidentiality
Integrity
Availability

6.9.1   Confidentiality

Confidential information means information that is "*private or secret carried out or revealed in the expectations that anything done or revealed will be kept private...for a select group not available to the public, e.g. because it is commercially or industrially sensitive or concerns matters of national security....*"[5] ISO17799 defines confidentiality as "*ensuring that information is accessible only to those authorised to have access.*"

Confidential information is only given on a NTK basis. Using this model as a subset of IA means that the goal is for obtaining reasonable assurance that the information stored, processed or transmitted by an information system will not be revealed to anyone who has not been identified as authorised to receive that information.

6.9.2   Integrity

As it relates to information, integrity means that the information is adhering to "*professional standards...the state of being complete or undivided...sound or undamaged.*"[6] ISO17799 defines Integrity as "*safeguarding the accuracy and completeness of information and processing methods.*" Thus, there is some reasonable assurance that the information is accurate and can be relied on to be factual and not modified or otherwise changed without going through a formal process to ensure that integrity is maintained.

6.9.3   Availability

Availability means that one is assured, with reasonable confidence and certainty, that the information and the information systems are always available when

---

[5] *Encarta World English Dictionary*; St. Martin's Press: New York, 1999, p.380.
[6] Ibid. p. 933.

needed. ISO17799 defines availability as *"ensuring that authorised users have access to information and associated assets when required."*

In summary, one can see the importance of this model as it relates to IA. In fact, it is the baseline, the heart of any IA process, system or program. The model when successfully implemented ensures that the information is accurate and can be relied on to be available only to those who need that information when it is needed.

6.10   The Protect-Detect-React-Deter Model

The protect-detect-react-deter (PDRD) model has just recently been formalised into a working model. Bits and pieces of it have been around since the inception of information systems security but not as a formal concept. However, in the past, and especially since the advent of the IA concept, IA professionals have begun more and more to look at the entire spectrum of IAs as one complete system or process.

The PDRD is a true system, a holistic approach to the issue of IAs. Let us dissect this model into its four basic components and see how they work and interact.

6.10.1   Protect

When discussing protection and defence of information, one must be sure to define exactly what is meant. For example, does protection include physical safeguards of the information systems themselves? The hardcopy output of the information stored, processed and transmitted by those systems? The answer is yes, if you want it to. After all, you can use this model in any way that logically suits your information environment. However, we will use it here to look only at the protection of the automated information. The logic is this: if the systems are destroyed by fire, flood, earthquakes or some other disasters, and assuming adequate back-up of the files as part of a disaster recovery-contingency planning program, then one can say that the physical destruction of the hardware or even software programs is not an issue.

So in this case, protection, as stated earlier in this book, deals with the issues of ensuring the integrity, reliability, etc. of information. Hardcopy is not an issue in this model as once it has been printed; it is a matter of physical security of the printed material.

6.10.2   Detect

Detection is an interesting and somewhat new aspect of IAs. Yes, detecting unauthorised access – attackers – has been, generally speaking, the reason why audit trail records of systems were to be reviewed. However, that is always after the fact. The detection aspect of IAs is now widely not considered a lone aspect of IA but labelled as "intrusion detection", and should be viewed in real-time to be truly useful.

What is intrusion detection? Quite simply, an intruder is a person attempting to gain unauthorised access, or has gained unauthorised access, to an information system and/or information residing on the system. Intrusion detection is the ability to detect the intruder, e.g. through the unauthorised actions of the intruder. This is obviously important because:

- Information may be stolen
- Information may be deleted
- Misinformation may be entered
- Systems may be compromised
- Use of the systems may be denied

Over the last several years, intrusion detection software has become more sophisticated in nature and in its ability to identify attacks. However, as of this date, it is not as good at the global attackers harassing our information systems. As with most IA-related products, it is always one step behind the attackers' latest techniques.

To understand intrusion detection as part of this model or any model, one must be able to profile the potential intruders, their methods, the software programs they use and the like. These intruders may be anyone and include:

- Computer and telecommunications fraudsters
- Organised crime
- White-collar workers
- Drug dealers
- People in debt
- People wanting revenge
- Greedy people
- Hackers, crackers, phreakers
- Economic and industrial espionage agents
- Disgruntled and ex-employees
- Vendors/suppliers
- Customers
- Business partners
- Military info warriors
- Political activists
- Animal rights activists
- Competitors
- Foreign government agents
- Subcontractors
- Terrorists
- Contractors, e.g. maintenance personnel
- Outside auditors
- Consultants
- Anyone under the right circumstances

All that is needed is a target, motive, opportunity and the skills to be success-ful. The intruders have become more prevalent because of:

- More distributed computing environment
- More standardised systems and programs
- More networking nationally and internationally
- Blurring of computers and telecommunication systems
- Remote systems maintenance
- Internet
- Electronic Commerce
- General standardisation, e.g. UNIX and Windows NT
- UNIX, NT and other platforms have known vulnerabilities
- More attackers.

The basic intruder approach is to:

- Research target organisation
- Gather documentation
- Systematic dial-up scanning, website attacks and penetrations or any number of methods depending on their target
- Once inside, set up a secure foothold
- Erase evidence of intrusion in audit logs
- Attack internal systems
- Search for target system

The intrusion detection model does not include such non-penetration attempt techniques as "dumpster diving" or scavenging (stealing document); social engi-neering, e.g. intimidation, manipulation; and the "more human" techniques used to gather information. It is based on the use of software programs and methods.

6.10.3   Case Example – Do not Rush to Judgement

When one is concerned with what appears to be attempted or actual unautho-rised access, how does one know it is some form of malicious attack that adversely impacts IAs? One must consider the affects of human error and mis-configuration of systems may have on the issue. To illustrate the point, the fol-lowing actual event is described:

"A large international corporation called in an information systems security con-sultant and explained that they were under attack by their competitor who was head-quartered in another country. They were ready to file a lawsuit against that competitor who appeared to be accessing their systems without authorisation and possibly also performing a denial of service attack against them. Furthermore, the attack appeared to be coming through a third party in a third country in an apparent attempt to hide the origin of the attacks. This of course is not unusual and was con-sidered a further indication of the covert attacks by the competitor. The consultant

travelled to both other countries, talked to law enforcement authorities on the best course of action. The consultant also discussed the matter with the apparently unwitting third party whose systems were being used as the conduit for the attacks. While collecting audit trail evidence and conducting detailed analysis of the third party's system configuration, it was determined that the third party had a business relationship and was networked with both parties. It was further determined that the systems were mis-configured in such a manner as to cause the problems being experienced. Thus, it was not an attack at all! Can you imagine the consequences of a lawsuit if the 'victim' corporation had hastily filed the lawsuit and the subsequent causes of the attacks were determined?"

6.10.4   React

How one reacts to attacks is based primarily on the corporate culture, which is generally spelled out in the corporate policy on IA and the like. Is the corporate culture one of a "campus atmosphere" where one is more open? Is the culture a more closed environment with more emphasis on protecting the information assets of the corporation as a high priority in order to protect its competitive edge in a volatile and globally competitive marketplace? How one should react then should be determined ahead of time and integrated into the corporate culture, or at least with the corporate culture in mind.

Reaction may be based on the development of an aggressive defence. Such a defence, however, should still be based on IA processes as its first line of defence.

Sometimes the best defence is an aggressive offence, once the attackers have been identified "beyond the shadow of a doubt". However, this may be dangerous and in fact a violation of law. The wrong approach may lead to attacking the wrong site as was possible in the case stated above. There are serious ramifications with the philosophy that "the best defence is a good offence".

As part of reacting, the first step may be to report anomalies occurring on discrete components (sub-networks) of the private or public network to a corporate "centralised analysis centre". If the major components of this model are successfully installed, it is possible to achieve awareness of these anomalies on a grand scale. Then when processed, this data may yield a practical warning system for attacks. Such a model entails correlation of the anomalies, disturbances, outages and penetrations.

One may react by examination of the resulting database for interdependencies (overlaps), as well as gaps in order that the IA professional can summarise what was known and inventory what was not known. The utilisation of the resulting database can then be used to determine and document baseline trends, expected behaviours and deviations from the baseline. Then the IA professional can correlate the exception or trend data between the various sub-nets.

This approach offers the benefits of providing a holistic perspective; may be combined with similar data from others; may be used as input for an inductive process that would combine this data with knowledge of intruders as a means of investigating incidents.

6.10.5   Deter

Deterrence is probably one of the most difficult components of this model. If the model thus far has been properly implemented and aggressively maintained, e.g. kept current at all times, then one may deter attacks by using one or more of the following methods:

- The corporation maintains a low profile (not usually practical if one is to sell products on a national or global scale, e.g. one must aggressively advertise).
- The corporation has a publicly known policy of aggressively pursuing and supporting prosecution of attackers.
- The corporation implements an IA program based on the multiple models described in this chapter and thus makes it too time consuming and difficult for an attacker to penetrate the system.

6.10.6   Questions and Some Answers to Think About

When developing an IA program, the IA professionals should consider the following:

- *Question*: How do you know you are actually under attack and not the victim of mis-configured systems? *Answer*: You may not know until it is too late; you may never know; you may know, but can't stop it.
- *Question*: What are the warning signs of potential or actual attacks? *Answer*: There may not be any.
- *Question*: Is it possible to know of pending attacks? *Answer*: Yes. No. Maybe depending on conditions.
- *Question*: What can you do to set up an "imminent" attack warning system? *Answer*: Base it on history; latest techniques identified in CERTs; on target visibility; on your defences; on your countermeasures; on your use of technology; and on vendor products.
- *Question*: What is the basis for deploying intrusion detection to assist in countering the attacks? *Answer*: What is normal activity? What is abnormal? Compare activity against known attack methods; establish countermeasures; and one must have, as a minimum, an IA policy, procedures, and awareness program.
- *Question*: What must be considered when deploying the intrusion detection system and processes? *Answer*: Any available tools should be adapted to your unique environment. The intrusion detection process must always be secure, operating and "foolproof". It must detect all anomalies and misuse; must have audit-based systems for history; must have real-time monitoring and warnings; provide for immediate action based on each unique attack; and one must know what to do if attacked.
- *Question*: Any other things to consider? *Answer*: Audit entry ports especially to critical areas; prioritise processes, shutdown others; isolate the problem; and establish alternate routing paths. One can never have too many intrusion detection "bells and whistles".

6.11   IA Success Considerations

To be successful, the IA professional, as a minimum, should:

- Develop and maintain a threat toolkit containing strategies, software, tactics, tools and methodologies used to attack systems
- Continuously maintain a current IA toolkit and methodologies that can defend information systems against attacks
- Model the capabilities of the potential intruders against real-time defences
- Collect information related to the corporation's information systems' vulnerabilities
- Establish, implement and maintain an aggressive IA program

6.12   Summary

The primary purpose of an IA is to minimise the probability of an IA vulnerability, minimise the damage if an attack occurred and provide a method to quickly recover in the event of a successful attack. There are many models that can be used to assist in that endeavour. All of them have some value and should be considered for integrating into a corporate IA program. The IA professional must also consider the cost and benefits of such implementations.

7

The Role of Policy in Information Assurance

Information assurance (IA) is based on concepts of confidentiality, integrity and availability. The role of policy in IA is to support these concepts in the content of an organisation's computer-networked environment.

7.1 Introduction

The term policy can be used to cover a multitude of sins; it can also be used to mean guidelines and best practice. For the purpose of this book the term policy is defined as:

"A written principle or rule to guide decision-making."

Within the context of information assurance (IA), a policy is used to guide and inform an individual. It is also used to define allowed and disallowed actions. For example, an acceptable usage policy (AUP) might define that the use of peer-to-peer file sharing is allowed on the network. A policy can function at the technical, socio-technical and social levels.

At the technical level, a policy will function to define the specification and configuration of a piece of hardware/software. For example, an organisation might have a standard policy governing the precise specification of the standard workstations that a user would normally use. This specification could even be vendor specific.

At the socio-technical level, a policy functions to govern the behaviour of an individual when interacting with a computer system. An AUP can be seen as a socio-technical policy as it defines how a user might use an organisation's IT infrastructure.

At the social level, the policy can function to define a level of technical competence for the system administrator or the rules governing the disclosure of information to a third party.

7.2 A Model of Policy Development

An IA policy needs to be seen as a living, breathing document that evolves and changes over time in response to various social and technical stimuli. Figure 7.1

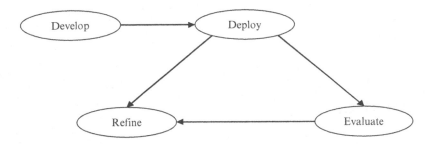

FIGURE 7.1. A Model of Policy Development

depicts a simple model of processes involved in developing and deploying a policy. The IA standards, such as BS7799 and ISO17799, view a security policy as a living document that has to be supported and championed at board level within an organisation in order for it to be effective.

Before the initial development of a security policy can begin, a set of requirements must be defined that the policy is required to meet. In addition, the security policy must also have a defined champion whose responsibility is to fight for the policy. Once a set of security requirements have been defined and the security policy developed, it must be deployed within an organisation. The process of deployment will involve an element of education of the user-base of the policy.

Once a policy has been deployed, its performance must be evaluated. As a part of the development process, a clear set of evaluation criteria and methods must be defined. The evaluation criteria should be:

- *Simple*: The criteria should be as simple as possible so as to ensure that a measurement can be taken.
- *Measurable*: The criteria should be specified in units that can be measured.
- *Accurate*: The criteria should be an accurate representation of the requirements that the policy is attempting to achieve.
- *Relevant*: The criteria should reflect the requirements that the policy is attempting to achieve.
- *Timely*: Within a certain time frame it should be possible to take a measurement.

Once the policy has been evaluated, the organisation needs to reflect on the policy and answer questions such as: (a) Is it still relevant to the organisation, (b) Does it still meet its requirements and (c) Have the requirements changed. Once these questions have been answered, the organisation can create a new security policy and start the process all over again.

7.3 Types of IA Policies

Within the context of IA there are a number of policies that an organisation can develop and deploy, for example:

- *Acceptable encryption policy*: Defines requirements for encryption algorithms used within the organisation
- *Acceptable use policy*: Defines acceptable use of equipment and computing services, and the appropriate employee security measures to protect the organisation's corporate resources and proprietary information
- *Analog/ISDN line policy*: Defines standards for the use of analog/ISDN lines for Fax sending and receiving and for connection to computers
- *Anti-virus process*: Defines guidelines for effectively reducing the threat of computer viruses on the organisation's network
- *Application service provider (ASP) policy*: Defines minimum-security criteria that an ASP must execute in order to be considered for use on a project by the organisation
- *ASP standards*: Outlines the minimum-security standards for the ASP. This policy is referred to in the ASP policy above
- *Acquisition assessment policy*: Defines responsibilities regarding corporate acquisitions, and the minimum requirements of an acquisition assessment to be completed by the information security group.
- *Audit vulnerability scanning policy*: Defines the requirements and provides the authority for the information security team to conduct audits and risk assessments to ensure integrity of information/resources, to investigate incidents, to ensure conformance to security policies or to monitor user/system activity where appropriate
- *Automatically forwarded e-mail policy*: Documents the requirement that no e-mail will be automatically forwarded to an external destination without prior approval from the appropriate manager or director
- *Database credentials coding policy*: Defines requirements for securely storing and retrieving database usernames and passwords
- *Dial-in access policy*: Defines appropriate dial-in access and its use by authorised personnel
- *DMZ lab security policy*: Defines standards for all networks and equipment deployed in labs located in the "Demilitarised Zone" or external network segments
- *E-mail policy*: Defines standards to prevent tarnishing the public image of the organisation.
- *E-mail retention*: This policy is intended to help employees determine what information sent or received by e-mail should be retained and for how long
- *Ethics policy*: Defines the means to establish a culture of openness, trust and integrity in business practices
- *Extranet Policy*: Defines the requirement that third-party organisations requiring access to the organisation's networks must sign a third-party connection agreement.
- *Information sensitivity policy*: Defines the requirements for classifying and securing the organisation's information in a manner appropriate to its sensitivity level
- *Internal lab security policy*: Defines requirements for internal labs to ensure that confidential information and technologies are not compromised and that

production services and interests of the organisation are protected from lab activities

- *Internet demilitarised zone equipment policy*: Defines the standards to be met by all equipment owned and/or operated by the organisation that is located outside the organisation's Internet firewalls (the demilitarised zone or DMZ)
- *Lab anti-virus policy*: Defines requirements that must be met by all computers connected to the organisation's lab networks to ensure effective virus detection and prevention
- *Password protection policy*: Defines standards for creating, protecting and changing strong passwords
- *Remote access policy*: Defines standards for connecting to the organisation's network from any host or network external to the organisation
- *Risk assessment policy*: Defines the requirements and provides the authority to the information security team to identify, assess and remediate risks to the organisation's information infrastructure associated with conducting business
- *Router security policy*: Defines standards for minimal security configuration for routers and switches inside a production network or used in a production capacity
- *Security incident management/computer forensics*: Defines how a security incident is to be managed and who is to be involved. It also defines how the computer forensic investigation is to be undertaken. It will also define how the evidence is to be secured and handled
- *Server security policy*: Defines standards for minimal security configuration for servers inside the organisation's production network, or used in a production capacity
- *The third-party network connection agreement*: Defines the standards and requirements, including legal requirements, needed in order to interconnect a third-party organisation's network to the production network. This agreement must be signed by both the parties
- *VPN security policy*: Defines the requirements for Remote Access IPSec or L2TP Virtual Private Network (VPN) connections to the organisation's network
- *Wireless communication policy*: Defines standards for wireless systems used to connect to the organisation's networks

7.4   Acceptable Usage Policy

The role and function of an AUP is to define the behaviour that a user may and may not engage in. The best way to achieve this is to specify that all behaviour is unacceptable except, and then specify the allowable behaviour.

An AUP is the front line tool in helping an organisation secure its networks and IT infrastructure. Its purpose is to educate the users of an organisation's IT infrastructure on what behaviour is acceptable and what is not, and also how to report any security incident and obtain help. In general, an AUP should include the following sections:

- *Overview*: The role of the overview section of the AUP is to define at the strategic level, the role and function of the AUP and to set the AUP in the operational context of the day-to-day activities of the organisation.
- *Purpose*: This section states that the purpose of the AUP is to define acceptable usage of the organisation's IT infrastructure.
- *Scope*: This section defines the scope of the policy. In particular, it should define in measurable terms that who the policy does and does not apply to. It should have a clear statement that all activities not covered under "Policy" of the AUP are unacceptable.
- *Policy*: This section defines the various detail complements of the policy, such as:

  - E-mail and communication activities
  - The World Wide Web
  - Authentication
  - Access to system resources
  - Incident reporting and incident management
  - Information retention and disclosure
  - Intellectual property rights

- *Enforcement*: This section states that any employee found to have violated this policy may be subject to disciplinary action, up to and including termination of employment. It should also define the fact that the organisation reserves the right to monitor all network traffic/activity for lawful purposes.
- *Contact points*: The name, address, phone and e-mail address of a person responsible for the AUP.
- *Definitions*: A clear definition of the terms used in the AUP.
- *Revision history*: The dates and times when the AUP was re-issued.

7.5 Summary

The primary purpose of a security policy is to define a principal/rule for decision-making. Within the context of IA, the most important policy is that of the AUP. The role and function of the AUP is to define the role, responsibilities and duties of a user of an organisation's IT infrastructure.

Section 2

IA in the World of Corporations

This section begins with a discussion of the duties and responsibilities of the Corporate Security Officer (CSO) in Chapter 8. The CSO plays a major role in the information assurance (IA) since he is responsible for the protection of the corporation's assets that include information and information systems.

This discussion continues in Chapter 9 where the functions of the CSO are discussed in detail and shown how they are an integral part of a corporate IA program. This is followed by a look at the IA in the nation-state's national security sector in Chapter 10. In the national security sector, information protection and defence is taken much more seriously. After all, the fate of the nation-state is at stake if the IA is not properly addressed.

In Chapters 10 and 11, the need for a corporate position as Corporate Information Assurance Officer is discussed. Although many corporations have yet to recognise the need for such a position, a few corporations, e.g. Microsoft Corporation, and government agencies are taking the initiative to appoint people to such positions. These chapters discuss the basic qualifications, duties, responsibilities and possible organisational structures and functions of an IA person and supporting organisation.

Chapter 12 focuses on the IA functions that are required within a corporation's IA organizational structure in order for it to function and implement security. Finally, in Chapter 13 the methods and tools for incident management and response are discussed.

8

The Corporate Security Officer

The corporate security officer (CSO) is responsible for the protection of corporate assets. Since information and information systems are some of the most vital corporate assets, the duties of the CSO also include some aspects of their protection.

This chapter addresses the CSO's responsibilities for the protection of corporate assets and the CSO's relationship to an information assurance.

8.1 A Short History of the World of Corporate Security

Corporate security has come a long way over the years. Obviously, corporate security began when corporations began. However, before that there was always some form of security. By security we mean the job, tasks and profession of dealing with the protection of assets.[1]

Ever since the age of the cave dwellers – the hunter-gatherers – there was always someone who wanted to take what belonged to someone else and wanted to do so without providing just compensation to the property's owner. Therefore, there was always someone delegated with the task of guarding the property of the cave clan while others went out for their business of hunting, gathering and so forth.

As human beings evolved, so did their belongings (assets) (see Figure 8.1). Humans developed more and more goods and services over the years, but as did the ancestors of the world's miscreants, there were always some people who wanted to take the goods of others without paying a fair compensation to the owners. Figure 8.1 depicts the evolution of the human ages showing some examples of assets needing protection.

Since these owners were too busy making the goods and providing services or working some other jobs, they did not have time to spend their working hours

---

[1] For purposes of discussion, the term "corporate security" used in this book, except where otherwise noted, encompasses all entities, to include non-profit businesses, proprietary businesses and government agencies. So, when the term "corporate security" is used, think of it as a "short-cut" instead of mentioning each in the series of these other entities.

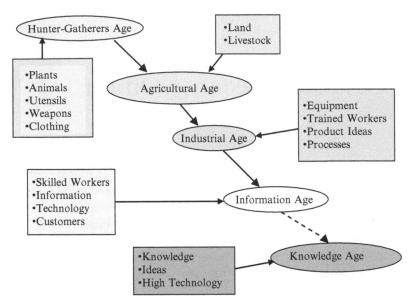

FIGURE 8.1. The Evolution of the Human Ages Showing Some Examples of Assets Needing Protection

watching their assets. They needed someone to guard their possessions for them – someone they could trust. In the beginning, it was family members and perhaps some other relatives, possibly friends. Later, some entrepreneurs probably saw a business opportunity here and decided to provide professional security services. So, as humans and what humans produced evolved, so did the profession of security – of assets protection.

What are these things we call "assets"? Whether you are talking about corporate assets or any assets, they can be categorised into the distinct groups of the following.

- People
- Information
- Physical things such as facilities

Some people look at information as a physical thing since generally it is "on or in" something like paper or disks, except, of course, when transmitted verbally. However, most of the times, information is considered as a separate entity, especially today due in part to its importance in our world.

As stated earlier, the duties and responsibilities of the corporate security department revolve around the protection of corporate assets. When one thinks of assets, remember that one generally thinks of people, information and things. People, of course, do not "belong" to a corporation; however, a corporation employs them. Thus, the corporation considers them to be valuable assets while information and things do belong to a corporation.

As assets, they all have value to the corporation. Thus, they must be protected from those who want to take the assets for their own use, destroy them, modify them or the like.

In addition, over the years, government agencies have become involved in assets protection from the viewpoint of laws and regulations. As more and more employees and management of a corporation are caught stealing corporate assets, executive management has become more and more personally responsible for the protection of the corporate assets. The reason is that the stockholders or other owners of a business actually own the assets. The executive management is responsible for protecting these assets as they go about making business decisions that affect these assets in one way or another – even profits are a form of assets.

For many decades, the security profession basically was one dominated by the function of physical security. The security personnel protected the physical property of their owners. Even personnel, company employees were protected from physical harm through the physical environment of the security and safety functions.

The security personnel were often thought of by management and other employees as those of less intelligence and/or those who could not get a "real" job. Furthermore, many were ex-military or ex-police personnel or those retired from the military, law enforcement or some other profession. They were thought of as ones looking for a "retirement job". Thus, the reputation of the security professional took a long time to improve and must still improve.

Over the decades, such things as global competition, high technology (i.e. technology based on the microprocessor) and more sophisticated threats to assets, their increased vulnerabilities and increased risks, have driven the need for more sophisticated assets protection. This, in turn, has caused the sophistication of the profession of security, of assets protection, to increase as well (see Figure 8.2).

The primary purpose of a corporate security officer (CSO) is to lead the corporation in the protection of corporate assets and manage the organisation and security staff who report to the CSO.

There are various titles given to people in such positions, such as Director of Security, Security Manager, Business Security Manager, Director of Industrial Security, even Vice President for Security, and so on. However, no matter what their title is, they have one basic responsibility and that is to protect the assets of their employer, e.g. the corporation. Figure 8.2 shows the basic corporate assets protection concept.

The corporate executive management establishes the CSO position and the corporate security budget. The CSO management is then charged with leading and the responsibility for protecting the assets of the corporation. As was alluded to above mentioned, the primary responsibility for the protection of any of the corporate assets generally meant that some form of physical security was required so the assets could not be stolen. The guards usually accomplished this form of assets protection. When it came to the protection of information, this was also the

FIGURE 8.2. The Basic Corporate Assets Protection Concept

case as even in centuries past, the guards were the ones who safeguarded and transported documents containing valuable information.

Gradually, we have seen that information has grown in importance as the corporations and nation-states entered deeper into the information age. However, what has really changed is the environment in which information flows. This, coupled with our almost complete dependency on information and information systems, and the expansion of responsibilities for their protection and defence, have made the task of protecting these valuable assets more complicated and difficult.

8.2   The Corporate Security Officer

It is the duty and responsibility of the CSO to provide the management leadership, based on the CSO's expertise, to cost-effectively safeguard the corporate assets. Therefore, the CSO has certain responsibilities vis-à-vis the information assurance (IA).

The reporting structure for the CSO varies based on the desires and decisions of the corporation's executive management. Some CSOs report directly to the corporate president or chief executive officer (CEO), others report to the head of the Legal Department or the head of the Human Resources Department. The CSO is accountable for providing direction for the corporation and overall responsibility for ensuring that all the security functions are performed in a manner that is cost-effective, meets employee, corporate and customers' needs/requirements and complies with corporate policies, applicable laws and regulations. Thus, the CSO is vested with the authority to carry out assigned duties in accordance with the responsibilities assigned and delegated by executive management through the corporate assets protection policy and/or the CSOs charter of duties and responsibilities.

The CSO is therefore responsible for overseeing the development and implementation of security processes that are designed to protect the people, property and *information* of the corporation.

8.3   Corporate Security Duties and Responsibilities

Although each corporation establishes its own unique form of assets protection and IA processes, the responsibilities identified later provide an example of those responsibilities as these relate to the CSO (see Figure 8.3).

- Develop methodologies and implement processes to evaluate current security requirements, and project future requirements on new business proposals and future contracts.
- Develop and oversee the implementation of a long range, corporate-wide security plan that details the efficient and cost-effective utilisation of security resources.
- Provide overall management direction for all security activities within the corporation focusing on centralised delivery on a corporate-wide basis, maximising the development of regional and corporate-shared services.
- Interface with the directors of environmental, health, safety, medical and others as appropriate to resolve issues involving the security of assets by the business sectors.
- Act to ensure that security processes are performed in full compliance with all customers, contractual and regulatory security requirements.
- Oversee the development of a corporate-wide information security program to protect corporate and customer information.
- Oversee the development of a corporate-wide crisis management program.
- Work with regional security managers to ensure the identification and implementation of common processes, shared services and best practices.
- Work with the sector managers of environmental, safety, health, medical and facilities to ensure an integration of functions to provide a productive and safe working environment for sector employees.
- Oversee the development and implementation of a corporate security measurement systemthat permits evaluation of the effectiveness of the security program, based on the factors of cost, customer satisfaction and compliance.
- Perform common managerial accountabilities and tasks in accordance with established corporate guidelines.
- Provide a physically secure environment for the corporate office to protect property, people and information.

- Direct the development and implementation of security processes that comply with government requirements.
- Provide guidance to corporate management regarding security policy and the interpretation, intent or application of security-related laws and regulations.
- Provide additional support to the corporate elements as required.
- Maintain active liaison with government security agencies in order to participate in the development of security policy, and represent the corporation in professional and industrial associations to influence the interpretation and implementation of that policy.
- Work with other corporate departments to develop and implement company policies and procedures that have important security implications for the company.
- Manage the development and implementation of an integrated, company-wide contingency plan.
- Ensure that the corporate crisis management room is maintained in a state of constant readiness, and provide the resources required to operate the room during actual emergencies and simulations.
- Develop, implement and maintain a company-wide security measurement system that permits evaluation of the effectiveness of each company element security program, the total company security programs and benchmarking with security programs of comparable companies.
- Liaisons with federal, state and local law enforcement, investigative and fire agencies.
- Chair the Corporate Security Council to develop a common company-wide approach to address security processes and problems.
- Develop corporate security policy and procedures to address the security functions.

Figure 8.3 depicts a sample security organisation for a corporation.

8.4   Corporate Security Support Tools and Processes

The CSO and the security organisational staff rely on the information technology (IT) organisation to provide the formation systems and applications that meet their needs. In that respect, the security organisation is no different than that of any other department within a corporation – they are internal customers of the IT professionals. However, the systems that they use are some of the most important, if not the most important, systems within a corporation for they have to do with the safety and security of the corporation. The following are a few examples.

- Today's corporations use badge readers to replace guards when controlling access to a facility, area or room. That system is computer based and relies on specific application software to properly work. That system, including the hardware, firmware, database of information and software, must meet an IA criterion in order to assure it works as required. If not, the system may allow unauthorised physical access to the facility, or it may not allow anyone access. In either case, it could adversely impact the system and the system must continuously work as expected.

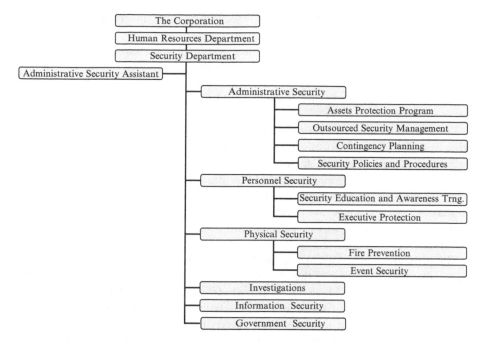

FIGURE 8.3. A Sample Security Organisation for a Corporation

- Often the CSO's responsibilities include fire protection and other emergency services. Fire alarms are based on microprocessors to set off an alarm and report that alarm to the fire department. Such a system must also meet specific IA criterion in order to safeguard the lives of the corporate employees and property of the corporation.
- The security awareness program processes and other functional processes are often automated, thus making the CSO's job more efficient and hopefully effective. However, in doing so, the IA requirements must be strictly enforced so as not to compromise security of the corporation, thus placing its assets at risk.

The more a CSO relies on information and information systems to assist in successfully accomplishing the assigned security tasks, the more that IA is a factor. It then stands to reason this need, and their assets protection role makes that profession a logical choice for the IA leadership role. However, many of them do not seem to be up to the challenge or do not want the added responsibility. Therefore, the IA leadership, as well as basic information systems security (InfoSec) within today's corporations is divided among the several professions of security, IT and auditors.

8.5   The More Things Change the More They Don't

The job of the security professional has grown from one of primarily physical security to more sophisticated protection requirements brought on by high technology and the dependency on information and information systems. However, we have now gone full circle.

Many of the security professionals have re-prioritised their assets protection tasks to once again emphasise the need for more sophisticated physical security. This change has been driven by the increased threats of terrorism. Terrorists are interested in the destruction of property and killing of people, the more the better as they see it.

Therefore, the security professional has been placed in a position of re-evaluating the physical security needs of the corporation so that the facilities and people are protected against such terrorist threats as car bombs, kidnappings of employees and other physically related threats. Keep in mind that this may also adversely impact the IA objectives of a corporation in that what may be blown up may include the corporate buildings housing the major information systems, backup power stations, as well as the employees with the technical expertise to maintain or even rebuild the systems.

The protection of information, the CSO's role in IA, continues to be part of their responsibilities, while the threats posed by terrorists to information at this time is rather low. Most of the threats from terrorists related to information come in the form of some Website destructions, use of viruses or worms. Even these information warfare (IW) threats have not been their weapons of choice. They primary use high technology to set off remote car bombs and communicate with each other via Websites and e-mails.

However, the day may not be that far off when the terrorists will realise that the way to truly damage a modern nation-state or corporations that are so dependent on information and information systems is to attack those systems. Before that happens, those involved in the protection of information-based assets must prepare their defences now so that terrorists' attacks in the future, whether they are physical and digital, will not be successful.

So, IAs, defences against sophisticated terrorists, are something that one must consider as a low to medium risk at this time, which may be elevated to a high risk in the not so distant future – of course, depending on your location, corporation and nation-state. If your corporation and employees are in the Middle East, your employees and information assets are, of course, more susceptible to the threats in that region.

8.6   Information Assurance: Whose Responsibility Is It?

Information permeates corporations at all levels. All employees in today's modern, information-dependent corporations depend on the information systems and the information that the systems store, display, process and transmit to successfully accomplish their assigned jobs. In addition, many professionals within a corporation are responsible for various aspects of IA, not the least of these is the CSO.

Like the InfoSec issues, there continues to be ongoing discussions centring on the issue of IA responsibilities. Since automated information permeates all aspects of a corporation, everyone shares some responsibility for IA, e.g. ensuring that the corporate sensitive information and information systems are protected and defended. There are very few arguments about that these days. However, in any bureaucracy, someone must take on the responsibility for providing the leadership and guidance for IA, but who? This is the crux of the issue. Should that responsibility fall on the IT people, the corporate security people, auditors or some guru of IA?

As for auditors assuming the IA leadership role, no, they are not qualified. Their entire profession is based on compliance and auditing for compliance. The IT personnel may have the InfoSec responsibility in some corporations, and since the IA incorporates InfoSec, perhaps they should provide the IA leadership? No, even their InfoSec responsibilities are a conflict of interest. How can one set the InfoSec policy and then audit objectively to ensure that he/she is adequate? One can see that InfoSec under the IT has not worked for decades. One just has to look at the successful attacks against corporate systems, their Web pages and the like.

In order to answer that question of the IA leadership, a short history of the evolution of InfoSec, which has led to IA, is necessary:

"IT personnel usually do not understand basic security principles, or true InfoSec. Their concept of security and InfoSec is usually a software program that controls access to the systems. Many corporations, however, still rely on IT personnel to resolve InfoSec problems. They do not have a choice. Who else is currently up to the challenge?"

8.7   Is IA a Corporate Security Responsibility?

The primary responsibility of the CSO is to protect the corporation's assets.[2] There is no doubt that the information and the information systems are some of the corporation's most valuable assets. Yet, other than physical security, the CSOs of today's modern corporations have generally not been involved in InfoSec, let alone IA.

Although many of modern CSOs have some understanding of InfoSec and IA, they do not have the knowledge, the skills and, in many cases, even the desire to deal with the InfoSec and now the problems associated with the IA, which is even more complex.

How did this happen? Why did this happen? Can anything be done by corporate security personnel to enhance the IA in a more effective and efficient way than is now the case? This is a topic of many debates between and within professions. As Dr Gerald L. Kovacich has said:

---

[2] If the reader is interested in learning more about the corporate security profession, see the American Society for Industrial Security's (an international association of security professionals) website at http://www.asisonline.org

"When modern-day automated information systems (AIS) were first developed, they were not user friendly. They occupied large rooms with air conditioners set at extremely low temperatures so the heat of the vacuum tubes would not melt the system. To turn the machine on, one needed a 'PhD in physics, electrical engineering and/or mathematics'. Besides, no one worried about security because the system only crunched numbers.

"All that was needed was a lock or a security officer at the door to the computer room with an access list noting who was authorised entrance into the computer room. The main security concern was someone stealing the hardware and because of its size, even that was unlikely.

"Gradually, over the last several decades, AIS became more powerful, cheaper, easier to use and more user-friendly. Nowadays, children are using AIS before they enter kindergarten.

"Unfortunately, security professionals are looking at AIS security as we did in the 1950s. We are still locking the door so no one steals the hardware. In today's technological world, however, hardware is not nearly as important as the information used by those computers.

"After more than 40 years of security neglect, an industrial security specialist today would have a difficult time wrestling the AIS security functions away from the information technology department, or others. IT people know the systems better than anyone. After all, they interact with them on a technical level on a daily basis. So is it wrong for the IT staff to be responsible for such things as InfoSec and information assurances?

"Let me answer that question with two questions: Would a farmer want a fox to guard his hen house? Are IT people trained security personnel?

"The answer to both questions is No! IT people have taken on the responsibility for information security and IA because security professionals did not. The IT staff's primary function is to operate the computers and provide the necessary support to enable systems' users to perform their assigned tasks.

"Protecting information requires a triad approach:

the primary responsibility for the protection of information and IA rests with the owner of that information;

it is up to the IT personnel to provide the necessary technical service and support; and

it is the responsibility of corporate security specialists to provide the leadership, policies, procedures, awareness training, inspections, and risk assessment for protecting the corporation's systems and information. In most corporations, the security specialist's portion is missing and they fall short of their responsibilities.

"Some security people say the process has worked well so far and why take on this extra and large burden? The situation has not been going along fine. IT people sometimes come to the security office and say that information in the systems are not secure, that they have problems on the systems affecting security of the information, or that they took off audit trails because it slowed down the system's performance over the weekend.

"It takes a security professional with that bit of paranoia and a questioning attitude to provide the overall security and information assurances required for those corporate assets.

"The function and responsibility of the corporation's security personnel is to protect corporate assets. AIS and the information are today's corporation's most valuable assets. It then follows that the security and IA is the security department's responsibility. Security personnel must take the leadership role. We owe it to our corporation, our profession, and ourselves it we are to truly consider ourselves security professionals."

It is acknowledged that a CSO has certain responsibilities for providing the leadership for protecting corporate assets; however, they are light-years away from assuming the professional responsibility for leading a corporate-wide IA program. However, they are now sharing some of that leadership role with the IT professionals. It is hoped that one day the InfoSec profession matures to an IA role that is led by one specialising in information protection and defences, regardless of the information environment, e.g. non-information systems environment.

8.8   Summary

Since automated information permeates all aspects of a corporation or government agency, everyone shares some responsibility for InfoSec and IA, e.g. ensuring that concept of confidentiality, integrity and availability are maintained. There are very few arguments about this. However, in any bureaucracy, someone must take on the responsibility for providing the leadership and guidance for IA, but who? This is the crux of the issue. Should that responsibility fall on the IT staff, the corporate security staff, internal auditors or others?

In today's corporate information environment, IA tasks seem to be shared between corporate security, IT and auditors. However, the leadership for IA seems to be lacking from a corporate, holistic viewpoint with several professions having some piecemeal responsibility.

The function and responsibility of the corporation's security personnel is to protect corporate assets. Information systems and the information that they store, process and transmit are some of the most valuable assets. It then follows that the IA is the security department's responsibility. Should security personnel take the IA leadership role? Yes. Will they? This is unlikely.

9

Corporate Security Functions

This chapter identifies and describes the basic security functions of a corporation's security organisation that is led by the corporate security officer. It includes a description and discussion of those functions that are an integral part of any corporation's assets protection program and also an information assurance (IA) program.

9.1   Introduction

The executive management of a corporation is ultimately responsible for the corporation's assets protection program (CAPP). They are accountable to the stockholders or other business owners for the protection of those assets. The corporate security officer (CSO) is the security professional on whom executive management relies to lead the assets protection efforts through the related security functions as well as has responsibility for the CAPP.

The corporate security functions and the CAPP must be driven by the philosophy of providing an effective (good) and efficient (cheap) use of corporate resources. The protection of assets must be based on security policies, procedures, processes, plans and projects based on assets protection or security "drivers" – those things that drive the security functions and the CAPP.

Security or assets protection as well as information assurance (IA) drivers usually include such things as (see Figure 9.1):

- Laws
- Regulations
- Executive management decisions
- Corporate policies

Figure 9.1 shows the flow of assets protection and security drivers through policies, plans, procedures, processes and projects.

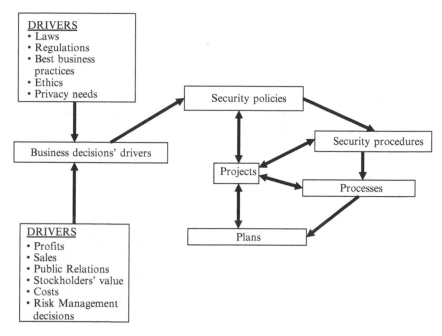

FIGURE 9.1. Shows the flow of assets protection and security drivers through policies, procedures, processes, plans and projects.

9.2   Corporate Security IA-Related Functions

Although each corporation establishes its own unique asset protection program, to include IA-related functions, there is a common thread that runs through most of these corporate asset protection functions. Using the CSO duties and responsibilities noted later, the functions related to IA will be identified and discussed. The assumption here is that the CSO does not have direct IA functional responsibility except those generally known as corporate security functions, e.g. physical security, personnel security and administrative security.

9.2.1   Evaluate Current Security Requirements

"Develop methodologies and implement processes to evaluate current security requirements and project future requirements on new business proposals and future contracts."

In evaluating the current security and future requirements, those of information and information systems should also be addressed. This would require the CSO to gain input from those responsible for IA so as to be able to evaluate the security requirements based on a holistic corporate assets protection requirements approach. The source of the requirements, known as requirements' drivers, would have to be established, and then a process developed to ensure requirements was updated based on the drivers from the requirements being changed, e.g. drivers such as changes in laws, contracts.

In order to project future requirements, a different approach would be needed, one that the CSO is generally not accustomed to dealing with. Corporate security officers generally establish a basic corporate assets protection program and then usually maintain a reactive posture. To be able to begin to do trend analyses, see where the main drivers are headed 2–5 years from now, requires a different process.

Since technology advances are a driving force in IA, the CSO must rely on the IA staff to provide this information. Unfortunately, most of those responsible for IA also seem to be in a reactive mode and seldom have time (at least that is a usual excuse) to look at the future trends, as they are too busy with fighting today's battles. If that is not bad enough, the CSO must understand business trends, especially in the industry that the corporation is in. For example, e-commerce or business and global market information would be needed. After that is in place, CSOs must then be able to look in the "crystal ball" to determine where they are today, vis-à-vis security requirements, and where they must be tomorrow. Furthermore, the CSOs must develop a process for getting there.

9.2.2   Corporate Security Plan

"Develop and oversee the implementation of a long range, corporate-wide security plan that details the efficient and cost-effective utilisation of security resources."

Incorporating the information developed in trend analyses (see Section 9.2.1), the CSO would be in a better position while developing a corporate-wide security plan. The plan must also look at the IA issues since the plan encompasses the entire corporation. Furthermore, it is very difficult to provide an efficient and cost-effective use of security resources without considering the security aspects of information and information systems. After all, somewhere within the corporation there are personnel responsible for IA. If one were to ignore their input and fail to integrate their requirements, concerns, functions and processes, the CSO would be ignoring some of the main assets of the corporation, which require protection. In doing so, the CSO could not successfully accomplish the task.

While at the same time, it is believed that most CSOs tasked with accomplishing this project only consider those tasks under their authority. Thus, if they do not have responsibility for IA, they will ignore that aspect while developing their plan. The security resources of all organisations must be considered and their input solicited.

9.2.3   Management Direction for Security Activities

"Provide overall management direction for all security activities within the corporation focusing on centralised delivery on a corporate-wide basis, maximising the development of regional and corporate-shared services."

The key is *overall management direction*. This does not mean that the IA functions are under the CSO; however, the CSO can make a case for leading the IA efforts of the corporation. While at the same time, the focus on providing a *centralised delivery* would seem to give the CSO the mandate for absorbing those IA resources and functions necessary to accomplish this function.

If politically and culturally feasible within the corporation, the CSO should establish a project to identify all the IA resources within the corporation, determine their current costs and the cost-benefits of centralisation under the security organisation. If it is determined to be cost-effective, the corporate executive management should be briefed with the intent of gaining its approval to consolidate the IA functions, personnel and other resources. If the executive management disapproves, then the CSO should request that this function be modified to exclude the IA functions.

The CSO would not be very smart to leave the function as written and then not have the authority to manage those aspects of the function. Management responsibility without authority to manage is not a position any CSOs would want to be in as they can get blamed when things are not going right but have no authority to make things right.

9.2.4   Interface with Other Directors

"Interface with the directors of environmental, health, safety, medical and others as appropriate to resolve issues involving the security of assets by the business sectors."

This is not an IA type of function *per se*; however, these directors have information, databases and information systems that as a minimum must be protected and defended if for no other reasons than those of privacy and liability concerns.

These directors and their organisations support the entire corporation, and it appears that these functions fall under the responsibility of the CSO. Therefore, the CSO must act as a mediator between these directors and the business sectors of the corporation.

9.2.5   Comply with Contractual, Customer and Regulatory Requirements

"Act to ensure that security processes are performed in full compliance with all customers, contractual and regulatory security requirements."

As with the other functions identified previously, this function has some very important IA concerns. There are very serious liability issues and non-compliance with contract specification issues that may develop. One can begin to see an obvious trend that the CSO cannot perform those functions identified in this chapter without having some management responsibility relative to IA. How can a CSO ensure that the customers' information and even the customers' information systems interfacing with the corporate information systems are being properly protected and defended against attacks and human errors that may damage the customers' information systems and information?

The CSO can co-ordinate this function with the audit staff and request that the auditors verify and validate compliance with these requirements. The difficulty is how and when that audit is performed. Generally, the audit staff is very busy with meeting audit requirements of their own. They may not have the resources to support this activity, and if they did, then should not that function then be transferred to the audit department? This is an option to be considered. The other option is for the CSO to have his staff conduct security compliance surveys or inspections.

The term audit should not be used as this could be confused with the audit organisation's use of the term. Furthermore, it would be more of a security compliance process that is somewhat different from an audit. It would not only evaluate for compliance, but also at the same time would be considered as part of a risk assessment so that one can cost effectively consider accomplishing a task for two different purposes with little extra effort.

The term inspection has a harsher tone to it and may not be considered, from a "public relations" or "political" viewpoint, the best way to proceed. However, the term "survey" seems less intrusive and less threatening. The choice of terms when dealing within the political and cultural reality of a corporation can make a difference. One must always approach such issues from a non-threatening standpoint as much as possible.

9.2.6   Corporate-Wide InfoSec Program

"Oversee the development of a corporate-wide information security program to protect corporate and customer information."

Here again, there is a case to make for the CSO to have the authority to manage the IA functions. However, the word *oversee* provides the CSO with an "out" as such functions vis-à-vis IA can be done by the CSO developing an overall corporate security policy. The CSO could then leave the procedural matters to the various organisations having the IA responsibilities within the corporation. The other option is a matrix management approach in which the CSO assigns security resources to assist other organisations. However, the success of a matrix management approach is always dependent on the personality of the manager who owns the resources being "loaned" to another manager's organisation as well as the budget availability of both managers. For example, one must relinquish the budget for the time and money to be expended for someone to support a given function, e.g. IA, in another's organisation?

9.2.7   Corporate-Wide Crisis Management Program

"Oversee the development of a corporate-wide Crisis Management Program."

The CSO having this responsibility would undoubtedly have representatives from the various corporate organisations as part of the crisis management team responding to a crisis. When a crisis was identified, which met the crisis criteria definition established earlier by the CSO and then the parties would meet to handle the crisis. Such a crisis could include such incidents as a successful denial of service attack, the destruction of databases and theft of sensitive corporate information. Such matters as incident response teams' emergency procedures and the like would also be part of the crisis management program.

9.2.8   Establish Common Security Processes

"Work with regional security managers to ensure the identification and implementation of common processes, shared services, and best practices."

As it relates to assets protection, this responsibility would be a matter of distributing those related processes that are used at the corporate location to the regional offices, to include the IA processes and the best practices. After all, it would be cost-effective to do so. Why reinvent the wheel so to speak.

The problem that may, and often does, arise is that regional offices consider themselves autonomous, and more so the further they are from the corporate headquarters. This attitude must be considered and the regional input to all processes to be identified as common processes must be considered. Management support and personalities play a major role here. However, an attitude of teaming and cost-benefits must be used by all. The bottom line is this: what is best for the corporation, not individual "empires" whether they be corporate or regional, must apply.

9.2.9   Provide Productive and Safe Working Environment

"Work with the sector managers of environmental, safety, health, medical, and facilities to ensure an integration of functions to provide a productive and safe working environment for sector employees."

The employees of these organisations cannot be productive if they rely on information systems, for example, and these systems are not accessible due to some virus, human error or attack.

This responsibility is not directly related to IA except that a case can be made for the CSO to assist the IA staff to ensure that the sector managers comply with the IA requirements established by the corporate staff responsible for IA.

9.2.10   Corporate Security Measurement System

"Oversee the development and implementation of a corporate security measurement system, which permits evaluation of the effectiveness of the security program, based on the factors of cost, customer satisfaction, and compliance."

Again, this would apply only to those functions that are under the authority of the CSO. As it relates to IA, the CSO may ask for but cannot require a measurement system to be established and results provided to the security staff if those functions are not under the direct control of the CSO.

A CSO should develop a security metrics management program (SMMP) in order to measure the costs, benefits, successes and failures of an assets protection program as well as to measure the effectiveness and efficiencies of the security staff.[1]

For example, one valuable metric would be to quantify the access control violations on systems that contain proprietary information. The data collection would include the names, organisations and the information to which unauthorised access was attempted.

The staff responsible for conducting non-compliance inquiries (NCI) would evaluate the violations. Say, for example, the majority of access violations were determined to be due to lack of proper awareness training concerning what access privileges the users had.

Let us assume that special emphasis was placed on providing that information through perhaps a mass e-mailing to users, through the briefings for new-hires and corporate newsletters. Then the access violations would continue to be tracked and hopefully show a decline.

Thus, those responsible for access control and NCIs would be able to spend more time on other matters, and the access control violators would decrease. Thus, these users would be more productive in that they would not be locked out of the systems and could spend more time doing what they were hired to do (see Figure 9.2).

9.2.11   Common Managerial Accountabilities

"*Perform common managerial accountabilities and tasks in accordance with established corporate guidelines.*"

This is a normal managerial responsibility and usually concerns such managerial matters as meeting goals, establishing and managing organisational budgets, career development of assigned personnel, conducting performance reviews and the like. Therefore, these are not directly related to IA. However, if a corporation were truly supportive of IA and security, then the managerial responsibilities identified would include supporting and complying with IA and security policy, protecting corporate assets and the like.

9.2.12   Physically Secure Environment

"*Provide a physically secure environment for the corporate office to protect property, people and information.*"

This is definitely one function that undoubtedly has been, is and will continue to be performed by the CSO. However, if we look at IA, as we should (but usually do not), we must consider information in every conceivable environment in which it flows. This would include an electronic media, hardcopies, videos or

---

[1] A SMMP detailed discussion is beyond the scope of this book; however, if the reader is interested in additional information on this topic, it is available in Dr Kovacich's book, *Security Metrics Management*, to be published by Butterworth-Heinemann in the winter, 2005.

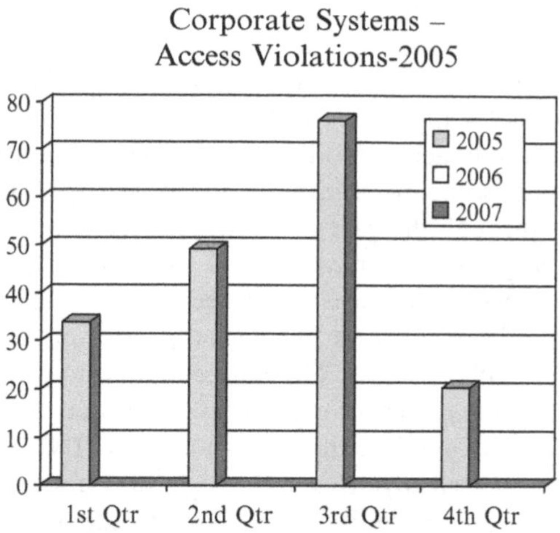

Corporate Systems –
Access Violations-2005

FIGURE 9.2. Corporate Systems–Access Violation-2005. It shows a metrics chart of systems access violations. *Note*: The legend box indicates that the metric measurement will take place for the next 3 years.

by whatever means. However, that aside, physical security will always be an important and basic defence against information theft.

When one thinks of physical security, one thinks of the human access controls and the guards stationed at entrances to facilities, areas and even some rooms or offices. However, in some corporations, the receptionists and administrative personnel at the visitors' entrances or entrance to a particular suite of offices, for example, are also controlling access.

When one enters a visitor's lobby, there may be a uniform guard behind the desk, or the guard may be wearing business attire with perhaps a corporate logo on the breast pocket of the sport coat. If the corporation has outsourced its guard force duties to an outside agency, the logo of the guard company may be on the breast pocket. In some corporations, the executive management has decided that a guard force was not necessary or is cost-prohibitive; thus, it uses administrative support personnel, such as receptionists and secretaries, to double as access controllers. Regardless, these individuals are required to ensure that only authorised personnel have access to the facility.

Besides the human element of physical access controls, there are the mechanical access controls. Some forms of mechanical access controls include:

- *Fences and walls*: One often sees fences surrounding a corporation. These physical barriers range from chain-link fences topped with barbed wire to concrete walls. The fences are used to control access by making it difficult for intruders to proceed beyond that barrier and also to guide personnel to the gates.

- *Gates*: The gates are established to control access by controlling physical access to an area, facility and the like. Guards may be stationed at the gates, or they may require the use of a device such as a special badge to "swipe" through a badge reader in order to allow access beyond that point. Often these entrances can only accommodate one individual at a time through the portal. This prevents someone from allowing others to "piggyback" by also following them in through the gate without having a proper badge.
- *Badge readers*: Badge readers have gained in popularity and are used to control physical access and eliminate the need for a guard to control access. Thus, the badge reader provides a more "foolproof" physical access control method at usually much less cost. The badge reader may allow the holder to just swipe it through the reader to gain access, or it may also require the user to enter a group or personal identification number (PIN).
- *Facility*: The facility itself by its very design may form a physical access barrier, e.g. no windows on the first floor, bars on the windows, etc.

Physical security is always the first line of defence; however, keeping unauthorised personnel out is only one process. Another is how to keep information and information systems from leaving the facility in an unauthorised manner. With today's Internet accesses; small, removable electronic media; and the ability to make copies and print sensitive documents with little control; this is almost an impossible task.

9.2.13   Government Compliance Requirements

"Direct the development and implementation of security processes that comply with government requirements."

Since the inception of the nation-state, there have been governments who try to influence, regulate or otherwise control information and its usage. In addition, there is information that is related to the national security of a nation-state. This has always been under the purview of the CSO for government contractors or for any business that must comply with various requirements of the nation-states' government agencies. The issue of privacy is one that comes to mind as one of the government's requirements.

While the staff responsible for IA is involved at the implementation level, the CSO has historically been in the leadership role in such instances, when security issues are involved. However, this responsibility can also be assigned to others, e.g. the corporate legal staff.

This function can be accomplished through a teaming, project plan effort to develop and establish a process of accomplishing this task. In addition, the use of security surveys can assist in assuring compliance.

9.2.14   Corporate Management Guidance

"Provide guidance to corporate management regarding security policy and the interpretation, intent, or application of security-related laws and regulations; provide additional support to the corporate elements as required."

Corporate management looks to the CSO as the in-house consultant for security matters; however, that may or may not apply to IA. On these occasions, the matter may be IA related, and thus when the word "security" comes up, the CSO is usually the first one to be contacted. However, on matters that involve anything to do with information systems and IA, the CSO is generally not even considered.

The corporate management will usually turn to the information technology (IT) executive for guidance, who is probably also the corporate information officer (CIO). When considering the IT executive as the CIO, the corporation's executive management either considers all its information being on information systems or misses the point. The CIO/IT executives generally have no experience in information as such but in systems. Furthermore, they usually lack experience and management authority over non-systems processed, stored and transmitted information. Therefore, they are not true CIOs as the term implies. It seems corporate management continues to miss the point – it is not about information systems but about information in any environment! Is it any wonder that we have the problems that we do?

9.2.15 Security Liaison Activities

"Maintain active liaison with government security agencies in order to participate in the development of security policy and represent the corporation in professional and industrial associations to influence the interpretation and implementation of that policy."

Within a corporation, it is better to have only one focal point when dealing with the government security agencies. That focal point is usually the CSO. In many corporations, the CSO is a retired military or government agency security officer or law enforcement officer. Thus, that the CSO usually understands how government security agencies operate, making the liaison task not only easier but also more successful. Even if an issue relative to IA is concerned, the communications link is through the CSO and not directly to those responsible for IA within a corporation.

9.2.16 Co-ordinate Corporate Security Policies and Procedures

"Work with other corporate departments to develop and implement company policies and procedures that have important security implications for the company."

It is inconceivable (but true) that today's CSOs in information-dependent corporations do not include the IA requirements and needed policy as part of the corporate security policies and procedures.

While the CSO would be more interested in the document, personnel and physical security aspects, these processes also impact how IA is conducted. Therefore, whatever direction is pursued by the CSO in order to accomplish this task, IA will be impacted.

In this case, the CSO would identify all the assets that required protection and identify those organisations responsible for those assets. A project would be

established and a project team made up of representatives from all those organisations that have responsibility for those assets. The project would be led by the
CSO. The project team would establish those requirements.

The goal would be to ensure that as much as possible the protection requirements would be standardised and consistent for all assets. Variations would only
be allowed where the asset was unique and required different protection requirements. The requirements would be documented and that documentation would be
the baseline for a corporate assets protection policy. Procedures for implementing
and complying with that policy would be established within individual organisations at more detailed level. For example, the policy may require access control,
both physical and logical. It may be more cost-effective to have a security guard in
some areas, while others used badge readers, biometric devices and the like.

A CSO should co-ordinate and team with those responsible for IA to develop
all-inclusive security policies that also consider information and information
systems. Thus, provide the CSO with the opportunity to influence the IA policies and procedures to ensure that he/she is not only consistent with the total
information asset protection needs of the corporation but also meets the generally accepted security standards for the protection of corporate assets.

9.2.17   Corporate-Wide Contingency Plan

"*Manage the development and implementation of an integrated, company-wide
contingency plan.*"

No contingency plan in any information-dependent corporation can be completed without addressing the issues of information and information systems as
part of the overall corporate contingency plan. In order to do so, the CSO must
integrate the IA contingency planning details into the overall plan.

To accomplish the function, the CSO must establish a project team with all
organisations represented. This is because contingencies are about more than just
security or IA. These are about dealing with emergencies, disasters and other issues
that require a contingency plan so that one can get back to normal business as soon
as possible with the least impact on the business. The project team led by the CSO
would be responsible for establishing a contingency plan. This plan would
undoubtedly consider all the information and information systems issues, e.g. IA.
The IA specialists' input must be a mandatory requirement to ensure that such a
plan was developed using a corporate holistic philosophy and methodology.

One also must remember that within contingency planning, there may be as
many as three distinct subsystems:

- *Emergency response*: This is self-explanatory; however, one should remember
  that the security, fire, environmental and medical processes play the biggest
  role in this effort.
- *Crisis management*: Managing a crisis is a team effort usually made up of at
  least the representatives of the emergency response components, human
  resources, facilities engineers and executive management.

- *Business continuity*: Generally consists of the disaster recovery components, with IT and the IA staffs usually playing a major role, along with business resumption elements. The business staff establishes the priorities and leads this effort, supported by IT, IA, user community and the like. In this effort, security may serve as an "integrator" of processes to successfully meet the challenges imposed by an emergency or a crisis.

9.2.18   Corporate Crisis Management Room

"Ensure the corporate crisis management room is maintained in a state of constant readiness and provide the resources required to operate the room during actual emergencies and simulations."

This is an extension of the crisis management function described in Section 9.2.7. Therefore, there is no need to further address it here, except to say that those issues related to IA that are to be addressed by the IA specialists and others should be as team players. They should undoubtedly be authorised to use this room as needed for their response teams, etc.

9.2.19   Corporate-Wide Security Measurement System

"Develop, implement and maintain a company-wide security measurement system that permits evaluation of the effectiveness of each company element security program, the total company security programs and benchmarking with security programs of comparable companies."

In order to accomplish this function throughout the corporation, the CSO must have integrated by whatever means, e.g. matrix management, teaming and the IA processes at the CSO level. If not, it would be difficult to view the total company security functions and accurately benchmark them.

9.2.20   Law Enforcement Liaison

"Liaisons with federal, state and local law enforcement, investigative and fire agencies."

The same process that applies for liaison with security personnel in government agencies applies.

9.2.21   Chair Corporate Security Council

"Chair the corporate Security Council to develop a common company-wide approach to address security processes and problems."

The CSO can use this opportunity that the issues of IA are addressed by ensuring that members of the Council include those responsible for IA within the corporation. However, this may not be the case. The CSO would usually include representatives of the legal, audit, human resources and others but may often neglect those with some of the most important roles related to corporate assets protection – the IA staff.

9.2.22   Corporate Security Policy and Procedures

"Develop corporate security policy and procedures to address the following security processes: Security quality and oversight; Personnel security; Information security; Physical security; Investigations; Fire protection; and Contingency planning."

The corporate security policy must be based on specific requirements. These requirements must come from somewhere. After all, the CSO, or anyone for that matter, should not just make them up as something that seems to be good to do. Such an approach would cause the establishment of requirements and subsequently policy and procedures that may not be necessary or cost-effective.

Requirements should be traced back to the authoritative sources such as audit standards, security standards, contractual requirements, laws, etc. Once these were identified, their intent could be discerned; and based on that information a security policy to include information protection and defence can be developed. Once developed with input from all those who have asset protection responsibility, the corporate security policy document would be one that met the requirements from the authoritative sources. This provides a process for establishing only the minimum security necessary for the protection of all corporate assets. From that policy, procedures would be developed by lower level organisations that would implement the policy and meet the various mandated requirements.

Taking that one step lower, the following addresses the specific functions noted previously and how they relate to IA:

- *Security quality and oversight*: The corporate policy and procedures requirements for this function provide that the CSO would be responsible for leading the overall corporate security and assets protection program and ensuring that it was done in a cost-effective, quality manner.
- *Personnel security*: The policy would require that all employees undergo a minimum background check prior to employment; with those in positions identified as sensitive, such as operations staff, programmers, IA personnel would require more in-depth background check.
- *Information security:* This policy and subsequent procedures would undoubtedly require the input from the IA staff; however, it must cover more than that. It must cover information that is neither automated nor related to information systems.
- *Physical security*: The policy must not only address the physical access to facilities, areas and the like, but also how electronic media, videos and documents containing sensitive information are to be physically protected.
- *Investigations (non-compliance inquiries)*: How one would conduct investigations relating to information systems attacks, theft and destruction of information and the like must also be addressed. This policy would obviously provide the leadership under the CSO but should include forensic support from the IA staff or those in IT. Regardless, an investigation related to information systems would undoubtedly be due to a breach in protection and therefore of serious concern to the IA staff who must be involved in such investigations as integral members of the investigative team.

- *Fire protection*: Fire protection plays an important role in protecting information and information systems. No policy or procedures can be complete without an IA input.
- *Contingency planning*: As stated earlier, contingency planning policy must also address the IA issues, and input from IT and IA staffs are mandatory if it is to be done right.

9.2.23   CSO as IA Leader

One can easily see that almost all of the functions of a CSO have a direct impact and relationship with the IA functions. It stands to reason that the CSO should also be the IA leader. However, this will never be possible if the CSOs continue to neglect their professional responsibilities and fail to understand information systems. Until that professional responsibility is accepted by CSOs, the IA responsibility will continue to elude them and fall under the purview of the IT staff.

As one can understand after reading the above, there is also too much opportunity for conflicts on how best to proceed in doing the IA functions in a manner that is best for the corporation. The way the CSO believes that the IA functions should be accomplished to be cost-beneficial and best for the corporation is often different from the approaches by the IT staff. Under such conditions, teaming is difficult as office politics come into play. Furthermore, the IA suffers and will continue to suffer under such conditions. Is it any wonder that surviving in the information environment is so difficult?

9.3   Summary

The CSO and the corporate security functions under the CSO's purview, all have some impact on how the IA functions are performed. Since the IA functions are normally not a corporate security function but usually an IT function, there must be continuous communication and co-operation between the two professions. This is not always the case. The CSO should be in the corporate leadership position when it comes to the corporate assets protection program and that includes the IA functions.

10

IA in the Interest of National Security

This chapter identifies and explains the information assurance (IA) requirements, specifically those related to information systems (ISs), in the national
security environment of a government-related corporation. This chapter also
discusses the philosophy and processes that can be adapted to the IA programs
in the world of business.[1]

10.1   Introduction

One may wonder why discuss national security in the context of information
assurance (IA). There are several reasons for this as noted below:[2]

- National security obviously impacts government agencies. However, it also
  impacts individuals and businesses of every size and type. This also includes
  other nation-states, thus foreign governments, as well as foreign businesses
  and citizens from other nations.
- In today's global marketplace and information environment, what happens in
  one nation often impacts the same in other nations. In this age of information
  warfare, one has many examples of national security affecting other nations
  and businesses. The defacing of government and business Websites and
  denial-of-service (DoS) attacks between the Chinese in mainland China and
  those on Taiwan; the Israeli–Arab incidents and the Serb–NATO incidents,
  just to name a few.

---

[1] The reader who does not work for a company or university with government contracts
may want to skip this chapter. However, many of the requirements set forth by various
government agencies for the protection of their (the government's) information, and IA
can cost-effectively be applied to the protection of non-government information. Also,
one never knows whom they may be working for from time-to-time. Thus, the information presented in this chapter may provide some future value.
[2] Note that in approximately 4 years since the First Edition of this book was published,
the information provided here remains valid.

- If national security is impacted, businesses are impacted. One can look to World War II and see the bombing of industrial plants – commercial businesses – by the other's adversaries. In any incident, police action or war, in which a nation's security is adversely impacted, the businesses of that nation are also impacted in the same manner. Therefore, it is obvious that in case of any conflict between nations, in which at least one of the nations is information dependent, attacks will be made against telecommunication systems, Websites, Internet accesses and the like. These are for the most part of the non-government systems. Furthermore, in today's global, competitive marketplace, economic power is being emphasised more than military power. Therefore, in order for an adversary to weaken a nation, the former would undoubtedly attack the economic might of a nation – its economic might is derived from its businesses. So, virus attacks, DoS attacks, theft of sensitive information, placing misinformation on corporate networks, etc. are very likely to be used.
- In every modern nation and especially information-based nations of the world, corporations are under contract to research, design, develop and produce weapons that can be used for the protection of the nation-state. In today's modern, information-based nations; there are literally thousands of universities and corporations under contract to government agencies. These businesses may exist solely for developing products for government agencies or may be producing various products for government agencies and also producing products for commercial use. They may be accomplishing these projects using the same information systems (ISs), application programs and even the same information. Corporations do many of the current government-sponsored research projects under contract. These not only can and will be used to assist government agencies, but also eventually can be used by businesses. The research into information-based defensive weapons is of such a nature.
- A cyber-attack on a corporation can also be viewed as an attack against national security. Nations are preparing to attack other nation's information infrastructures, which are generally private businesses.
- The modern world is rapidly becoming one integrated supply chain. Corporations for government agencies, other corporations that may be involved in the defence industry or for commercial businesses and customers, are producing products. Some of these may even be of a foreign nature. This inter-relationship means that what may happen to one corporation or nation may adversely impact other corporations on a global scale. Since these modern corporations are information dependent and information based, the IA plays an important role. One just has to look at the devastating earthquake in Kobe, Japan, and its effect on worldwide supply of chips, to see this global dependency.

10.1.1   IA: A Definition

One of the leading countries dealing with issues of IA is of course USA. This stands to reason since it relies so largely on high technology and automated information. The US Department of Defence's (DoD) National Security

Telecommunications and Information Systems Security Committee (NSTISSC), which has changed its name to the Committee on National Security Systems (CNSS) defines IA as:

> *Measures that protect and defend information and information systems by ensuring their availability, integrity, authentication, confidentiality, and non-repudiation.*

Their document[3] goes on to state that. ... *These measures include providing for restoration of information systems by incorporating protection, detection, and reaction capabilities....*

10.1.2   Levels of Protection

The US DoD document referenced above also states: ... *Levels of protection – Extent to which protection measures, techniques, and procedures must be applied to ISs and networks based on risk, threat, vulnerability, system interconnectivity considerations and IA needs... Levels of protection are:*

1. *Basic – IS and networks requiring implementation of standard minimum security countermeasures.*
2. *Medium – IS and networks requiring layering additional safeguards above the standard minimum security requirements.*
3. *High – IS and networks requiring the most stringent protection and rigorous security countermeasures.*

10.1.3   System Assurance

As part of national security of information and ISs that processes, stores, displays and transmits information of a sensitive or classified nature, requirements are set forth and must be met by the government contractor. This includes the following requirements:[4]

• Access to protection functions
• Protection documentation
• Periodic validation or System Assurance (SysAssur)
• System isolation

10.2   National Security Classified Information

When one thinks of information valuation in the national security arena, one has just as difficult a time determining its value as is the case in the corporate world. However, there is no doubt that the value of information of national security inter-

---

[3] www.NSTISSC.gov/assets/pdf/4009.pdf
[4] This information is contained in Chapter 8, Information System Security of the National Industrial Security Operating Manual (NISPOM), Defense Security Service, US DoD.

est is obviously much greater than that of any corporation. If a corporation's information is not adequately protected and defended, that corporation may go out of business. However, if the same thing were to happen to a nation's national security information, the nation may cease to exist except as part of another nation.

National security classified information is one of the most important categories of information which must be safeguarded by all in the interest of national security. It is mentioned here briefly because the process used to place a value on that information goes through more stringent analyses than personal, private and business information.

In USA, as an example, national security classified information is generally divided into three basic categories:

- **Confidential**: Loss of this information can cause damage to national security
- **Secret**: Loss of this information can cause serious damage to national security
- **Top secret**: Loss of this information can cause grave damage to national security

There is also national security information that is not classified as stated above, but requires some lesser degree of control and protection because it has lesser value. These include:

- For official use only
- Unclassified but sensitive information
- Unclassified information

There is also a category of classified information that is considered "black" or "compartmented". Such information is further protected by not only requiring a security clearance and the need-to-know (NTK), but also often an additonal background investigation and special briefing. Such efforts are often called "Special Access Required information," "Special Access Program information" and "Sensitive Compartmented information". In these compartments, the IA must include some of the most stringent processes as this information can truly be considered the "crown jewels" of a nation.

Using the UK as another example, security is treated in a similar fashion, as it is by most other nations. The following is quoted from referenced Website[5] to give some idea to the thinking surrounding national security information and its value:

"The Prime Minister: In recent years, the nature of the threats to Government security has changed. While some of the traditional threats to national security may have somewhat reduced, others have not. The security of Government is also increasingly threatened by, for example, theft, copying and electronic surveillance, as well as by terrorism.

"To ensure that their approach to security reflects current threats, the Government have recently completed a review of their arrangements for the management of protective security in Departments and agencies. This has recom-

---

[5] http://www.parliament.the-stationery-office.co.uk/pa/cm199394/cmhansrd/1994-03-23/Writtens-4.html

mended a new protective marking system for documents which will help identify more precisely those which need protecting, enabling them to be protected more effectively according to their value. The new system will also be more closely related to the code of practice on Government information announced in the Government's White Paper on openness.

"In addition, the review has concluded that existing security measures should be examined closely to ensure they are necessary in relation to today's threats; that commercially available security equipment should be more widely used; and that personnel vetting enquiries should be streamlined particularly in routine cases. Overall, the aim is to give Departments and agencies, and management units within them, greater responsibility for assessing the nature of the risks they face and for making decisions, within a framework of common standards of protection, about the security measures they need to put in place. Substantial cost savings will result.

"The first stage of the implementation of the proposals of this review will be the introduction of a new protective marking system with effect from 4 April 1994 alongside the code of practice on access to Government information. The new definitions, which will allow fewer Government documents to be classified, particularly at the higher levels, are set out. The other elements of the new approach to protective security will be put in place in due course. The four categories of protective marking: Definitions The markings to be allocated to any asset, including information, will be determined primarily by reference to the practical consequences that are likely to result from the compromise of that asset or information. The levels in the new protective marking system are defined as follows:

- *"**Top secret**: The compromise of this information or material would be likely: to threaten directly the internal stability of the United Kingdom or friendly countries; to lead directly to widespread loss of life; to cause exceptionally grave damage to the effectiveness or security of United Kingdom or Allied Forces or to the continuing effectiveness of extremely valuable security or intelligence operations; to cause exceptionally grave damage to relations with friendly governments; to cause severe long-term damage to the United Kingdom economy.*
- *"**Secret**: The compromise of this information or material would be likely: to raise international tension; to damage seriously relations with friendly governments; to threaten life directly, or seriously prejudice public order, or individual security or liberty; to cause serious damage to the operational effectiveness or security of United Kingdom or Allied Forces or the continuing effectiveness of highly valuable security or intelligence operations; to cause substantial material damage to national finances or economic and commercial interests.*
- *"**Confidential**: The compromise of this information or material would be likely: materially to damage diplomatic relations (i.e. cause formal protest or other sanction); to prejudice individual security or liberty; to cause damage to the operational effectiveness or security of United Kingdom or Allied Forces or the effectiveness of valuable security or intelligence operations; to work substantially against national finances or economic and commercial interests; substantially to undermine the financial viability of major organisations; to impede the investigation or facilitate the commission of serious crime; to impede seriously*

the development or operation of major government policies; to shut down or otherwise substantially disrupt significant national operations.

- *"**Restricted**: The compromise of this information or material would be likely: to affect diplomatic relations adversely; to cause substantial distress to individuals; to make it more difficult to maintain the operational effectiveness or security of United Kingdom or Allied Forces; to cause financial loss or loss of earning potential to or facilitate improper gain or advantage for individuals or companies; to prejudice the investigation or facilitate the commission of crime; to breach proper undertakings to maintain the confidence of information provided by third parties; to impede the effective development or operation of government policies; to breach statutory restrictions on disclosure of information; to disadvantage government in commercial or policy negotiations with others; to undermine the proper management of the public sector and its operation."*

10.2.1   An Example of National Security Information Impact

When looking at the impact of IA failure in the national security arena, there are more serious consequences than just losing the corporate competitive advantage. The following example by Mr Perry Luzwick, an IA expert at Logicon Corporation in USA, put it this way:

"What is the cost to replace the information, and the cost of lost business/profits or national security? Here's an example of perceived value. The Department of Defence sends a roll-on/roll-off (RORO) ship with 100 M1A1 Abrams main battle tanks to South Korea. The ship encounters bad weather in the North Pacific, suffers damage from mechanical problems and cargo which became unsecured, takes on water, and sinks. The nation bemoans the loss of life, Military Sea Lift Command calculates sealift shortfall workarounds, and Materiel Command orders more tanks. The value of the tanks, ship, and loss of life can be accurately calculated by traditional accounting methods.

"Change the scenario. North Korean actions indicate probable conflict. The United States wishes to show its resolve and support for an ally, so it sends a RORO with 100 M1A1s to meet activated Army and Marine Corps Reservists airlifted to South Korea. The ship sinks. What is the value of the tanks? The perceived value is definitely higher than the accounting value. What is the value of the information the ship sunk to the North Koreans?"

There are many more examples that can be given; however, the point is made: national security information impacts nation-states and corporations.

10.3   IA Requirements in the National Security Arena

There are many similarities between the IA requirements in the corporate world and the world of national security as practised by government agencies and defence industry-related corporations. Such things as initial and recurring background investigations of employees are more stringent as well as physical security requirements and the implementation of the NTK principle. This section will concentrate on those directly related to information and ISs protection and defence requirements. The ISs are sometimes called automated information systems (AIS).

In the case of a defence industry-related corporation, the IA requirements are incorporated into the contract between the government agency and the contractor. A defence industry-related corporation would then include such IA requirements into contracts with subcontractors, associated contractors, team members, etc. where those businesses will also be handling government information. This is logical as it does no good to provide the IA in one corporation while another uses the same information and is not required to do likewise.

The main emphasis of IA deals with compromise of national security information. Unless there is a state of war, information destroyed or inappropriately modified may be reconstructed, albeit possibly taking a great deal of time. However, the compromise of national security information may make the product being developed of little use since the adversary has the information and can build like products or products of a defensive nature. The worst-case scenario is when a compromise occurs and no one knows that it has occurred. Thus, time, money and other resources are expended that will be of little use if they are needed since, as noted earlier, using the compromised information, the adversary has developed defensive systems that make the other nation's products useless. So, the IA requirements are implemented so that:

National security information is to be protected from compromise that would allow an adversary to compete in building like systems, developing countermeasures or delaying operational use of the systems.

The compromise or delays in product development would be accomplished through man-made, hostile acts of:

Espionage through authorised or unauthorised accesses to information, e.g. theft

Sabotage through fire (destruction), water (destruction) or software (e.g. destruction, theft, manipulation) using such malicious codes as Trojan horses, viruses and logic bombs

The IA in a national security environment must also protect and defend against natural acts such as fire, water, earthquakes, windstorms and the like.

It is the responsibility of the IA specialist to understand the national security requirements, especially those specified in the contract. The IA specialist must be able to provide an IA program for the defence industry-related corporation that includes increasing awareness of the need for an effective IA program in the government environment and also provide basic guidance and understanding necessary for the development of the IA program in that environment.

The fundamental national IA requirements are:

- *IA policy*: The set of laws, rules, and practices that regulate how a defence industry-related corporation manages, protects, defends and distributes national security information.

- *Accountability*: Individual and information accountability is the key to protecting, defending and controlling any system that processes, stores and transmits national security information on behalf of the individuals or groups of individuals.
- *Assurance*: Guarantees or provides confidence that the IA policy has been implemented correctly and the IA elements of the system accurately mediate and enforce that policy.
- *Documentation*: Development documentation records how a system is structured and what it is supposed to do and gives the background information on which the design is founded. Control documentation records the resources used in developing and implementing a system that will process, store and transmit national security information.

10.3.1 IA Objective in the National Security Environment

The overall objective of the IA in the national security environment is to prevent unauthorised access to classified information during or resulting from information processing and prevent unauthorised manipulation that could result in national security information being compromised. This is done by:

- Protecting and defending information stored, processed and transmitted by an AIS
- Preventing unauthorised access, modification, damage, destruction or DoS
- Providing assurances of:
- Compliance with government and contractual obligations and agreements
- Confidentiality of private, sensitive and classified information
- Integrity of information and related processes
- Availability, when required, of information
- Use for authorised business and by authorised personnel only of information and AIS
- Identification and elimination of fraud, waste and abuse

10.3.2 Responsibilities

The responsibilities for compliance with the AIS security requirements in the world of national security are similar to those of the corporate world. Management is responsible for ensuring compliance with the IA requirements, policies and procedures as well as ensuring the reporting of violations. All employees are, of course, responsible for understanding their responsibilities as well as complying and reporting violations to management. However, in this case, the seriousness of the information and its implications, due to loss or compromise, requires that violations be immediately reported and inquiries conducted. The disciplinary action taken against violators is usually more severe.

10.3.3   Collective IA Controls

The IA controls that must be considered for any national security environment include:

- Individual accountability
- Physical controls
- System controls
- System stability
- Data continuity
- Least privilege[6]
- Communications security
- National security information controls

These controls are based on the contractual and non-contractual requirements and generally established national security principles. The IA program that includes the objectives and controls noted above are usually approved by the government security officer responsible for the security of the corporation's contractual efforts. In fact, each system that is considered for use to process, store and transmit national security-related information must be approved by the government's security officer for the contract. The entire effort often has a name designated for it by the government customer, and it is also called a program instead of a contract, e.g. Widget Program.

10.3.4   Government Customer Approval Process

In order to process national security information, the government customer must approve each AIS prior to authorising its use to process, store or transmit national security information. Furthermore, a "Master Information Systems Security Plan" (Master SSP) is required. In that plan, the information required for each certification for an IS to be accredited under this plan must be identified.

In order to gain that approval, the government customer requires that the government contractor (e.g. business, university) provide an SSP. That SSP will contain[7]:

- System identification
- System owner
- Systems description
- System requirement specifications

---

[6] "Least privilege" means that the user or program can only access that information needed and no more. Furthermore, the user does not have any authority that is not absolutely necessary to perform the work assigned, e.g. add, delete and modify databases or information.

[7] This information is contained in Chapter 8, Information System Security of the National Information Protection Operating Manual (NISPOM), Defence Security Service, US Department of Defence.

- Sensitivity and classification levels
- Levels of concern for confidentiality, integrity and availability
- Protection measures
- Variances from protection measure requirements
- System-specific risks and vulnerabilities
- System configuration
- Connections to separately accredited networks and systems
- Security support structure
- Certification and accreditation documentation is also required and consists of:
- Security testing and test plans
- Documentation
- Certification
- Accreditation documentation

10.3.5   AIS Modes of Operation

There are a number of modes of operation that can be used to process, transmit and store various types of national security information. The mode used is authorised by the government customer based on the authorised variations in the AIS IA environment. It is based on the personal security clearances of the users and national security information access needs, e.g. secret clearance held by the users and their need to use that information to accomplish the contractual tasks assigned. It is also based on the automated and manual information protection and defence controls that will be used.

The modes of operation that are used generally fall into four distinct categories:

- *Dedicated*: The users all have a personal clearance equal to the highest level of national security information being processed, stored and transmitted by the AIS and an NTK for all the information on that AIS.
- *Systems high*: All the users have a personal clearance but not an NTK for all the information on the AIS. The users must be separately identified and controlled. This is generally done through passwords, identification devices and add-on software packages.
- *Partitioned*: All users have a personal clearance for the highest level of national security information processed, but not necessarily they have had a special briefing and an NTK for all the information on the AIS. The general controls include a separate identity and password for each user, possibly a special briefing and an NTK. The AIS is partitioned to include possibly two or more CPUs in the same "box" using the same communication links.
- *Multilevel*: This mode permits concurrent processing of various separate national security-related, multi-contractual programs' information. This is the highest level, most costly and least flexible of the security modes and seldom used. Users on these AIS may or may not have a personal security clearance or an NTK for all the information on the AIS. Thus, someone with no national security background check or clearance can use the system

containing national security information. This is possible because the system is so secure that it prevents the user from accessing national security information or national security information of a higher level than the user is cleared to access.

10.3.6   The Appointment of the Defence Industry-Related Corporation's Focal Point for IA

Gaining approval to process, store and transmit national security information usually requires the approval of the government customer security officer. As with any such process, documentation is required on which to base that approval. The types, format and specific requirements will vary depending on the customer and the classification of the information, e.g. top secret, secret and confidential.

This IA-related document usually requires that the defence industry-related corporation appoints a focal point with the responsibility for ensuring that the national security information is protected in accordance with the contract and applicable related laws, regulations and other provisions as specified by the government customer.

The responsibilities of the IA leader[8] include:

- Directing the IA program for the contract
- Ensuring that the personal clearance and NTK of users is in place and enforced
- Ensuring that the users receive national security briefings and training
- Ensuring audit trails are in place and audit records reviewed in a timely manner
- Ensuring the AIS is operating as approved by the government customer
- Ensuring that any IA-related problems are promptly handled
- Designating IA custodians for each AIS who are responsible for the day-to-day IA program for the specified AIS

10.3.7   Documenting and Gaining Government Customer Approval for Processing, Storing and Transmitting National Security Information

As mentioned earlier, many government customers require that they approve individual AIS or groups of similar AISs that will be used to process, store and transmit national security information. However, this approval may be delegated to the corporate IA leader. The approval is considered after reviewing the

---

[8] The individual appointed may have a different title than the IA depending on the government customer, nation-state or defence industry-related corporation. That person may be known as the Corporate IA Officer, the Corporate Information Security Officer, the Widget Program IA Officer, etc. Furthermore, the need for documentation, type, etc. will vary not only by nation but also by government agencies within a nation.

AIS IA-related documentation in a format that they specify and which is usually stated in the contract.

The documentation requirement can be very detailed or general in nature, depending on the AIS and the government customer's requirements. The government customers using the government-approved document for that AIS written by the defence industry-related corporation may then periodically inspect the AIS. Regardless of the format, what is of primary importance is that the IA-related issues be addressed and documented.

The following is an example describing the various IA-related issues that may be addressed in documentation:

- *Identification*: Identify the specific AIS or AISs (if they are all identical, e.g. desktop computers, local area network (LAN) with workstations). This would include their make, model, serial numbers, physical location and mode of operation.
- *Summary of system usage*: This section would include the level of national security information to be processed, any local and remote capabilities, hours of national security information processing and the percentage of information on the AIS that is considered national security, classified information.
- *AIS hardware*: The specific hardware must be identified and include a floor plan, schematic, disconnect methods if networked and any switching devices for disabling the AIS.
- *AIS software*: The name, type, versions of the software and how they are safeguarded to ensure that they were not replaced with another version. This includes protection and defence software such as those used for access control, intrusion detection, etc.
- *Communications*: This section would include the identification of the equipment and transmission lines, disconnect methods, configurations and interfaces, remote devices, protection procedures and physical controls on the lines.
- *Personnel*: Their IA responsibilities, controls to restrict access, visitor and maintenance personnel controls.
- *Physical controls*: This section would include a description of the physical safeguards and characteristics to include any computer facilities and remote areas.
- *General access controls*: Described herein would be how passwords were used, logon and logoff procedures, and how users with various national security clearances and NTK were segregated.
- *AIS operations*: This section would describe how systems were started, used and shutdown to include how they were reconfigured if used at different times for different government programs.
- *Information storage, protection controls*: This section would be used to describe how information was controlled, handled, marked, stored (using what type of accountability system), declassifying the information, such as process used to downgrade information (e.g. from Secret to Restricted), and how the information will be destroyed when required. This section not only deals with the hardcopies coming off the systems but also the electronic media used as storage devices.

- *Audit trails and records*: This section would be used to describe the various types of manual and automated audit trail programs and records that would be used. Included herein would be samples of each as well as their analyses processes.
- *Emergency plan*: This section would describe the procedures to be used in the event of any emergency to include a security violation, system crash or other emergencies that may be possible depending on the information environment.

Remember, the level of description and details documented would be based on the national security requirements as specified in the contract.

10.4   Summary

Thousands of universities, as well as large and small corporations have government contracts. These contracts vary from research and development contracts to production contracts. Most of them rely heavily on ISs and the use of national security information.

These corporations are targets of attacks by other corporations, as well as a nation's adversaries. This includes some of its "allies" who are allies in a military sense but adversaries in an economic sense and also want to gain that competitive edge in economic and military development. Furthermore, they want to do so without paying the high costs of research and development. It is cheaper to steal the information than to develop it on one's own.

A defence industry-related corporation whose systems will process, store and transmit national security information has a responsibility not only to the corporation but also to the nation and its citizens. How well the corporation implements an IA program that will be used to safeguard the national security information has a direct bearing on the security of the nation.

The IA-related requirements and the processes implemented to meet those requirements, although having more serious consequences than that of corporate sensitive information, really is not much different than those of a corporation's IA program.

Establishing an IA focal point, establishing IA controls, documenting how systems will operate and how information and systems will be protected, is always a good practice regardless of the type of sensitive information processed, stored and transmitted.

A Case Study

Section 9 Intrusion Detection Systems

5-900. General
This section specifies the minimum standards for an approved intrusion detection system (IDS) when supplemental protection is required for top secret and secret material. The IDS shall be connected to, and monitored by, a central monitoring station. Alarm system installation shall conform to the requirements of this section or to the standards set forth in Director of Central Intelligence Directive (DCID) 1/21 (Physical Security Standards for Sensitive Compartmented Information Facilities). The Cognizant Security Authority (CSA) will approve contingency protection procedures in the event of the IDS malfunction.

5-901. CSA Approval
The CSA approval is required before installing an IDS. Approval of a new IDS shall be based on the criteria of the DCID 1/21 or UL Standard 2050, as determined by the CSA. The IDSs currently in use that do not meet either of these standards, such as those certified to meet Grade A service and those installed by a non-UL listed company, may continue in use until 1 January 2002.

5-902. Central Monitoring Station
a. The central monitoring station may be located at a UL listed:
   (1) Defence (Government) contractor monitoring station (DCMS or GCMS), formerly called a proprietary central station; (2) cleared commercial central station; (3) cleared protective signal service station (e.g. fire alarm monitor); or (4) cleared residential monitoring station. For the purpose of monitoring alarms, all provide an equivalent level of monitoring service.
b. Trained alarm monitors, cleared to the SECRET level shall be in attendance at the alarm monitoring station at all times when the IDS is in operation.
c. The central monitoring station shall be required to indicate whether or not the system is in working order and tampering with any element of the system. Necessary repairs shall be made as soon as practical. Until repairs are completed, periodic patrols shall be conducted during non-working hours, unless a secret cleared employee is stationed at the alarmed site.
d. When an IDS is used, it shall be activated immediately at the close of business at the alarmed area or container. This may require that the last person who departs the controlled area or checks the security container notify the central monitoring station to set the alarm. A record shall be maintained to identify the person responsible for setting and deactivating the IDS. Each failure to activate or deactivate shall be reported to the FSO. Such records shall be maintained for 30 days.
e. Records shall be maintained for 90 days indicating time of receipt of alarm; name(s) of security force personnel responding; time dispatched to facility/area; time security force personnel arrived; nature of alarm; and what follow-up actions were accomplished.

5-903. Investigative Response to Alarms

a. The following resources may be used to investigate alarms: proprietary security force personnel, central station guards and a subcontracted guard service.

   (1) For a DCMS or GCMS, trained proprietary security force personnel, cleared to the SECRET level and sufficient in number to be dispatched immediately to investigate each alarm, shall be available at all times when the IDS is in operation.

   (2) For a commercial central station, protective signaling service station or residential monitoring station, guards dispatched shall be cleared only if they have the ability and responsibility to access the area or container(s) housing classified material; i.e. keys to the facility have been provided or the personnel are authorized to enter the building or check the container or area that contains classified material.

   (3) Uncleared guards dispatched by a commercial central station, protective signaling service station or residential monitoring station to an alarm shall remain on the premises until a designated, cleared representative of the facility arrives, or for a period of not less than 1 hour, whichever comes first. If a cleared representative of the facility does not arrive within 1 hour following the arrival of the guard, the central control station must provide the CSA with a report of the incident that includes the name of the subscriber facility, the date and time of the alarm and the name of the subscriber's representative who was contacted to respond. A report shall be submitted to the CSA within 24 hours of the next working day. (Note: The primary purpose of any alarm response team is to ascertain if intrusion has occurred and, if possible, assist in the apprehension of the individual. If an alarm activation resets in a reasonable amount of time and no physical penetration of the area or container is visible, then entrance into the area or container is not required. Therefore, the initial response team may consist of uncleared personnel. If the alarm activation does not reset or physical penetration is observed, then a cleared response team must be dispatched. The initial uncleared response team must stay on station until relieved by the cleared response team. If a cleared response team does not arrive within 1 hour, then a report to the CSA must be made by the close of the next business day.)

   (4) Subcontracted guards must be under contract with either the installing alarm company or the cleared facility.

b. The response time shall not exceed 15 minutes. When environmental factors (e.g. traffic, distance) legitimately prevent a 15-minute response time, the CSA may authorize up to a 30-minute response time. The CSA authorization shall be in writing and noted on the alarm certificate. (Note: The UL standard for response within the time limits is 80%, i.e. the minimum allowable on-time response rate. Anything less than 80% is unacceptable. However, in all cases, a guard or cleared employee must arrive at the alarmed premises.)

5-904.   Installation

The IDS at the facility, area or container shall be installed by a UL listed alarm installing company or a company approved by the CSA. When connected to a commercial central station, a DCMS or GCMS protective signaling service or residential monitoring station, the service provided shall include line security (i.e. the connecting lines are electronically supervised to detect evidence of tampering or malfunction). If line security is not available, then two independent means of transmission of the alarm signal from the alarmed area to the monitoring station must be provided. In all cases, the extent of protection for a container shall be "Complete" and for an alarmed area shall be "Extent No. 3".

5-905.   Certification of Compliance

Evidence of compliance with the requirements of this section will consist of a valid (current) UL Certificate for the appropriate category of service. This certificate will have been issued to the protected facility by UL, through the alarm installing company. The certificate serves as evidence that the alarm installing company: (a) is listed as furnishing security systems of the category indicated; (b) is authorized to issue the certificate of installation as representation that the equipment is in compliance with requirements established by UL for the class and (c) is subject to the UL field countercheck program whereby periodic inspections are made of representative alarm installations by UL personnel to verify the correctness of certification practices.

5-906.   Exceptional Cases

a. If the requirements set forth above cannot be met due to extenuating circumstances, the contractor may request the CSA approval for an alarm system that is:
   (1) Monitored by a central control station but responded to by a local (municipal, county, state) law enforcement organization
   (2) Connected by direct wire to alarm receiving equipment located in a local (municipal, county, state) police station or public emergency service dispatch center. This alarm system is activated and deactivated by employees of the contractor, but the alarm is monitored and responded to by personnel of the monitoring police or emergency service dispatch organization. Personnel monitoring alarm signals at police stations or dispatch centers do not require PCL's. Police department response systems may be requested only when: (a) the contractor facility is located in an area where central control station services are not available with line security and/or proprietary security force personnel, or a contractually dispatched response to an alarm signal cannot be achieved within the time limits required by the CSA and (b) it is impractical for the contractor to establish a DCMS or proprietary guard force at that location. Nonetheless, installation of these type systems must use UL-listed equipment and be accomplished by an alarm installation company that is listed by UL for any of the following categories:

1. Defense (National) industrial security systems
2. Proprietary alarm systems
3. Central station burglar alarm systems
4. Police station connected burglar alarm systems

b. An installation proposal explaining how the system would operate shall be submitted to the CSA. The proposal must include sufficient justification for the granting of an exception and the full name and address of the police department that will monitor the system and provide the required response. The name and address of the UL-listed company that will install the system, and inspect, maintain and repair the equipment, shall also be furnished.

c. The contractor shall require a 15-minute response time from the police department. Arrangements shall be made with the police to immediately notify a contractor representative on receipt of the alarm. The contractor representative is required to go immediately to the facility to investigate the alarm and to take appropriate measures to secure the classified material.

d. In exceptional cases where central station monitoring service is available, but no proprietary security force of central station or subcontracted guard response is available, and where the police department does not agree to respond to alarms, and no other manner of investigative response is available, the CSA may approve cleared employees as the sole means of response.

http://www.dss.mil/isec/chapter5.htm#section%209

11

The Corporate IA Officer

The need for a corporate information assurance officer is discussed in this chapter. The topics discussed include the required basic qualifications for a person in that position as well as the duties and responsibilities needed to lead an information assurance program for the 21st century corporation.

11.1   The Corporate Information Assurance Officer[1]

The information assurance (IA) profession seems to have a difficult time being considered other than an information systems security profession. In addition, some consider the entire IA topic as one used by people like the US government, primarily Department of Defence personnel.

The position of the corporate information assurance officer (CIAO) is a relatively new but necessary position. It is more than that of the corporate security officer (CSO) or the corporate information systems security officer (CISSO) because the IA functions are much more than that of the "old" information systems security or corporate security professions. The discussion of the position of a CIAO will be based on what it should be as there are only a few such positions today.

However, it is felt that when one looks at the totality of the IA and information systems security administration and management functions, one can see the need for such a position. In addition, this position in today's information-dependent environment includes issues related to privacy and liability. This is a logical progression of the professional CSO and CISSO to a CIAO. This is because the issues of privacy and liability have a direct bearing on why a formal IA program is necessary and the ability of the CIAO to provide adequate IA.

---

[1] Some of the information provided are excerpts from Dr. Kovacich's book, *Information Systems Security Officer's Guide: Establishing and Managing an Information Protection Program*, First and Second Editions published by Butterworth-Heinemann, and reprinted with permission.

11.1.1 CIAO Position

The CIAO's position requires someone with education and experience that is much more than that of "just a computer techie". In fact, it is believed that the CIAO's duties are somewhere between 75% management and 25% of actual IA work. Therefore, whoever assumes that position should generally have the following education and experience:

- **Education**: A combination of undergraduate and graduate degrees in computer science/information systems, criminal justice/criminology, information systems security/business security, social science, investigations, psychology, business management and related fields. An MBA in international business or related graduate degree would be a plus. One may ask, why an MBA? The rationale for this is that at the corporate level, the individual in the position of the CIAO must have a good understanding of business, especially global business these days, because each IA-related decision made by the CIAO will have an impact on resource allocations, budgets, productivity and the like. One can have the best IA program in the world but if it stifles productivity and dramatically increases business costs, then the corporation may not be able to compete effectively, thus losing their market share. This may even lead to a corporation going out of business. Perhaps such a statement is a little overly dramatic but the point is made. For those in government agencies, the same would apply since there is little difference these days in managing a government agency and a business organisation from the standpoint of information dependencies, resource allocations, budget and the like.
- **Certifications**: The CIAO should be, as a minimum, a certified information systems security professional (CISSP). Additional certifications, such as a Certified Information Systems Auditor, Certified Fraud Examiner, Certified Protection Professional, help ensure that the individual filling the position of a CIAO understands the issue of IA from a holistic perspective.
- **Experience**: The CIAO should have a minimum 10-year experience managing an IA, information systems security or corporate security organisation, to include experience in formal project management, budgeting, people-skills, team building, total quality management/continuous process improvement, matrix management, time management, problem-solving and other related management experiences.

11.1.2 CIAO Duties and Responsibilities

In concert with the executive management of the corporation, the CIAO should develop and receive approval for formally establishing a charter of the CIAO duties and responsibilities. The following charter example is provided:

Summary of the purpose of the corporation's CIAO position: *develop, implement, maintain, manage and administer a corporate-wide IA program to include all plans, policies, procedures, processes, assessments, and authorisations necessary to protect and defend the corporation's information and information systems. This*

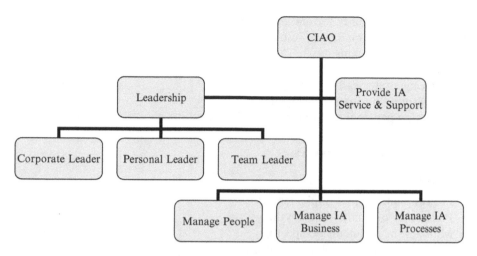

FIGURE 11.1. Shows the Duties and Responsibilities of the CIAO

includes ensuring their availability, integrity, authentication, confidentiality, non-repudiation, as well as also providing for restoration of information and information systems by incorporating protection, detection and reaction.[2]

Since the CIAO is also assumed to be a manager and manage an IA organisation, the CIAO's duties and responsibilities should include few tasks as described in the following sections (see Figure 11.1).

11.1.2.1   Managing People

- Managing people includes:
- Building a reputation of professional integrity
- Maintaining excellent business relationships
- Dealing with changes
- Communicating
- Developing people
- Influencing people in a positive way
- Building a teamwork environment
- Developing people through performance management, e.g. help IA staff to be result oriented.

11.1.2.2   Managing the Business of IA

This consists of:
- A commitment to results
- Being customer/supplier focused

---

[2] The CIAO position summary is taken from US directive NSTISSI 4009 that defines the IA. The definition is used because it not only defines the IA but also describes what the CIAO is directed to do.

- Taking responsibility for making decisions
- Developing and managing resource allocations
- Planning and organising
- Being a problem solver
- Thinking strategically
- Using sound business judgement
- Accepting personal accountability and ownership

11.1.2.3   Managing IA processes

This includes:

- Project planning and implementation
- Persistence of quality in everything
- Maintaining a systems perspective
- Maintaining current job knowledge

11.1.3   Goals and Objectives

The CIAO must have goals and objectives. These must directly support the goals and objectives of the corporation. Since any IA program for a corporation is centred on providing service and support to meeting the corporation's goals and objective, this is quite logical.

11.1.3.1   The CIAO's Goal

The CIAO's primary goal should be to administer an innovative IA program that minimises risks to information and liability risks at least impact to costs and schedules, while meeting all of the corporation's and customers' (internal and external) reasonable expectations. This goal sounds very bureaucratic, "managerial" and possibly even a little "academic". All that may or may not be true. However, as a goal, it sets the direction of an IA program for the corporation and assists the CIAO in focusing on doing what must be done to attain that goal. Let us dissect that goal and see why it is so. *Administer an innovative program* means that the CIAO manages a program that must be flexible and have the ability to rapidly change to meet the needs of the corporation.

The idea of innovation means that just because it has not been done in a certain way before does not mean that it should not be tried. Such ideas, as brainstorming with others and "thinking outside the box", are integrated into solving problems and implementing processes to meet the corporate needs.

Minimises risks to information and liability risks at least impact to costs and schedules means that all processes integrated into the IA program and all decisions made must be considered on the basis of ensuring that the minimal amount of risks is taken. In addition, what must also be considered and decided is how to do that and how to obtain that "perfect balance" between minimal risks while at the same time of having the least impact. By least impact we mean impact on people's productivity, additional costs to projects and the business and also without adversely impacting the project and business schedules of the corporation.

It is extremely important that such decisions incorporate this thought process, whether this is a formally established goal. The CIAO may even want to use a checklist identifying such items when making a decision. As a minimum, when such decisions are implemented or submitted to management for approval, such information will greatly assist the decision makers in supporting a CIAO's decision.

While meeting all of the corporation's and customers' (internal and external) reasonable expectations means that the IA processes, IA program and IA-related decisions accomplish what is expected of the CIAO and the IA program in terms of IA. Internal customers means that the management and employees of a corporation whom the CIAO provides IA services and support are considered customers and should be treated as such. Additionally, external customers are those identified as customers by the corporation, which possibly include suppliers, associates, subcontractors and the like.

Sometimes the CIAO is placed in a difficult position by trying to meet this goal. Management may disapprove of a particular IA approach, but then the CIAO is held responsible for any adverse impact to information, even though the proposal by the CIAO, if it had been implemented, would have mitigated the problem. Such is the life of a CIAO!

11.1.3.2   The CIAO's Objective

It is assumed that the CIAO will be responsible for managing an IA organisation in order to meet the needs of the corporation. The CIAO's objectives should include the following:

- Enhance the quality, efficiency, and effectiveness of the IA organisation
- Identify potential problem areas and strive to mitigate them before the corporate management and/or customers identify them
- Enhance the corporation's ability to attract customers because of the ability to efficiently and effectively protect information
- Establish the IA organisation as the IA leader in its industry

11.1.4   Leadership Position

The CIAO must be in a leadership position. In that position, it is extremely important that the CIAO understands what a leader is and how a leader is to act. According to the definition of *Leadership* found in numerous dictionaries and management books, it is basically about the position or guidance of a leader, the ability to lead, the leader of a group; a person that leads; directing, commanding, or guiding head, as of a group or activity. As a *leader*, the corporation's CIAO must set the example; create and foster an information protection "consciousness" within the corporation.

- As a *corporate leader*, the CIAO must communicate the corporation's community involvement, eliminate unnecessary expenses, inspire corporate pride and find ways to increase profitability.
- As a *team leader*, the CIAO must encourage teamwork, communicate clear direction, create an IA environment conducive to teaming, treat others as peers and team members not as competitors and recognise their needs also.
- As a *personal leader*, the CIAO must improve personal leadership skills, accept and learn from constructive criticism, take ownership and responsibility for decisions, make decisions in a timely manner and demonstrate self-confidence.

11.1.4.1   Providing IA Service and Support

As the CIAO and leader of an IA service and support organisation, the CIAO must be especially tuned to the needs, wants and desires of the corporation's customers.

To provide service and support to the corporation's external customers, the CIAO must:

- Identify their information protection needs
- Meet their reasonable expectations
- Show by example that the IA program can meet their protection expectations
- Treat customer satisfaction as top priority
- Encourage feedback and listen
- Understand their needs and expectations
- Treat customer requirements as an important part of the job
- Establish measures to assure customer satisfaction
- Provide honest feedback to customers

To provide service and support to the corporation's internal customers, the CIAO must:

- Support their business needs
- Add value to their services
- Minimise IA impact on current processes
- Follow the same guidelines as for external customers

The CIAO will also be dealing with suppliers of IA products. These suppliers are a valuable ally because they can explain to the CIAO many new IA problems being discovered and how their products mitigate those problems, and generally they can keep the CIAO up-to-date on the latest news within the CIAO/IA profession.

In dealing with suppliers of IA-related products, the CIAO should:

- Advise them of the corporation's needs and what types of products can help
- Assist them in understanding the corporation's requirements and products that the corporations may want from them, to include what modifications they must make to their products before the corporation is willing to purchase them
- Direct them in the support and assistance they are to provide the corporation

- Respect them as team members
- Value their contributions
- Require quality products and high standards of performance from them

11.1.4.2   Use Team Concepts

It is important that the CIAO understands that the IA Program is a corporate program. To be successful, the CIAO cannot operate independently but as a team leader, with a team of others who also have a vested interest in the protection of the company's information and information systems.

It is important to remember that if the IA functions are divided between two or more organisations, there will naturally be a tendency for less communication and co-ordination. If that occurs, the CIAO must be sensitive to this division of functions and ensure that even more communication and co-ordination occurs between all the departments concerned.

The IA program must be "sold" to the management and staff of the corporation. If it is presented as a law that must be followed or else, then it will be doomed to failure. The CIAO will never have enough staff to monitor everyone all the time, and that is what will be needed. For as soon as the CIAO's back is turned, the employees will go back to doing it the way they want to do it. Everyone must do it the right IA way because they know it is the best way and in their own interests, as well as in the interest of the corporation.

In the corporation, as in many companies today, success can only be achieved through continuous inter-departmental communication, co-operation and specialists from various organisations formed into integrated project teams to solve company problems. The CIAO should keep it in mind that teaming and success go together in today's modern corporation.

11.1.5   Vision, Mission and Quality Statements

Many of today's modern corporations have developed vision, mission and quality statements using a hierarchical process. In other words, they flow up and down the management chain. The statements should link all levels in the management and organisational chain. The statements of the lower levels should be written and used to support the upper levels and vice versa.

The following examples can be used by the CIAO to develop such statements, if they are necessary.

11.1.5.1   Vision Statements

In many of today's businesses, management develops a vision statement. The vision statement is usually a short paragraph that attempts to set the strategic goal, objective or direction of the company. It is:

- Clear, concise and understandable by the employees
- Connected to ethics, values and behaviours

- States where the corporation wants to be (long term)
- Sets the tone
- Sets the direction for the corporation

An IA vision statement may be to: Provide the most efficient and effective IA program for the corporation, which adds value to the corporation's products and services, as a recognised leader in the financial industry.

11.1.5.2   Mission Statements

Mission statements are declarations as to the purpose of a business or government agency.

An IA mission statement may be to: Administer an innovative IA program that minimises security risks at least impact to cost and schedule, while meeting all of the corporation's and customers' IA requirements.

11.1.5.3   Quality Statements

Quality is what adds value to the corporation's products and services. It is what the corporation's internal and external customers should also expect from the CIAO.

An IA quality statement may be to: Consistently provide quality IA professional services and support that meet the customers' requirements and reasonable expectations, in concert with good business practices and company guidelines.

11.1.5.4   Project and Risk Management Processes

Two basic processes that are an integral part of an IA program are project management and risk management concepts.

- *Project management concepts*: As the CIAO and IA program leader, the CIAO will also provide oversight of IA-related projects that are being worked by members of the CIAO staff. The criteria for a project should be as follows: formal projects, along with project management charts, will be initiated in which improvements or other changes will be accomplished, and that effort has an objective, beginning and ending dates, and will take longer than 30 days to complete. If the project will be accomplished in less than 30 days, a formal project management process is not needed. The rationale for this is that the projects of short duration are not worth the effort (costs in terms of hours to complete the project plan, charts, etc.) of such a formal process.
- *Risk management concepts*: To be cost-effective, the CIAO must apply risk management concepts (see Chapter 3 for risk management concepts) and identify:

Threats to the information and information systems
Vulnerabilities (information systems' weaknesses)
Risks
Countermeasures to mitigate those risks in a cost-effective way

11.2   Summary

The CIAO position is needed in today's information-driven and information-dependent corporation. The position requires someone who has the education and experience to lead a corporation's IA efforts. The position calls for someone who understands systems, security and business as well as the risks to information and how to cost-effectively mitigate those risks. The CIAO must be focused on the goals and objectives of the corporation and integrate an IA program into the corporation's processes that will assist (or at least not deter the corporation) in meeting those goals and objectives. The CIAO must be result oriented, use team concepts and project management techniques to be successful.

12

IA Organisational Functions

This chapter describes and discusses the establishment of a corporate information assurance organisation and its major functions. The corporate information assurance officer would manage the organisation.

12.1 Determining Major IA Functions

There are many information assurance (IA) functions, and these functions can be grouped and assigned to various organisations within the corporation. For example, the physical security function would undoubtedly remain within the corporate security organisation. The function of auditing for compliance to corporate policies would also undoubtedly remain within the audit department. To integrate those functions into an IA organisation would dilute the main tasks of the corporate information assurance officer (CIAO), as well as almost impossible politically. In addition, there should be some basic separations of functions, e.g. the organisation establishing an IA policy should not also be auditing that policy to ensure that it is adequate.

The CIAO's duties and responsibilities within any medium or large corporation cannot be successfully accomplished by the CIAO alone. Therefore, it is logical that specialists be assigned as staff to the CIAO. The size of that staff is driven by several factors. These factors include what is known as IA drivers. In other words, those factors that cause the CIAO's workload to increase and decrease. The following three drivers are offered as examples.

- *Number of systems*: More systems and their various configurations, type of hardware and software and the like, all have a bearing on the amount of information and systems activity going on within the corporation. Thus, the more information systems the greater the task of protection and defence.
- *Number of system users*: The number of system users has a direct bearing on the workload of the CIAO. The more users the more IA infractions that will occur and the more information on those systems that require protection.

- *Importance of information being stored, processed and transmitted*: The CIAO's workload is also driven by the sensitivity of the information being stored, processed and transmitted by the systems. For example, the IA is not an issue if the information is not important, and it is an important issue if the information is deemed sensitive and important to the corporation.

The CIAO and the IA organisations should have at least the following basic IA-related functions and processes under their authority:

- Requirements
- Policy
- Systems IA architecture
- Awareness and training
- Access control
- Security tests and evaluations
- Non-compliance inquiries
- Risk management
- Disaster recovery/contingency planning program

Figure 12.1 shows a sample IA functional organisation.

One must consider the office politics and related aspects of these functions. Each corporate culture is unique and the functions that should be performed by the IA organisation in lieu of another organisation within the corporation is generally solely based on the amount of support that is given to the CIAO by the corporation's executive management. Thus, the need for the CIAO to manage an IA program using team-building concepts and other management techniques as stated throughout Section 2 will determine whether or not the CIAO will be successful.

What is essential for the CIAO is to make a case to the corporation's executive management as to why certain functions belong within the IA organisation However, if that support is not forthcoming, the CIAO should concentrate on being successful in accomplishing the job assigned and not worry about obtaining the other functions regardless of their importance to the IA program. The next step would then be to co-ordinate IA-related interests with the managers assigned to the IA-related functions and try to integrate the IA interests into those functions.

An example is the awareness program. If that function is given to the corporate security officer's organisation, the CIAO should work with that manager to ensure that the IA interests are integrated into the overall corporate security awareness program. This has several advantages such as the IA staff does not have to develop an entirely new awareness program and does not require additional budget and the allocation of at least one dedicated individual to that function. It also eliminates the perception that the CIAO is neither a "team player" nor an "empire builder".

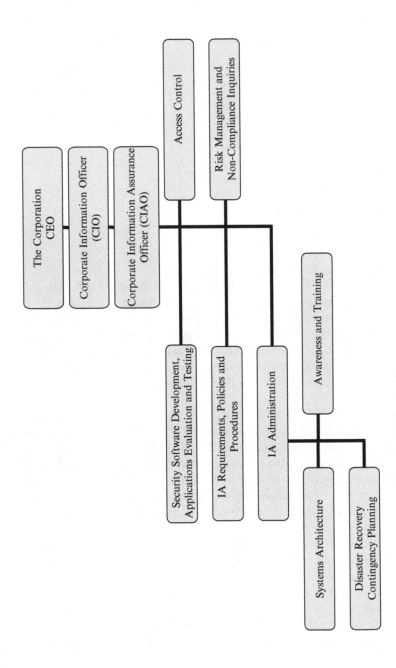

FIGURE 12.1. A Sample IA Functional Organisation

12.2   IA Functions and Process Development

Let us assume that the CIAO has been authorised and given an approved budget (a very key and necessary aspect of corporate life) by executive management to establish an IA organisation to meet the IA program needs of the corporation. Let us further assume that the basic IA functions noted above have been approved to be under the authority and responsibility of the CIAO. With that in mind, the CIAO can proceed to establish an IA organisation so that a corporate IA program can be established. It is not the intent of this book to delve into how to recruit and hire IA staff but only to address the functional aspects of an IA organisation.

Such functions should be established using an orderly and systematic method. In fact, this is the first IA project that should be formalised into a project plan, complete with objectives, tasks, dates for accomplishment, identify who will do each task and an estimated time for accomplishing the tasks. It is also important from a management aspect to formalise this project so that the project plan can be used to periodically brief executive management on the status of the project as well as to track the costs of the project. Remember the old saying "time is money". Well, that is certainly truer today than ever before. By costing out such projects, it will assist the CIAO in establishing the cost factors associated with developing, implementing and maintaining a cost-effective IA program. This, in turn, will provide a history on which to base future costs of functions and portions of the IA program, as well as to justify budget requirements.

All of these support and relate back to the goals and objectives stated through the vision, mission and quality statements noted in Chapter 10. By using those goals and objective statements, one can begin to see how a CIAO can focus on "doing it right the first time". In other words, the CIAO is beginning this effort from ground zero and thus can integrate good management practices as the IA program is developed. This is much easier than trying to integrate such methods and philosophies into an IA program after that program has matured.

In order to effectively and efficiently identify and establish the IA functions to be accomplished by the CIAO's IA organisation, a standard process should be developed. By establishing a process for each function as the first task, it will assist in ensuring that the functions will begin in a logical, systematic way that will lead to a cost-effective IA program. By identifying and using IA work drivers as noted above, the CIAO can begin to develop such a process. In addition, an experienced CIAO will know well what needs to be done usually in what order and how to accomplish those tasks. More than likely, the CIAO brings to this position the methods that have been successful in the past – at least one hopes that is the case.

12.2.1   IA Requirements Function

The CIAO has determined that one of the main drivers for any IA program is obviously the requirements for an IA. The requirements are the reason for the IA program. After all, if it were not required, it would not exist as the corporation has no intention of spending precious resources, e.g. money, on programs that are not needed. This is obvious, but sometimes it is necessary to state the obvious. This *need* is further identified and defined and subsequently met by the establishment of the IA functions.

So, to begin the functions' process identification, it is important to understand where the requirements and the needs come from. For most corporations, it includes the following:

- A need for an IA program as stated by the corporation's executive management to protect the corporation's competitive edge, which is based on information systems and the information that they store, process and transmit
- A requirement as specified in contracts with corporate customers, e.g. protect and defend their information
- A requirement as specified in contracts with corporate subcontractors, e.g. protect and defend their information
- A requirement as specified in contracts with corporate vendors, e.g. protect and defend their information
- The desire of the corporation to protect its information and systems from unauthorised access by customers and subcontractors, vendors, and others
- National and international laws that are applicable to the corporation, e.g. requirements to protect the privacy rights of individuals and corporations as these relate to the information stored, processed and transmitted by the corporation's systems

12.2.2   IA Policy Function

Based on the requirements and IA drivers as stated earlier, the CIAO must take the next step to develop an overall corporate IA policy, co-ordinate that policy with applicable department managers and gain executive management approval for that IA policy. That policy should be clear, concise and written at somewhat of a high level. It must conform to the corporate policy format of course. The IA policy should not get bogged down in details at a system identification level but set the IA guideline for the corporation. The IA policy should be distributed to all department managers and that distribution should be done through a cover letter, signed by the CEO, President and/or Chairman of the Board. The letter should basically state that the information is important to the corporation's well-being and competitive edge; the IA policy document provides the overall policy for protecting that competitive edge and obligates all of the corporate employees to support that policy.

The policy establishes the baseline for the corporation for the protection and defence of information and information systems. It must be the first function to be addressed after establishing the requirements because all other functions must flow from or derive their guidance from the policy function. If there is not a logical and cost-effective policy in place, a logical and cost-effective IA program cannot be established.

The IA policy should be set forth in a corporate IA Requirements and Policy Directive. The Directive should generally include the following:

- Introduction section that includes some history as needed for an IA
- Purpose section that describes why the document exists
- Scope section that defines the breadth of the directive
- Responsibilities section that defines and identifies the IA responsibilities at all levels to include executive management, organisational managers, systems custodians, IT personnel and users. The Directive should also include the requirements for customers', subcontractors', vendors' and other's access to the corporate systems and information.
- Requirements section that includes the requirements for:
- Identifying the value of the information
- Access to the information and to the systems
- Access to specific applications, databases and files
- Audit trails and their review
- Reporting responsibilities and action to be taken in the event of an indication of a possible violation
- Minimum protection requirements for the information, hardware, firmware and software
- A requirement for developing, implementing and maintaining current IA procedures at all levels of the corporation

12.2.3   IA Procedures Function

Based on the corporate IA policy, each organisation must establish procedures, based on its unique environment, number of systems, types of configurations, hardware, software, types of information and the value of the information under its responsibility. These organisational IA procedures provide detailed direction as to how each organisation is to comply with and support the corporate IA policy.

This has several advantages that include the following:

- The individual organisational managers are in a better position to write the document and develop cost-effective procedures, which work for their organisation.
- It makes the department, especially managers, responsible for compliance with the IA policy. In other words, they have a shared investment in the IA program.
- It negates the managers' complaints that their situation was unique, and thus they could not comply with all aspects of an IA procedure as written (if one had been written by the CIAO staff).
- It also relieves the CIAO of dealing with this large magnitude of procedures throughout the corporation and places it squarely where it belongs – on the individual organisational managers and employees.

12.2.4   Systems IA Architecture Function

One of the primary functions of any IA program should be the systems IA architecture function. This function ensures that IA requirements are met through integration of IA architecture into the systems architecture of each corporate IT project. Furthermore, it is imperative that this function be integrated into the total corporate systems architecture. When the IA architecture requirements are met, it will automatically comply with the IA policy. Therefore, IA systems architecture specialist(s), assigned to the IA organisation should be involved as a team member of each new systems development project. The philosophy is as follows:

Design it to protect and defend information and information systems
Build it to protect and defend information and information systems
Test it to protect and defend information and information systems
Implement it to protect and defend information and information systems
Maintain it to protect and defend information and information systems

12.2.5   IA Awareness and Training Function

It naturally follows that once the IA policy has published there must be some process to make the corporate employees aware of the IA requirements. There must be a process to:

- Advise new employees of the IA policy
- Advise non-employees who use the systems and information of the IA policy
- Advise all users of the information and systems of changes in that policy
- Provide reminders to users as to that policy
- Gain the support of everyone by explaining the need for such a policy and requirements

The awareness program process can be broken into the following four major parts.

- Awareness briefings for new employees
- Awareness briefings for non-employees but users of the corporate information and systems
- Recurring, e.g. annual, awareness briefings
- An IA training for the IA staff members and those employees with some IA responsibilities

12.2.5.1   Awareness Briefings

The IA awareness briefings in some corporations are integrated into new-hire orientation briefings and also into security-related briefings. As mentioned earlier, it may be required to integrate the IA awareness material to be used for an IA briefing into the other corporate briefings. If that is the case, there is a concern that the personnel giving the briefings do not understand the IA concepts in sufficient detail to give the briefings and answer questions relative to IA – or worse yet, provide erroneous information. Another concern is that the IA portion of any of the other briefings does not allow sufficient time to adequately inform the attendees of all the pertinent IA information that they should know. If an IA awareness briefing must be integrated into other briefings, it may be possible for an IA specialist to provide that portion of the briefing.

Ideally, the IA awareness briefings should be tailored, based on the unique jobs of the specific audiences as follows:

- All new hires, whether they used a system. The rationale is that they all handle information and come in contact with computer and telecommunication systems in one form or another
- Managers
- System users
- Information technology department personnel
- Engineers
- Manufacturers
- Accounting and finance personnel
- Procurement personnel
- Human resources personnel
- Security and audit personnel
- The system IA custodians (those that would be given day-to-day responsibility to ensure that the systems and information were protected in accordance with the IA policy and procedures, e.g. access control administrators, firewall administrators audit trail records reviewers

A process should be established to identify these personnel, input their profile information into a database and using a standard format track their awareness briefings attendance, their initial briefings and any annual re-briefings, etc. That information could also be used to provide them, through the corporate e-mail system, with additional awareness material.

As part of the IA awareness process, those attending such a briefing should acknowledge in writing that they understand their responsibilities and agree to comply with the requirements and policy.

It is well understood that all users and others must understand the IA requirements and policy in order to support the protection and defence of information and information systems. However, another key element supporting the need for the IA awareness briefings is to hold the users accountable for their actions if they are subsequently identified as violating the IA policy. Such violations may be the cause for not only disciplinary action but civil or criminal action as well. In any case, a basic requirement that must be presented as evidence in any proceedings is as follows:

- A current IA policy exists.
- The IA policy was violated.
- The person was made aware of that policy.

- The person acknowledged in writing that the IA policy was understood and would be followed.
- The person acted with intent to violate that IA policy.

Most of the violations will probably be due to human error. Even if human error and no malicious intent are identified, it still has an impact on the protection and defence of the corporation's sensitive information and information systems.

12.2.5.2   IA Awareness Material

One of the other means used to make systems users and others aware of the IA requirements, policy and their responsibilities is to provide reminders through various media. This should be done in a cost-effective manner. It is often difficult to quantify the cost-benefits of awareness material. However, it is still recommended as a good procedure to keep users aware of the IA matters, and it includes such material as:

- Annual calendars
- Posters
- Labels for systems and diskettes
- Articles published in the corporate news publications
- Logon notices and system broadcast messages, especially of IA changes

12.2.6   Access Control and Audit Records Analyses Functions

Once the IA requirements are identified, the IA policy published and everyone made aware of that policy, the next logical step would be to look at the processes used to control access to systems, applications and information. Access controls must be maintained on all systems and information that are considered sensitive. In other words, if the systems or information can be destroyed without adversely impacting the corporation's business, then access controls are not considered necessary – it may be prudent to still control access, but it is not an IA requirement. Access controls are expensive and require intensive amount of resources to adequately maintain them. Therefore, their use should always be based on IA requirements and IA policy. The requirements and policy are based on the value of the information and the information systems to the corporation.

12.2.6.1   Access Control

Access control is based on the need-to-know (NTK) principle. It means that access to information and information systems is only provided to those personnel with the need for access to information and systems. The criterion is that access is required in order for them to successfully function in their position within the corporation, or as non-employees to support the corporation as part of their contracts or other legal agreements. A basic principle of IA is that access is only provided to that information and systems required for the individual to complete their tasks – no more and no less. Thus, there is a need for access control processes.

As part of any access control function and process, there must be personnel in positions of authority who are the designated owners of the information and/or systems. These owners must authorise the identified personnel access to the information and/or systems. It is not the responsibility of an IA organisation to authorise access to information and/or systems but to either directly control access as an IA function or indirectly through various organisational personnel designated as access controllers and assigned to other organisations. For example, as part of the IA program, the CIAO, in co-ordination with other departments' managers, can establish a process for all corporate employees and others who require access to the systems.

The employees would obtain system access approval from the manager or designated representative who owned that system. The information owners' approval is based on a justified need-for-access as stated by the employee's manager. If the systems' owners and information owners agreed, access is granted. Thus, the access control process included a justification by an employee's manager stated not only what systems and why they needed access to them, but also what information they required access to in order to perform their jobs. An audit trail is then maintained of who approved access to whom, and for what purposes. It also helps provide a separation of functions, which is a vital component of any IA program, e.g. accounts payable personnel should not also have access to all the accounts receivable files.

12.2.6.2   Access Control Systems

Access control systems may be integrated hardware, firmware and/or software applications. They also may be an integrated manual and automated process or even an administrative and technical process. However it is established, the process must be safeguarded at the highest level because a compromise or successful attack against the access control systems means the heart of the IA goals of protection and defence have been violated. After all, these are the front-line defences of a corporation's systems and information. Access control systems must be thoroughly and often tested to validate and verify that they are operating as expected.

12.2.6.3   Audit Records Analyses

Having access control systems in place, no matter how good, does nothing to identify that an attack or probe of the access control systems was conducted. It is bad enough to be under attack but much worse not to even know that an attack is occurring until that fateful moment when it is successful, e.g. the systems are not available such as in a denial of service attack (DoS). What if the objective of the attack was to probe the system for weaknesses and when found steal the sensitive information? There would be no DoS, no missing or modified information. No one would even know that the probe had taken place and that it was successful and now the competitor of the corporation had the proprietary information that it had long sought.

It is amazing how many corporations do not require audit trail records or if so, place them in storage in either hardcopy or on electronic storage devices – without being reviewed. The rationale is that there is no time to review and analyse the records for indications of attacks and probes. In today's information environment this is unconscionable.

When an attack is discovered, often after the damage has been done, the audit records may be analysed to determine what happened. However, these are historical documents and cannot replace real-time monitoring where an attack may be identified and stopped before it can be successful. So, it would fall into the "too little, too late" category.

It is true that in major corporations, there are massive amounts of data that can and are collected that would give indications of attacks and probes. However, the problem is more complicated than just the vast amount of audit trail records available from systems. There are also other problems.

Audit records are unique to each system.

Audit records for each system provide different levels of information granularity in different ways and formats.

Reviewers of audit trail records are not trained on what to look for and what actions to take in the event certain, specific events were noted.

Audit records are not integrated into a database for analyses across the entire corporation to present an "IA picture" from a holistic point of view.

It is often a misconception that the reviewer should only look for unauthorised access attempts. That is only part of the issue. The unauthorised access attempts can and often do indicate attacks and probes against the systems, but what is often more important is a look at the authorised accesses. These indicate that someone using a valid user ID and password entered the system. But how can one know that the person was not using a stolen user ID and password?

What is needed if this basic concept of access control and audit records analyses is to work to develop an automated process to collect all the corporate systems' audit records. Then using artificial intelligence and neural networks, one can begin to truly conduct the analyses required. Integrated into this automated process would be the profile of what each user requires access to under the NTK concept, what they had been approved to access and profiles of all the users' activities, what they access, when, etc. Such an automated audit records analyses would compare the normal activity of the users and alert an IA personnel or access administrators to deviations from the norm. Such a system is urgently required in order to begin to establish a true IA program.

12.2.7   Evaluation of all Hardware, Firmware and Software Functions

After IA requirements have been identified, incorporated into an IA policy document, and the CIAO's staff of IA requirements and IA system architecture specialists are working with systems development project teams, it is imperative that the hardware, software and firmware be evaluated. These evaluations are needed to ensure that their vulnerabilities are identified and processes established to mitigate those vulnerabilities using such processes as the risk management methodologies noted in Chapter 3.

The evaluations can be done by various methods. The key is to know what the vulnerabilities are for each system. Some of the evaluation methods are as follows:

• Contact the supplier of the product and identify the vulnerabilities and seek their advice on how to mitigate them. It should be noted that they may not be completely honest; however, that is why a rapport and trust must be developed with the suppliers as noted in Chapter 11 concerning the CIAO and suppliers/vendors.
• Establish an in-house team of specialists that are intimately familiar with the product and determine the product vulnerabilities and how to mitigate them.
• Contact other professionals in the field to get their opinions and advices on the product's vulnerabilities and how to mitigate them.
• Review magazines, Websites and computer emergency response team (CERT) announcements related to the products and their vulnerabilities and how to mitigate them.
• Outsource vulnerability testing to a company with the expertise to identify product vulnerabilities and how to mitigate them.

The objective is to build systems that meet at least the minimal protection and defence requirements as established by the corporation's IA program. One must also remember that the systems currently in place must also be evaluated in a similar fashion. This process is not limited to systems in development.

An additional process that may be helpful is to establish an IA baseline checklist that would be completed by the prospective suppliers of the product, in concert with the IA staff. The process would include a technical evaluation by IA personnel in concert with IT personnel. If the product was considered *risk acceptable*, it can be approved for purchase. If not risk acceptable, the risk management process would be used to identify countermeasures. If the risks were unacceptable and weighed using a cost-benefit-risk methodology and the products were still to be purchased, executive management should be called upon to make the final decision of acceptable and unacceptable risks.

Some items may have an unacceptable level of risk but would still be accepted due to its value to the corporation and its competitive edge. In those instances, special audit trails should be considered to monitor the use of the product with the goal of identifying threat agents that could take advantage of the products' vulnerabilities. In any case, it is better to at least know that a system is vulnerable than to not know the vulnerability existed until it was too late.

12.2.8   *Applying Risk Management Principles and Establishing a Risk Management Function*

Although Chapter 3 discussed the risk management principles and methodologies, it is a process that permeates the entire IA program and should be the basis for all decisions made to protect and defend information and information systems. Thus, its application and summary information is stated here.

Remember the objective of an IA program's risk management process is to maximise information protection and defences, and minimise cost through risk management.

What Is Risk Management? In order to understand the risk management methodology, one must first understand what risk management means. Risk management is defined as the total process of identifying, controlling and eliminating or minimising uncertain events that may affect corporate information and information system resources. It includes risk assessments, risk analyses including cost-benefit analyses, target selection, implementation and test, security evaluation of safeguards and overall IA review.

12.2.8.1   Risk Management Process Goals

The goal of the risk management process is to provide the best protection and defence of systems and the information they store, process and/or transmit at least cost consistent with the value of the systems and the information.

12.2.8.2   Risk Management Process

Remember that the IA program is a corporate program made up of IA professionals and others who provide service and support to their corporation. Therefore, the risk management process must be based on the needs of the corporation, its customers and not on the needs of the CIAO, staff or IA program. It is also important that one should be sure that the risk management concepts, program and processes are informally and formally used in all aspects of the IA program to include when and how to do awareness briefings, the impact of information systems security policies and procedures on the employees, etc.

The following steps should be considered above and beyond the "normal" risk management approach in the risk management process.

- *Management interest*: Identify IA areas that are of major interest to executive management and customers and approach from a business point of view. So, the process should begin with interviews of your internal customers to determine what areas of IA are adversely affecting their operations the most. Then, target those areas first as the starting point for the risk management program.
- *Identify specific targets*: Software applications, hardware, telecommunications, electronic media storage etc.
- *Input sources*: Users, system administrators, auditors, security officers, technical journals, technical bulletins, CERT alerts (Internet), risk assessment application programs, etc.

- *Identify potential threats*: Internal and external, natural or man-made.
- *Identify vulnerabilities*: Through interviews, experience, history and testing.
- *Risk identification*: Match threats to vulnerabilities with existing countermeasures, verify and validate.
- *Assess risks*: Acceptable or not acceptable, identify residual risk, then certify the process and gain approval. If the risks are not acceptable, then:

- Identify countermeasures
- Identify each countermeasures' costs
- Compare countermeasures, risks and costs to mitigated risks

12.2.8.3   Recommendations to Management

When the risk assessment is completed, the CIAO must make recommendations to management. Remember in making recommendations to think from a business point of view – cost, benefits, profits, public relations, etc.

12.2.8.4   Risk Management Reports

A briefing that includes a formal, written report is the vehicle to bring the risks to management's attention. The report should include identifying areas that need improvement, areas that are performing well and recommended actions for improvement to include costs and benefits.

Remember that it is management's decision to either accept or mitigate the risks, and how much to spend to do so. The CIAO and IA staff are the specialists, the in-house consultants. It is management's responsibility to decide what to do. They may follow the CIAO's recommendations, ignore them, or take some other action. In any case, the CIAO has provided the service and support required.

If the decision is made that no action will be taken, there is still a benefit to conducting the analyses. The CIAO at least now has a better understanding of the environment, as well as an understanding of some of the vulnerabilities. This information will still help in managing an IA program.

12.2.9   IA Tests and Evaluations Function

The IA tests and evaluations (T&E) is a required function to be used in the testing phases of new system development as part of the normal system development lifecycle. It is also an integral part of the product evaluation process and risk management function. Tests and evaluation functions should be done using formal project management techniques and a formal testing and evaluation approach. A minimum criterion for testing should be established as a baseline.

This criterion should be based on the IA requirements and IA policy. For example, the T&E would include obtaining a userid on a system with various access privileges. The IA staff member, using that identification would violate that system and attempt to gain unauthorised access to various files, databases and systems. That information would be analysed in conjunction with a comparison of the systems' audit trails; thus, profiling the IA of an information system. Also, the T&E would include a review of records and prior audit trail documents to help establish the "IA environment" being tested and evaluated.

12.2.10   IA Non-Compliance Inquiries Process

When users or other employees do not follow established IA policy and procedures, there must be a process in place to determine the who, where, when, why and how of the incident. An auditor, a corporate security investigator or a member of the IA staff can be designated to complete that function. There are advantages and disadvantages of each. For example:

- The auditor may know how to audit for compliance and some knowledge of audit-related interview techniques; however, they are not investigative specialists familiar with collection of evidence techniques, interrogation techniques and related laws.
- The corporate security investigator may have a good understanding of evidence collection, laws and interrogation techniques, but limited knowledge in computer forensics and systems in general.
- The IA specialist may know information protection and defences, systems in general and computer forensics, but is limited in knowledge of relative laws, interrogations and evidence collection. In order to conduct non-compliance inquiries (NCIs) in a professional manner, the CIAO should be responsible for a preliminary review of the incident and a decision made to refer it to corporate security investigators based on a pre-determined criteria.

The corporate security investigator with an IA staff member identified to assist should conduct the inquiries into matters referred to them by the CIAO. The IA staff member would conduct the computer forensics (e.g. electronic media searches for evidence) portions of the investigation, under the guidance of the investigator. Non-compliance inquiries are at least 75% accomplished using the normal investigative techniques. What is different is the "scene of the crime". Thus, there is the need for an IA staff specialist assistance.

In addition, the IA staff specialist, while working with the investigator, can obtain information that will assist in determining the impact of the incident on the IA program. For example, new vulnerabilities and threat agent techniques may be identified and the IA policy may need to be updated. Such information must also feed back into the other IA processes and considered when conducting T&Es, awareness briefings, access control system configurations and the like. It is imperative that each IA process supplements and supports the other IA processes.

Regardless of who takes the lead in conducting NCIs, there must be a process to at least conduct them in a professional and expeditious manner. In addition, they should be done in a confidential manner in order to protect the privacy of those involved. Remember not everyone accused of a violation is guilty of that violation.

To call such incidents inquiries instead of investigations are done for a specific purpose. The term "investigation" generally is considered more serious. Law enforcement agents with badges and guns who investigate violations of laws normally conduct them. This is considerably different to an "investigation" into whether or not someone shares his or her password with another. Thus, when an investigation is being conducted within a corporation, one can differentiate between the two. Furthermore, when someone outside the corporation hears the world "investigation" they are more inclined to think of it as a serious incident and not one where passwords were shared. Such matters when heard by the news media and stockholders provide for very bad public relations.

12.2.11   IA Contingency Planning and Disaster Recovery Function

Establishing an IA contingency planning and disaster recovery function is one of the least difficult programs to establish, and yet, always seems to be a difficult task to accomplish. With the change in information systems' environments and configurations, e.g. client-server, LAN, distributed processing, etc., this problem may be getting worse.

Prior to discussing contingency planning and disaster recovery (CP-DR) function, it is important to understand why it is needed. It is really a very important aspect of an IA program and its most vital function if the protection and defences fail. The CIAO must remember that the purpose of IA is to:

- Minimise the probability of an information and systems protection vulnerability
- Minimise the damage if vulnerability is exploited
- Provide a method to quickly recover efficiently and effectively from the damage

12.2.11.1   What Is it?

Contingency planning is a plan for responding to emergencies, back-up operations and recovering after a disaster; it addresses what action will be taken to return to normal operations. Emergencies requiring action would include such natural acts as floods, earthquakes, human-caused acts of fires, hacker attacks causing denial of services, etc. Disaster recovery is the restoration of the information and/or information systems, facility or other related assets following a significant disruption of services.

12.2.11.2   Why Do It?

The question of why do it is a question often asked, primarily by users, e.g. why should I back-up my information? Why is a CP-DR program necessary? Everyone associated with using, protecting, maintaining information systems and the information that they store, process and/or transmit must understand the need for such a program. It is:

- To assist in protecting vital and sensitive information
- To minimise adverse impact on productivity
- To stay in business

12.2.11.3   How Do You Do It?

Each CP-DR program is unique to the environment, culture and philosophy of each business or government agency. However, the basic program, regardless of business or agency, requires the development and maintenance of a CP-DR plan. It must be periodically tested, problems identified, corrected and processes changed to minimise the chances of adverse events happening again.

12.2.11.4   CP-DR Plan

The CP-DR plan should be written based on the standard format for writing plans used by the corporation. The following generic format is offered for consideration.

- *Purpose*: State the reason for the plan and its objective. This should be specific enough so that it is clear to all who read it why it has been written.
- *Scope*: State the scope and applicability of the plan. Does it include all systems, locations and subcontractors?
- *Assumptions*: State the priorities, the support promised and the incidents to be included and excluded. For example, if the area does not have typhoons, will you assume that typhoons, as a potential disaster threat, will not be considered?
- *Responsibilities*: State who is to be responsible for taking what actions. This should be stated clearly so that everyone knows who is responsible for what. Consider a generic breakdown such as managers, systems administrators, users, etc. Also, specific authority and responsibility should be listed by a person's title and not necessarily their name. This approach will save time in updating the plan due to people changes.
- *Strategy*: Discuss back-up requirements, how often they should be accomplished based on the sensitivity of the information and state how it will be recovered, etc.
- *Personnel*: Maintain an accurate, complete and current list of key CP-DR personnel to include addresses, phone numbers, pager numbers, cellular phone numbers, etc. Be sure to establish an emergency prioritised, notification listing and a listing of response team's members and how to contact them in an emergency.
- *Information*: Maintain an on-site inventory listing and an off-site inventory listing; identify the rotation process to ensure a history and current inventory of files. Identify vital information. This information must come from the owners of that information and must be classified according to its importance, based on approved guidelines.
- *Hardware*: Maintain an inventory listing; to include suppliers, name, serial number, property identification number, etc.; ensure emergency replacement contracts are in place; maintain hardcopies of applicable documents on- and off-site.
- *Software*: Identify and maintain back-up operating systems and application systems software. This should include original software and at least one back-up copy of each. Be sure to identify the version numbers, etc. In this way, you

can compare what is listed in the plan and what is actually installed. It would not be the first time that software back-ups were not kept current and compatible with the hardware. Thus, the systems may not able to work together to process, store and transmit much-needed information.

- **Documentation**: All important documentation should be identified, listed, inventoried and maintained current in both on- and off-site locations.
- **Telecommunications**: The identification and maintenance of telecommunications hardware and software listings are vital if the corporation is operating in any type of network environment. Many systems today cannot operate in a standalone configuration. Thus, the telecommunications lines, back-ups, schematics, etc. are of vital importance to getting back in operation within the time period required. As with other documentation, their identification, listing, etc. should be maintained at multiple on- and off-site locations. The CIAO should be sure to identify all emergency requirements and all alternate communication methods.
- **Supplies**: Supplies are often forgotten when establishing a CP-DR plan as they often take a "back-seat" to hardware and software. However, a listing and maintenance of vital supplies are required to include the name, address, telephone numbers and contact information, concerning the suppliers of those supplies. The CIAO should also be sure to store sufficient quantities at appropriate locations on- and off-site. If the CIAO does not think this is an important matter, try using a printer when its toner cartridge has dried out or is empty and others are not available. Physical supplies for consideration should include plastic tarpaulins to cover systems from water damage in the event of a fire where sprinkler systems are activated.
- **Transportation and equipment**: The CIAO should also determine if a back-up facility is needed or whether or not to obtain back-up copies of software for storage at that facility, etc. The CIAO obviously must have transportation and the applicable equipment (e.g. a dolly for hauling heavy items) to do the job. Therefore, the CIAO must plan for such things to include: listing emergency transportation needs and sources, stating how emergency transportation and equipment will be obtained and which routes and alternate routes to take to off-site location(s). The CIAO must also be sure to include maps in the vehicles and also in the plan; and there are fully charged, hand-held fire extinguishers available, which will work on various types of fires, e.g. electrical, paper, chemicals.
- **Processing locations**: Many businesses and agencies sign contractual agreements to ensure that they have an appropriate off-site location to be used in the event their facility is not capable of supporting their activities. Also one must ensure that emergency processing agreements are in place, which will provide you with priority service and support in the event of an emergency or disaster. Even then, you may have a difficult time using the facility if it is a massive disaster and others have also contracted for the facility. The facility should also be periodically used to ensure that one can process, store and/or transmit information at that location. It is also a good idea to identify on-site locations, which can be used or converted for use in the event of other than a total, major disaster.

- *Utilities*: Identify on-site and off-site emergency power needs and locations. Do not forget that these requirements change as facilities, equipment and hardware change. Battery power and un-interrupted power might not be able to carry the load or are too old to even work. These must be periodically tested. For as with the printer cartridge supplies, systems without power are useless. Besides power, one should not forget the air conditioning requirements. It would be important to know how long a system can process without air conditioning based on certain temperature and humidity readings.
- *Documentation*: Identify all related documentation, store it in multiple on- and off-site locations and be sure to include the CP-DR plan!
- *Other*: Miscellaneous items not covered earlier.

12.2.11.5   Test the Plan

There is no use in having a plan that has not been tested, for only through testing can the CIAO determine that the plan has any chance of working when required. Therefore, it must be periodically tested. It needs not be tested all at once because that would probably cause a loss of productivity by the employees that would not be cost-effective.

It is best to test the plan in increments, relying on all the pieces to fit together when all parts have been tested. Regardless of when and how one would test the plan, which is a management decision, it must be tested. Probably the best way to determine how and what to test, and in what order, is to prioritise testing based on prioritised assets.

When testing, the scenarios used should be as realistic as possible. This should include emergency response, testing back-up applications, systems and recovery operations. Thorough testing, documenting the problems and vulnerabilities identification must be done. Also, why problems occurred must be determined and formal projects established to fix each problem. Additionally, the CIAO and other team members should make whatever cost-effective process changes are necessary to ensure that the same problem would not happen again, or the chance of it happening is minimised.

12.3   Summary

The CIAO and the IA organisational functions and processes will vary depending on the culture, management commitment and business of the corporation. However, a summary of these functions is provided as an example of what should be done as part of an IA program and thus by the CIAO and IA staff.

- Identify all government, customers and corporate IA requirements necessary for the protection and defence of all information processed, stored and/or transmitted by the corporation's information systems; interpret those requirements and develop, implement and administer plans, policies and procedures necessary to ensure compliance.

- Evaluate all hardware, firmware and software for impact on the protection and defence of the information and the information systems; direct and ensure their modification if requirements are not met; and authorise their purchase and use within the corporation and applicable customers, subcontractors, associates and other locations.
- If needed, establish and administer a technical security countermeasures program to support IA requirements. For example, this program would mitigate emanations across communications links that would cause "data leaks" across cables.
- Establish and administer an IA tests and evaluations program to ensure that the entire corporation's and applicable subcontractors', suppliers' and customers' information systems are operating in accordance with their contracts.
- Direct the use of, and co-ordinate: monitoring of the corporation's information systems access control software systems, analyses of all systems' protection and defence infractions/violations and reporting of the results to the CIAO for review and appropriate action.
- Identify information systems business practices and IA violations/infractions, support the conducting of inquiries, assess potential damage and implement/recommend corrective/preventive action.
- Develop, implement and administer a risk management program, provide analyses to management and modify IA requirements accordingly to ensure a least-cost IA program.
- Establish and administer an IA awareness program for all corporate employees and other users of the information systems to ensure they are cognisant of information systems threats, and IA policies and procedures necessary for the protection and defence of information and information systems.
- Direct and co-ordinate a corporate-wide information systems disaster recovery/contingency planning program to mitigate the possibility of loss of systems and information, and to assure the rapid recovery of information systems in the event of an emergency or disaster. This function should be co-ordinated and integrated into the Corporate Security's corporate CP-DR program.
- Support the Corporate Security organisation in conducting high-technology crime and abuse inquiries in which where there are indications of intent to damage, destroy, modify or release to unauthorised people, information of value to the corporation. (Note: the main task is to provide computer forensics and computer-related technical service and support.)
- Direct the development, acquisition, implementation and administration of IA software systems.
- Direct and establish a process to mitigate the potential for the corporation's systems' protection to cause liability and privacy issues that would adversely affect the corporation.
- Represent the corporation on all IA matters with customers, government agencies, suppliers and other outside entities.
- Provide advice, guidance and assistance to corporate management and employees relative to IA matters.

13

Incident Management and Response

Incident management and incident response is the process of managing and responding to a security incident. A security incident can be a technical, social or socio-technical breach in an organisation's security policy. Common examples of incidents include:

- A company's Website defaced by an intruder
- An employee at the company believed to be selling trade secrets
- A rival corporation believed to be dialling into a company's computer system and downloading financial data
- A computer virus spreading among employees by way of infected Microsoft Word documents shared via e-mail

The problem is only growing as in 1989 CERT CC reported 132 incidents, while in 2000 they reported 47,711 incidents. Incident response is the discipline of handling situations in a manner that is:

- *Cost effective*: Incident response by its very nature is not revenue generating. It is concerned with protecting an organisation's IT infrastructure and thus will consume some resources. It is therefore vital that the incident response process is managed in a cost efficient manner so as to maximise the return in investment.
- *Business-like*: In order to be accepted in the business – incident response must function like any other business unit.
- *Efficient*: Without efficiency, effort in incident management and response will be duplicated, and time/money will be lost in learning old lessons. It is therefore vital that the incident management/response is operated in an efficient manner so as to maximise productivity.
- *Repeatable*: The process of scientific reproducibility is vital to the incident management/response. Two similar incidents should be managed in the same way in every regard.
- *Predictable*: Incident management/response must be as predictable as possible. An organisation needs to be able to rely on incident response and to know what services and other support functions are to be expected.

It is 4:30 p.m. on Thursday and you receive a phone call from your computer support/help desk telling you that a computer has been compromised, and it is being used as an illegal FTP server for the distribution of pirated software. What do you do? The answer is *"Don't Panic"* and reaches for incident management policy that you have defined for your organisation/business unit. This policy will involve the activation of a computer security incident response team (CSIRT). The most common mistake that corporate security offices make is to logon to the computer system in question and start looking for evidence of a security breach. For a definition of best practice in this area, see RFC-2350.

A CSIRT must draw upon a variety of skills if it is to function correctly and must interact with other key players. These include:

- Senior executive IT staff
- General counsel
- Human resources
- Physical security
- IT department
- Law enforcement
- Public relations
- Board of directors
- The various business units of the organisation

The below diagram defines the triage, coordination and resolution process (Figure 13.1).

The first stage in incident management and response is called incident triage, the second stage is called incident coordination and the third stage is called incident resolution.

A decision that must be made at the start of this process is: "What is the goal of this process". For example, if the goal is that of bringing a criminal prosecution against the perpetrator, then all of the evidence of the incident must be secured and managed in a forensically sound manner that adheres to the rule of law. On the other hand, if the goal of the process is simply to bring a server back online, then the incident response team needs not to worry about management of evidence.

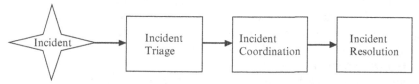

FIGURE 13.1. The Incident, Triage, Coordination and Resolution Process.

13.1   Incident Triage

The first stage in incident triage is to assess the report; this involves the interpretation of incoming incident reports, prioritising them and relating them to ongoing incidents and trends. This first stage includes confirming that the incident is real and not a hoax.

The second stage is to verify the report; this involves determining whether an incident has really occurred and if so its scope. The basic function of incident triage is to access/prioritise the report and confirm that the incident is not a hoax. Thus, incident triage is:

- Interpretation of the incident
- Prioritisation of the incident

Deploying a CSIRT is expensive in terms of both money and resources. Thus from a corporate security point of view, you need to be sure that this resource is properly utilised.

Large organisations may have security incidents happening all of the time; consequently, it is very important that when an incident occurs it is prioritised with reference to other ongoing investigations. Key questions that need to be addressed are (a) is that part of an ongoing attack and (b) is this a new attack and if so, do I wish to respond to it?

13.2   Incident Coordination

The real function of incident coordination is that of crisis management. The first stage in incident coordination is that of categorising the incident-related information (log-files, audit data, network logs, contact information, etc.) with respect to the information disclosure policy. The second stage is that of coordinating the notification of other involved parties on a need-to-know (NTK) basis as per the information disclosure policy. Before any incident management can begin, it is vitally important that an information disclosure policy is in place. Thus, incident coordination is:

- Categorisation of the incident
- Disclosure of the incident

It is important to note the role that the users play in the coordination activity. Within the incident management process, users can function as a force multiplier or as a force divider. An uneducated user is one of the most dangerous agents that you will encounter in the process of incident management. It is, therefore, vital that users are educated and taught (a) how to detect an incident and (b) how to respond to an incident.

Various open standards have emerged over the last few years to allow for the standard encoding of incident information and thus the sharing of information in a standard pre-defined format. Standards, such as INCH and IODEF, are all designed to allow for information relating to an attack to be encoded and shared in a standard format. Standards, for example IODEF, make use of encoding methods, such as XML, to facilitate communication across different organisations.

13.3   Incident Resolution

The process of incident resolution involves the technical analysis of the computer system in question along with the elimination of the cause of the security incident and the recovery of affected system. This may mean deploying a forensic process to capture and analyse the system in a forensically sound manner, or it may mean utilising pre-defined technically competent staff to analyse the system and any other information related to the incident. Thus, incident resolution is:

- Technical assistance with the incident
- Eradication/containment of the incident
- Recovery from the incident

The eradication of the incident involves the elimination of the cause of a security incident (the vulnerability exploited), and its effects (e.g. continuing access to the system by an intruder). The identification of the vulnerability used to gain unauthorised access to the system can be very difficult. It is important that at this stage we are using the term vulnerability to include both human and technical means of compromising security. For example, has an employee given his/her password to a partner and has that partner used this information to send an abusive e-mail to another employee?

The recovery of the system refers to the restoring of the affected system and services to their status before the security incident. This also includes any security patches required to ensure that the cause of the incident does not reoccur.

13.4   Proactive Activities

There are a number of activities that the corporate security officer (CSO) can engage in to ensure that an incident does not occur. These are:

- Information provision and sharing
- Security tools
- Education and training
- Product and services evaluation
- Site security auditing

13.4.1   Information Provision and Sharing

This can include information, such as an archive of known vulnerabilities (CVE/CAN), patches, security/advisory mailing lists (BUGTRAQ) and a knowledgebase consisting of resolutions to the past problems. Archives include the following:

Bugtraq and NTBugtraq
CVE/CAN numbers
80 Information Assurance: Servicing in the Information Environment
   Vulnerability archives such as packetstorm and security focus
Vendor security lists such as Microsoft Security Bulletins

The ability of organisations to document a problem and its solution allows them to learn from the past mistakes and adapt to new problems as these occur.

It is also important that security information, when identified, is shared within an organisation with those individuals that NTK it. At a time of crisis for an organisation, it is vital that the people who need the information have access to it.

13.4.2   Security Tools

One of the front-line tools that a CSO can use in the defence of an organisation's computer/network infrastructure is that of a well-trained and knowledgeable system administrator. A good system administrator will make regular use of security tools to identify the security state of an infrastructure, such as:

- Port scanners such as nmap
- Vulnerability scanners such as nessus, saint, statn and nikto
- Network packet capture tools such as tcpdump and ethereal, and
- Intrusion detection systems such as snort, dragon and NFR
- In identifying the security state, a system administrator can identify if any security updates/patches need to be applied.

13.4.3   Education and Training

Education and training has two roles to play in securing an organisation's infrastructure. The first is education of the users of the systems to that they can identify if/when a security breach has occurred. The users of the systems are the front-line troops in the battle against people wishing to compromise security as the users of the systems have the experience to know how the systems should behave. It is, therefore, vital that the users of the systems also know what to do when they think that a security breach has occurred.

The second is that of training of the individuals responsible for securing the systems and/or investigating any security breach. It is vitally important that these people have an up-to-date technical understanding of the networks and operating systems that are deployed within an organisation. This type of training also includes the use of fire drills to train staff how to respond to an incident.

13.4.4   Product and Services Evaluation

Most organisations today make use of outsourcing in some shapes/forms, whether it is outsourcing the IT infrastructure for an organisation or the cleaning services – these all have security implications, and it is vital that these are all evaluated.

13.4.5   Site Security Auditing

One of the ways that an organisation can measure the security state of its infrastructure is (a) via a third party performing a penetration test or (b) via an individual within the organisation's functioning as an independent evaluator of the organisation's infrastructure. The snapshot functions to allow the organisation to measure the effectiveness of its policy and procedures associated with the management and securing its infrastructure.

Section 3

Technical Aspects of IA

This section discusses the technical aspects of information assurance (IA) as it relates to information and information systems storing, processing and transmitting of information. No book, even one providing an introduction to the IA, can be complete without some discussion of operating systems, application software and their relationship to, and integral part of, an IA program. Chapter 14 provides that overview.

Since no IA program can provide any sort of protection without encryption, Chapter 15 discusses the use of cryptography, e.g. public key infrastructure, as a means of information protection in a corporate information-dependent environment. This section concludes with Chapter 16 looking at technical equipment that can be used to protect or attack an information system, e.g. transient electromagnetic pulse emanation standard, high energy radio frequency guns, electromagnetic pulse weapons.

Finally in Chapter 17 we explore the various security standards, such as ISO17799/BS7799, and common criteria that can be used to implement security at both the technical and management level.

14

IA and Software

No discussion of information assurance (IA) is complete without at least an overview of IA as it relates to operating systems and application software. This chapter will discuss IA problems and possible solutions as they relate to operating systems and application software. The discussion will include views on malicious codes such as viruses, logic bombs and Trojan horses along with the software that is now being deployed in network to implement secure communications and authentication.

14.1 Operating Systems and Trusted Systems

14.1.1 Security Policies

Mandatory access control (MAC) means that access control policy decisions are made beyond the control of the individual owner of an object. A central authority determines what information is to be accessible and by whom. With a MAC policy, a user cannot change their or another's access rights. A discretionary access control (DAC) leaves a certain amount of control to the discretion of the owner of an object. With this DAC, the owner of an object has the ability to define the access rights that are granted to a user. Commercial operating systems, such as NT and UNIX, use DACs to facilitate the accounting and auditing functions.

As stated earlier, a policy is a statement of the security that we expect the system to enforce. An operating system can only be trusted in relation to its security policy. The military policy of security is based on a need-to-know. Each asset is given a protective marking. The higher the protective marking the greater the need for security. In general, the military model of information security defines information security in terms of confidentiality. A person wishing to access an information asset must have been given the necessary clearances to access the information. A clearance is an indication that a person is trusted to access information up to a certain level of sensitivity. The most commonly used security model to analyse military security policy is the Bell-La Padula model.

The commercial world is less rigid and hierarchically structured than the military one. This has led to a set of alternative security policies being developed and utilised. Clark and Wilson proposed a security policy based on *well-formed transactions* that they assert are as important in the commercial domain as confidentiality is in the military domain. In terms of a business process, performing the actions in order, performing exactly the actions listed and authenticating the individuals who perform the actions constitute *a well-formed transaction*. Clark and Wilson present their policy in terms of *transformation procedures* that process *constrained data items*. A transformation procedure is a function that only operates on specific kinds of data items, and that data items are manipulated only by transformation procedures.

The *Chinese Wall Security Policy* is a policy that reflects certain commercial needs for information access protection. In order for this security policy to function we need to define three levels of abstraction:

- *Objects*: At the lowest level are elementary objects such as files. Each file contains information concerning only one corporation.
- *Corporation groups*: At the next level, all objects concerning each corporation are grouped together.
- *Conflict classes*: At the highest level, all groups of objects for competing companies are clustered.

Each object belongs to a unique corporation group, and each group is contained in a unique conflict class. The access control policy is rather simple. A person can access any information as long as he/she has never accessed information from a different corporation in the same conflict class. That is, access is allowed if either the object requested is in the same corporation group as the object that has been previously accessed or the object requested belongs to a conflict class that has never been accessed before.

14.1.2   Models of Security

The Bell-La Padula model is a formal description of the allowable paths of information flow in a secure system. The objective of the model is to identify allowable communication where it is important to maintain security. This model uses the following definitions:

- The *subject* refers to the entity that can access the information. A subject could be a computer, a program or a person.
- The *object* refers to the information that the subject is attempting to access.

The Bell-La Padula security model only allows a subject to access an object in two ways: *read* and *write*. The security class of an object "*o*" is denoted by the function $C(o)$. Typical security classes are Top-Secret, Secret, Confidential and Unclassified. This security model makes use of two axioms to characterise a secure information flow.

- **Simple security property**: Subject s may have *read* access to an object o only if $C(o) \leq C(s)$. This says that the security class (clearance) of someone receiving a piece of information must be at least as high as the class (classification) of the information.
- ***-Property**: Subject s who has *read* access to an object o may have *write* access to an object p only if $C(o) \geq C(p)$. This says that a person obtaining information at one level may pass that information only to people at levels no lower than the information. This property is to prevent write-down of information, which occurs when a subject with write access to high-level data transfers that data by writing it to a low-level object.

The implications of these two axioms are illustrated in Figure 14.1

The flow of information is generally horizontal, with information flowing to and from the same level. The security classification of subjects (represented as squares) and objects (represented as circles) is indicated by their position. As the classification of an item increases, its height on the diagram also increases.

In 1978, the Take-Grant model for the analysis of security was published. In this model there are only four primitive operations: *create, revoke, take* and *grant*. Let R be a set of rights, S be a set of subjects and O be a set of objects. It is important to note that objects can be either active (subjects) or passive (non-subject). Each subject or object is denoted by a node on a graph; the rights of a particular subject to a particular object denoted by a label direct from the subject to the object. This security model is most often used when designing and implementing modern operating system security.

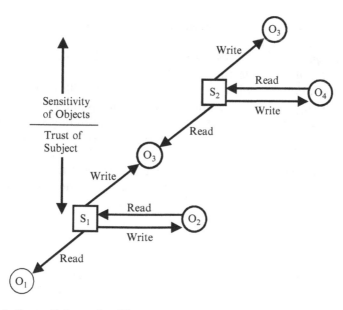

FIGURE 14.1. Secure Information Flow

Figure 14.2 depicts a simple Take-Grant model; the subject is depicted as a square and denoted using the letter S, while the object is depicted as a circle and denoted using the letter O. Finally, an access right that exists between S and O is depicted as an arrow and denoted by the letter R.

A description of the four primitive operations is given as follows:

- **Create** (o, r): A new node with label o is added to the graph. From s to o there is a directed edge with label r, denoting the rights of s on o.
- **Grant** (o, p, r): Subject s grants to o access rights r on p. A specific right is *grant*. Subject s can grant to o access rights r on p only if s has grant right on o, and s has r rights on p. Informally, s can grant (share) any of its rights with o, as long as s has the right to grant privileges to o. An edge from o to p is added; with label r. O is an active subject.
- **Revoke** (o, r): The right r is revoked from s on o. The edge from s to o was labeled $q \cup r$; the label is replaced by q. Informally, s can revoke its rights to do r on o.
- **Take** (o, p, r): Subject s takes from o access rights r on p. A specific right is *take*. Subject s can take from o access rights r on p only if s has take right on o, and o has r rights on p. Informally, s can take any rights o has, as long as s has the right to take privileges from o. An edge from s to p is added with label r.

14.1.3 Security Methods of Operating Systems

The basis of protection is separation, keeping one user's objects from another user. It should be noted that separation in an operating system could occur in several ways.

- **Physical separations**: In which processes use separate physical resources to store and access objects.
- **Temporal separation**: In which processes having different security requirements are executed at different times.
- **Logical separation**: In which users operate under the illusion that no other processes exist, as when an operating system controls and limits the access of a program executing on behaviour of a user. The operating system functions to ensure that the user is not allowed to access objects outside its permitted domain.
- **Cryptographic separation**: In which processes conceal their data and processes through the system of symmetric and asymmetric cryptographic algorithms.

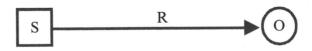

FIGURE 14.2. A Take-Grant Model

14.1.4   Typical Operating System Flaws

Typical security flaws that have been encountered in operating systems include:

- **Authentication of user**: The operating system must identify each user who requests access and ascertain that the user is actually who they purport to be. The most common authentication mechanism is password comparison.
- **Protection of memory**: Each user's program must run in a portion of memory protected against unauthorised accesses. The protection will certainly prevent outsiders' access, and it may also control a user's own access to restricted parts of the program space. Differential security access controls, such as read, write and execute, can be applied to the control of the user's memory space.
- **File and I/O device access control**: The operating system must protect user's and operating system's files from access and modification by unauthorised users.
- **Allocation and access to general objects**: General objects, such as constructs to permit concurrency and allow synchronisation, must be provided to users. However access and user of these objects must be strictly controlled so that no user is able to adversely affect the behaviour of another.
- **Enforcement of sharing**: Resources on most common operating systems need to be shared among users. Sharing of resources brings about the need to guarantee integrity and consistency. Integrity controls, such as monitors and transactions processors, are often used to support sharing controls.
- **Guarantee of fair service**: All users expect a fair share of the services offered and support by the operating system. No user should indefinably be starved from using and accessing a service. Hardware clocks and scheduling combine to ensure fairness.
- **Inter-process communication and synchronisation**: Executing processes sometimes need to communicate with each other. Operating system provides this service by acting as a bridge between communicating processes. Access control tables mediate inter-process communication.
- **Protection of operating system protection data**: The operating system must maintain data by which it can enforce security. This data must itself be protected from unauthorised access and modification. The operating system itself cannot provide enforcement of protection of this data, thus we must make use of other techniques such as encryption, hardware control and physical access controls.

14.2   Databases and Database Security

A database is a collection of data and a set of rules that organise the data by specifying certain relationships among the data. Within most organisations certain databases have become mission critical information systems. This means that without access to these databases and trust in the information contained in them, the organisation would cease to function. Consequently, the security and effective use and management of the organisational assets have become vital to the success and viability of an organisation.

The security requirements for a database are very similar to that for an operating system or any other organisational mission critical information system. The basic problems are as follows:

- *Physical database integrity*: Physical database integrity is concerned with the protection of data contained in a database from the effects of physical problems such as power failure.
- *Logical database integrity*: Logical database integrity is concerned with the protection of data at the logical level. For example, the modification of a piece of data in the database should not affect other pieces of data in that database.
- *Element integrity*: Element integrity is concerned with the protection of integrity of each element of data in the database.
- *Access control*: This is concerned with the policy that a user is allowed to access only authorised data and different users can be restricted to different modes of access such as read and/or write.
- *Auditability*: This is concerned with the tracking of who has accessed the database and/or modified elements in the database.
- *User authentication*: This is concerned with ensuring that every user is positively and uniquely identified, both for the audit trail and permission to access certain data.
- *Availability*: This is concerned with the availability of the database to be utilised by the users of the database in a useful and meaningful manner to the business process.

14.2.1   Physical Database Integrity

Physical database integrity is concerned with the protection of data contained in a database from the effects of physical problems such as power failure.

- *Non-natural vulnerabilities*: Intruders can break into your computing facilities. Once in they can sabotage and vandalise your computers and steal hardware, diskettes, printouts, etc. For example:
- A former cost estimator for Southeastern Color Lithographers in Athens, Georgia, was convicted of destroying billing and accounting data on a XENIX system. The lost data had the effect of disrupting the supply chain for the organisation. The conviction was based on an audit trail linking the delete commands to his terminal (but not necessarily to him). The employer claimed damages of $400,000 in lost business and downtime.
- *Natural vulnerabilities*: Computers are very vulnerable to natural disasters and environmental threats. Disasters, such as fire, flood, earthquakes and power loss, can wreck your computer and destroy data. For example, a squirrel caused a short circuit in a transformer, causing a power surge in Providence, Rhode Island, in October 1986. The surge affected numerous computers.

General tactics for the management of physical database integrity include:

- Risk transfer through the outsourcing or facilities management of the organisation's critical business information infrastructure. Thus, the identification and response to the IA problem should be included in any service level agreement (SLA).
- A comprehensive disaster recovery play that covers both natural and non-natural disasters such as fires, floods and theft. This type of plan only functions if it is adequately funded, tested and maintained.

For non-natural vulnerabilities one can adopt the following countermeasures:

- *Physical security on buildings and equipment*: This can be achieved using technologies such as biometrics. In addition, educating users and adopting clear desk policies also aid in minimising the risk of a security breach. The goal is to uniquely identify a user so that a complete audit trail exists for all security related actions of a user in such a way that when a breach in physical database integrity occurs you can identify how it happened, who made it happen and recover from the resulting loss.
- *Logical security on key information assets*: This can be achieved through the use of technologies such as cryptography key management and certification authorities. If, when data is stolen, it is encrypted using algorithms, such as triple DES, Blowfish and/or RSA, then it is unlikely that the unencrypted data can be accessed with a valid cryptographic key. In addition, the use of digital signatures or certification purposes strengthens logical security as signatures can be revoked and new signatures can be issued.

For natural vulnerabilities one can adopt the following counter measures:

- The use of online back-up devices and other devices in hot-stand-by mode. This can be achieved using various technologies that introduce redundancy into the system and consequently increase reliability. The goal is to run the systems in parallel so that when one system fails another system automatically compensates for the failure. Thus, availability is maintained.
- The use of a separate physical location and the duplication of all information storage and information processing capabilities. This option is extensive both in terms of physical cost and manpower costs.
- The use of off-line and off-site back-ups of key information assets.

14.2.2   Logical Database Integrity

Logical database integrity is concerned with the protection of data at the logical level. For example, the modification of a piece of data in the database should not affect other pieces of data in that database. This is achieved through the normalisation of the data in the database. For example, if a database is normalised into Boyce-Codd normal form (BCNF), then every element in every relation is only dependent on the primary key. In formal database terms, this is expressed as a relation as in BCNF if and only if every determinant is a candidate key. The term "determinant" refers to an attribute that is on the left-hand side of a functional dependency. If we have a relation, R, then the attribute R.B is functionally dependent on attribute R, if and only if each value of R.A is associated with exactly one value of R.B at any time.

```
Relation Dep: Product (Product ID, Price, Description)
   Functional Dep: Product ID → (Price, Description)
```

The above also tells us that the attribute Product ID is the primary key and the attributes Price and Description are functionally dependent on it.

14.2.3   Element Integrity

The term "element integrity" is used to refer to the correctness and accuracy of an element in a database. In principle, only authorised users should insert data into a database. When adding a database to a database, some database management systems (DBMS) also make it simple to ensure that the data is of the correct type to be inserted into that element. For example, a DBMS would not allow one to insert a string into an element that is of type number.

In an attempt to minimise the effect of a loss of element integrity, a database should have the data in it placed into relations and then the relationships should be normalised. In its simplest terms, a database is simply a set of relations. Relations (often referred to as tables) have a set of properties that attempt to ensure element integrity, and these are:

- Every relation in a database must have a distinct name. That name must be unique in the database.
- Every column in a relation must have a distinct name within the relation. Each column of a relation is also a set and hence should also be unambiguously named.
- All entries in a column must be of the same kind, i.e. from the same domain.
- The order of columns in a relation is not significant. The head of a relation – its list of column names – is also a mathematical set. Sets in mathematics are not ordered.
- The order of rows is not significant. There should be no implied order in the storage of rows in a relation. The body of a relation is a set.
- The row in a relation must be distinct. Duplicate rows are not allowed in a relation. In other words, a relation must have a primary key.
- Each cell or column/row intersection in a relation should contain only an atomic value. In other words, multi-values in a cell are not allowed.

The primary key of a relation is an attribute or composite attribute that has the properties of uniqueness and minimality. In a relation, we define which attribute is the primary key by underlining it. When manipulating a relation, the three types of entity integrity that concern us are as follows:

- The first is that when we are inserting some data into a relation we must ensure that the components we are inserting have a primary key associated with them.

- The second type is that when we remove the last element from a relation the relation should not disappear from the database.
- The third and final type is that when we update a database, we should ensure that all the elements needed to be updated are updated.

When entering data into a database, there are various checks that the organisation can perform to ensure element integrity. Even if the data entered into an element of a database is of the correct type (a DBMS will ensure this), there is no guarantee that the value of the data is correct. So an organisation may either enter the data twice and check to make sure that the two pieces of data entered are the same or if some property between data elements in a database can be identified, then a check can be executed to ensure that this property holds for all instances of the elements in the database.

14.2.4 Access Control

Databases are often logically separated by user access privileges. For example, within an organisation, users may not have access to the salary information associated with employees on the database. Access to that information may be restricted to the personnel department. When a database is being created, the database administrator should specify the areas of the database that the different users can see. In database design terms, this is called a user schema or view. In SQL-92, a view is conceptually a relation, but its records are taken from another relation. For example, suppose we had a relation defined as follows:

```
Employee-Data (Emp ID, Name, Job-Description, Salary)
```

Where EmpID is the primary key of the relation Employee-Details. For security reasons we may only want the personnel department to have access to the entity Salary. So we would define a view of the relation that excludes this attribute. In SQL-92, this would be expressed as follows:

```
CREATE VIEW Current-Employee-Details(EmpID, Name, Job)
    AS SELECT E.EmpID, E.Name, E.Job FROM Employee-Data
```

Most DBMSs use the Take-Grant model of security to implement access controls. SQL-92 supports DAC through the GRANT and REVOKE commands.

```
GRANT privileges ON object TO users
```

For our purposes an object is either a relation or a view of a relation. Several privileges can be specified:

- *Select*: The right to access (read) all columns of the table specified as object
- *Insert*: The right to insert rows with values in the named column of the table named as object
- *Delete*: The right to delete rows from the table named as object
- *References*: The right to define foreign keys (in other tables) that refer to the specified column of the table named as object

Suppose that Andrew has created a relation called Incident and there are two other users called Alison and Francesca. Some examples of the GRANT command that Andrew can execute are:

```
GRANT SELECT ON Incident TO Alison, Francesca
GRANT INSERT, DELETE ON Incident TO Francesca
```

14.2.5   Auditability

In some applications, it may be desirable to generate an audit record of all access (read or write) to a database. Such a record can help maintain the integrity of a database or at least discover, after the fact, who affected what values and when. The second advantage is that a user can make use of inferences to deduce information that they are not security cleared to know (this is called the Inference problem). An audit log of what actions a user has performed can allow an administrator to create a picture of what a user really knows. In database terms, this type of audit log is called a transaction log, and it records all the transactions that have been executed over a database since the database was last backed-up. The transaction log allows a database administrator to recover a database when, for whatever the reason, the database crashes and all information in it is lost.

The level of recording that is performed to create an audit log for a database is defined in the security policy for the database. Just as with most operating systems, a database can record every statement that every user executes in the database. For the purposes of a transaction log for a database, we are only concerned with those actions that create, modify or delete data from the database and those that create, modify or delete the access rights for a user of the database.

14.2.6   User Authentication

This is concerned with ensuring that every user is positively and uniquely identified both for the audit trail and the permission to access certain data. Most typical databases make use of a user name and password for every use, and when a user connects to the database, they are authenticated with reference to the user name and password. Typically, the user name and passwords are sorted in a special table in the database, and the DBMS makes use of a one-way hashing function to sort the passwords. Consequently, when a user is authenticated, the password that they entered is encrypted using the hashing function and compared with the stored hash of the password. If the two match, then the password is the same and the user is allowed access to the database.

From a security perspective, the biggest headache that the database administrator will have is with users not adequately managing their passwords. In addition, some DBMSs install default username and passwords on their systems for diagnostic purposes. Such usernames and passwords should be disabled as they form a back door for an intruder to enter the system.

14.2.7   Availability

This is concerned with the availability of the database to be utilised by the users of the database in a useful and meaningful manner relative to the business process. A database can only be used if the information contained within the database is available so the requirement of availability is high on the list of requirements relating to the implementation of a DBMS.

14.2.8   Database Case Study

Today's databases contain millions of pieces of information, and corporate databases themselves are probably extremely sensitive when viewed as a whole. However, individual elements of it may not be considered sensitive. Information classification management plays a large role in determining the sensitivity of information and then classifying it accordingly. However, in today's massive database environment the task is almost impossible.

From an IA standpoint, it is "easy" to protect the entire database; however, what about its individual elements? What if some elements were combined? The result is that some non-sensitive pieces of information not requiring protection may require protection when combined.

Due to the massive amounts of information contained in today's databases, it is almost impossible to establish and maintain the protection of such pieces of information when combined. It would require that each piece of information be integrated with all the other pieces of information in the database in an infinite number of combinations and then checked against some rule-based system to determine its sensitivity. To establish and maintain a current and cost-effective system for such a process is not within the capabilities of any IA professional. Moreover, systems are currently unavailable to accomplish such tasks. The result is that database information accessed piecemeal can provide extremely sensitive information. For example, a major US aerospace corporation was building missile warheads for the military. The number of warheads on each missile was classified Secret. An unclassified database was used to maintain information relative to warhead parts, etc. The information in the database included the total number of bolts used to hold all the warheads in place – unclassified information. Also, the total number of bolts used to hold down an individual warhead was included in the database – unclassified information. However, one can take the total number of warhead bolts for each missile, e.g. 12, and divide it by the number of individual warhead bolts, e.g. three, and one discovers that there are four warheads per missile – Secret information. This simple but true example indicates some of the difficulties in protecting individual pieces of information to the level of granularity required to be effective.

14.3   Application Software

Application software is second only to operating systems in its importance to information protection and IA. Application software must be protected to ensure that it is maintained as originally intended without being contaminated by malicious code or in any way modified in such a manner as to allow additional vulnerabilities and/or minimise its secure integration with other applications software, e.g. intrusion detection software.

Some of the most important application software that requires protection at the highest levels is the software used to protect information, e.g. intrusion detection, access control, audit trails recording, etc. If this software is compromised, then no information on the information systems will be protected. Ironically, security software is often given no more protection than an accounting software package.

Over the years, there have been more and more examples of malicious codes, e.g. viruses, logic bombs, Trojan horses, etc., being written and executed globally through the Internet and other networks.

14.3.1   Malicious Code

The following are definitions used to identify and categorise malicious software:

- **Back doors**: Sometimes called *trapdoors*, which allow unauthorised access to one's systems
- **Logic bombs**: Or hidden features in programs that are executed after certain conditions are met
- **Trojan horses**: Are programs that say they are doing one thing while they are doing another, e.g. a program hidden in a program
- **Viruses**: Or programs that modify other programs on a computer, inserting copies of themselves
- **Worms**: Programs that propagate from computer to computer on a network, without necessarily modifying other programs on the target machine
- **Bacteria**: Or *rabbit programs*, make copies of themselves to overwhelm a computer system's resources
- **Bots**: Or programs that allow a remote user to mount a distributed denial of service attack against another computer on the Internet

The following are all examples of logic bombs:

- **General dynamics logic bomb**: A programmer, Michael John Lauffenberger, was convicted of logic bombing General Dynamics' Atlas Rocket Database. He quit his job and hoped to be rehired at a premium when the logic bomb went off. However, another programmer discovered it.
- **Pandair logic bomb**: A contractor programmer, James McMahon, was accused of planting logic bombs in a Pandair Freight system in the United

Kingdom. One bomb locked up terminals, and another bomb was set to wipe out memory. He was cleared of all charges due to insufficient evidence.

- *Logic bomb deletes brokerage records*: Donald Gene Burleson was prosecuted on felony charges for planting a time bomb that, shortly after he was fired, deleted more than 168,000 brokerage records from the USPA in Fort Worth, Texas. He was convicted and jailed.

14.3.1.1   Trojan Horse Software

There has been a literal plague of what have been described as "Trojan horse" programs. These software tools are named in honour of the famous beast of history that allowed the mighty walls of the city of Troy to be breached by the cunning Greek warriors. Today's "Trojan" software is more likely to appear in the guise of a cute little attachment sent by what appears to be a friendly e-mail account. These programs represent a fundamental change in the threat matrix; they are particularly dangerous in the small- and medium-sized businesses in which there may not be any formal IA program.

All the various Trojan software provides a common core of functions which typically includes the following:

- Operate concealed, in "stealth mode" without any indication to the user of their presence. Nothing will be visible in the Windows system tray or will appear if the user activates the "close program" dialog box
- Open and close the CD-ROM drive
- Run programs already resident on the "target" system remotely without the user's intervention
- Capture (log) user keystrokes without alerting the user
- Capture screen shots
- Reboot the computer
- Upload (and execute) programs to the "target" computer without the user's knowledge
- Operate microphones, web cameras, modems and other peripherals to gain information, include remotely turning on computers, downloading their contents and turning them back off.

14.3.1.2   BackOrifice2000

The program which probably best exemplifies the large number of new software tools that are magnifying the IA risks is called "BackOrifice" (BO) which in its most current form is known as "BackOrifice2000" (BO2K). Named in a mocking double entendre to deride Microsoft's "BackOffice" with a teenager's sense of potty humour (the logo shows what one might infer to be human buttocks), the software itself is no laughing matter. The original software was developed by a hacker who goes by the name "Sir Dystic" in what he has claimed is an effort to get Microsoft to improve the security features of the widely used Windows operating systems. The original version was released by the hacker group the – Cult of the Dead Cow – at the annual DefCon hacker conference in Las Vegas in July 1998 and only operated under Windows 95. The BO2K version operates under Windows 95, 98 and NT 4.0 (sometimes). This most current version was released in July 1999 again at the DefCon conference.

The software is shareware and available for free to anyone, anywhere in the world with an Internet connection. By some estimates, several hundred thousand copies of this tool were downloaded in 1998 alone, and it continues to be very popular among hobbyists and hackers and others with interest in computer and network security.

The program has a number of features that set the standard for other tools to follow and also several unique features that distinguish it from the many "copy cat" utilities. Some of the features included in the software itself and described in the documentation that are of greatest interest for the application of the product to Netspionage (network-enabled espionage) include the following:

- Session and keystroke logging
- HTTP file system browsing and transfer
- Direct file browsing, transfer and management
- Multimedia support for audio/video capture and audio playback
- NT registry passwords and Win9x screensaver password dumping

A computer user must be running either Windows 95 or 98 to allow the Trojan to automatically infect a target machine. The software will not install itself automatically on an NT system. The software comes in two parts: the client and the server. The server is installed on a target computer system. The client is used from another computer to gain access to the server and control it. The client connects to the server via a network.[1]

Once connectivity is established it is possible to exercise considerable control over the server/target system. For example, the server (target) can be made to send an e-mail message to a designated address with key information about the system included in the message. It is also possible to connect to an Internet Relay Chat (IRC) server to inform all the users of a particular IRC channel that a specific computer is now available for remote operation and control.

What Does This Mean? If someone successfully installs BO or one of the many imitators on a target system, then they have at least as much control as the assigned owner/user. Anything the users could do while sitting at their keyboard can probably be done by the techno-spy sitting at their own computer that may be located in the same building as the target or on the other side of the world. The techno-spy running the client software is able to search through the file listings of the target system, find any that are of interest and copy, modify or delete them as desired or transmit them to another computer for future use. Cached passwords (e.g. passwords stored on the computer to login

---

[1] This information is derived from the BO documentation.

to a remote system or Internet service provider) can likewise be copied and transmitted. The keystroke logging allows the client to capture any passwords entered by the user (for instance, those that have not been cached) and use them later, perhaps to impersonate the authorised user and gain access to an important database system.

The fact that the BO product accommodates "plug-ins" provides more reasons to be aware of this tool. As if the basic functionality was not dangerous enough, there are extensions that allow even unsophisticated users to package BO *into* another program. What this does is allow BO to infect a target when the "doctored" program is executed. The plug-in called "*SilkRope*" also modifies BO, so it cannot be found with a common file scan. These tools are one reason why the various holiday executables can be a source of real danger. Although the "dancing Santas" or "happy Halloween ghosts" executable may be cute, it is a very simple matter to load BO into the file and send them out via e-mail to the desired target. When the target executes them, they enjoy the display, unaware of the infection and subsequent control over their system enjoyed by the operator of the client code.

These are features that are nearly ideal for the purposes of theft of sensitive information from computer and network systems. These tools are optimised for theft of passwords, documents and other materials right from under the noses of the often unsophisticated users, such as senior executives, managers and other less technical staff, which means they are ideal tools for attackers.

Although BO and its variants and imitators are potentially very dangerous; the makers of security and anti-virus software have largely neutralised the threat from unsophisticated use of these tools. Common anti-virus tools often detect them in their normal state and can even "disinfect" systems that have been attacked. However, in the hands of experts, one should not assume that "off the shelf" anti-virus tools alone are sufficient. It is possible for BO to be compiled in a manner that will change its file signature and thus defeat file comparison anti-virus software. The network operations group of the corporation should monitor network traffic for unusual transmissions using the UDP protocol that BO uses to communicate between the client and server.

Regardless of the current effectiveness of specific protective measures, there is a running arms race between the developers of such attack tools as BO and those who develop protective tools. The mere fact that the capability now exists ensures that some Netspionage agents and techno-spies will exploit the vulnerability.

Potentially, any one of the many Trojan software programs could be used by a techno-spy to steal sensitive files or modify or delete data, from any computer running Windows 95 or Windows 98 and many systems running Windows NT. However, there are a few factors limiting their effectiveness at present:

- First, each one of these programs requires some sort of server application to be first installed on the target machine that the techno-spy is seeking to plunder. Achieving this installation requires either physical access to the computer system or some way of convincing the authorised user to install it. Where physical access is not feasible, it is often possible to trick an unsuspecting user into installing the code by inserting it into some pretty executable and then sending it to the target via e-mail. Alternatively, the operator of a targeted system may be invited to a Website/URL to download a copy of the modified executable onto the target system. Once the unsuspecting user double clicks on the downloaded file he/she will unknowingly install a copy of the Trojan onto their system.

- Once a copy is installed, the attackers must then find the IP address of the target machine before the software can be activated and controlled remotely. The attacker can often use their client application to search through a range of possible IP addresses. However, this is a serious challenge if they do not have enough information about the network to limit the range of addresses to be searched because there are 4 billion possible IP addresses.

The installation of a properly configured firewall between the target machine and the attacker will probably make it impossible for the attacker to communicate with the target machine. Since many corporations install firewalls between their internal networks, computers and the Internet, this means that if the firewall operates correctly, there should not be any Trojan remote controlling internal systems via the Internet. More likely the use of a Trojan utility will occur inside the corporation since internal compartmentalisation of networks using internal firewalls is not common.

Although a leading anti-virus vendor advises that corporations can defend themselves from Trojan software problems by "following safe computing practices, for example: not downloading or running applications from unknown sources..."[2] this advice is too simplistic. Users are increasingly expected to do just that, download software from new and unknown sources and therefore remain vulnerable to these tools. And if the operator of the Trojan is a trained attacker who has infiltrated the corporation in the guise of a lowly temporary employee holding a position as a secretary, he or she would not be downloading anything, except possibly the crown jewels of the company via a Trojan utility.

14.3.1.3   Other Trojan Software

The BO is not the only sophisticated tool available. There are many others. An excellent listing of many additional "network Trojan" software programs can be found at http://xforce.iss.net/alerts/. The X-Force service, sponsored by ISS has documented more than 120 of them for the various versions of Windows. This site also provides a full technical description of how the software operates as well as techniques for detecting and removing them from computers.

The following is a short list of some of the most common additional tools and the special features associated with each one. Note that the feature described is not the only function the software performs; most of them have the full complement of basic features similar to BO but also other unique features:

---

[2] http://www.sarc. com/avcenter/venc/data/backorifice.html

- *NetBus pro*: Presents itself as a remote administration and spy tool
- *NetSphere*: Will operate the ICQ[3] real time messaging utility
- *SubSeven*: Uses IRC or ICQ to inform the attacker when a target is infected
  The following are all examples of Trojan horses:
- *Password-catching Trojan horses*: Beginning in autumn 1993, Trojan horses appeared in the network software of numerous Internet computers. In particular, Telnet, a program that permits people to connect from one machine to another, was altered so that all user names and passwords were logged for later illegal use.
- *Emergency system Trojan horse*: A former employee maliciously modified the software of the Community Alert Network installed in New York and San Jose, California. The software did not fail until it was needed in response to a chemical leak at Chevron's refinery in Richmond, California. The emergency system was then down for 10 h.
- *Beware of smart telephones*: A scam was detected involving third-party pay phones that could capture and record credit card numbers for later illegal use. This type of Trojan horse attack is also seen in ATM frauds.

The best example of what can happen when malicious code escapes onto the Internet happened in November 1988. In that month, the Internet Worm was released onto the Internet. This worm was a program that invaded Sun 3 and VAX Computers running versions of the Berkeley 4.3 UNIX Operating Systems and containing the TCP/IP Internet protocols. Robert T. Morris created this program. The worm used the following security vulnerabilities to replicate itself:

- Finder demon stack overflow to gain root access
- Sendmail debug option to gain root access
- Password cracking to gain access to a user and then replicating using its host's table

The net effect of the Internet Worm was that the Internet stopped functioning as people and organisations removed themselves from the Internet to stop the spread of the infection – a self-denial of service.

14.3.2   Viruses

A virus is a program that can pass on malicious code to other non-malicious programs by modifying them. In modifying the other programs, the virus is said to infect them. Some viruses have little to no effect on the machine that they have infected, while other viruses can have devastating consequences, e.g. reformatting the hard drive.

The *I love you* virus was released from a source in the Philippines in the year 2000. Within hours of its release, many information systems and

---

[3] ICQ is an instant messaging computer program and a play on the phrase "I Seek You".

networks were overwhelmed and ceased to function. It is estimated that this virus alone caused damages in the order of millions of US dollars to the global economy.

The only way to prevent infection by a virus is not to share executable code. Techniques for keeping you and your organisation free from viruses include:

- Use only commercial software acquired from reliable and trusted sources. Most large commercial organisations will go to great lengths to ensure that the software supplied to a customer is fit for its purpose and virus free.
- Test all new software in an isolated environment. If you must use software from non-trusted sources, then make sure that it is well tested before released into your network.
- Make and retain back-up copies of the operating system and any applications installed. This way, in the event of an infection you can remove infected files and reinstall them from clean and trusted back-up copies.
- Regularly use virus detection software and make sure that they are supplied from a reputable and trusted source. Also, be sure to protect them from modification and destruction.

14.3.3   Bots and Bot-Nets

A Bot is a program designed to mount a denial of service attack against a target on a network when instructed by a remote user or Bot-Master. A bot-master is the person (or group of people) who would run/maintain a herd of bots. A herd of bots is a collection of bots that can be used to mount a denial of service attack. A typical herd is 10,000+ bots.

Bot-Nets have been used by organised crime to extort money from online business such as online gambling. In 2004, the National High-Tech Crime Unit arrested a number of individuals for attempting to extort money from the online gambling company bluesq.com. These individuals have links with organised crime in Russia.

A typical bot on a bot-net functions by making a specific domain name system (DNS) look-up request. If the bot-master does not want the bot-net to do anything, then this request will return the IP address: 0.0.0.0. When the bot-master wants the bot to perform an action, then it will return a no-zero IP address, and this IP address is an IRC server. The bot then connects to the IRC server and receives commands from the bot-master. The use of an IRC channel is so that a bot-master can remain anonymous while controlling the herd. Modern bot are designed to allow for the uploading of software updates and the downloading of personnel information from the infected computer system. This way the herd master can ensure that these bots are up to date and contain the latest denial of service tools.

Typically a stolen credit card is used to pay for the DNS name registration and IP allocation. Thus, bot-nets are an example in which one type of crime is used to facilitate another. The growth of broad-band and the ability of home-users to have a 24×7 connection to the Internet is one of the factors that has allowed bot-masters to create such large herds.

14.4   Digital Tradecraft

Digital tradecraft combined with the global Internet accesses offer the IA professionals some of their greatest challenges. The following is a real-world look at some of those challenges.[4]

The Internet, specifically the Web, has now made available to the increasing numbers of people with widely varying legal, ethical and personal motivations and constraints the tools and technologies that are nearly ideal for the theft of the increasingly valuable digital assets of the typical corporation. The global reach, now afforded to prospective attackers by the expanding connectivity provided by the Internet, has created a situation of unparalleled opportunity for anyone who is willing to go after a corporation's assets.

The pages that follow describe software programs and utilities that allow even unsophisticated attackers to steal the prime assets of their own or other corporations and then safely transfer those assets to others. The focus in this section differs somewhat from a description of traditional hacker tools and how they have been used. Whereas a hacker may choose to engage in stealing sensitive information, e.g. Netspionage, it is also possible for a Netspionage agent to commit Netspionage without being an accomplished hacker. In fact, successful techno-spies may never need to engage some of the sophisticated technical tools such as port scanners and attack simulators. Such powerful software requires a great deal of technical knowledge and tends to be the hacker's weapons of choice for neutralising traditional information security technologies. Instead we will discuss a new application of software and technical tools that we describe as "digital tradecraft".

14.4.1   Digital Tradecraft Defined

Tradecraft is defined as "the technical skills used in espionage"[5] and typically might include knowledge of lock picking, clandestine photography, secret writing, surveillance and dead drops.[6] As one can deduce from such examples, a great deal of the traditional spy's life revolved around the means of acquiring information and then communicating it to the sponsoring agency for processing and analysis. It is obvious that such means are intended to allow the spy to operate in

---

[4] This section was excerpted from Dr Kovacich's co-authored book, *Netspionage: The Global Threat to Information*, published in September 2000 by and reprinted with permission of Butterworth-Heinemann, Woburn, Massachusetts, USA.
[5] Melton (1996) p. 159
[6] Ibid, p. 161

stealth and with anonymity, largely in hopes that they might continue to survive and perhaps even someday return safely to their homeland.

In many ways the objectives of Netspionage are exactly the same as they have been for traditional espionage. The new tools are intended to allow the "virtual agents" operating against online business corporations to penetrate the internal systems of the target. Once successfully "inside", they may obtain information without detection and then communicate it so that the sponsoring corporation may operate with the advantage of superior information while the attacked corporation remains blissfully unaware of the nature and extent of their losses.

14.4.2   Digital Dead Drop

Imagine you are a techno-spy and you need to set up a secure place where you can "stash" copies of the critical information you have obtained from the penetrated corporation. As you read this, identify techniques that you can use to stop the theft of sensitive information by this method.

As good as you are there is always the chance, no matter how small, that the authorities may raid your computer someday. If they find the copies of the stolen crown jewels on your company computer system, you are going to be in big trouble. One way to avoid such professional embarrassment is to load a "digital dead drop" with the copies of the stolen valuables and get them out of your system as quickly as possible.

There is no need to purchase a server and set up an Internet connection as there are already many services offering 10, 20, 30 or more megabytes of online storage for free. The most generous provides 300 MB of personal "Free Disk Space" on "secure servers".[7] All they require is some personal information about the subscriber, which of course could be completely fabricated, since the service apparently makes no effort to verify anything. The advantages to the techno-spy are obvious. They get a free online storage place that is accessible from anywhere on the Internet at any time of the day or night. Of course if they are especially careful, they will protect the valuable stolen contents by using one or more methods of cryptography, perhaps even steganography (see later) to ensure that even an examination of the files deposited in the dead drop will be fruitless for investigators. Those that use such services should also be aware that the sites might be excellent targets for the Netspionage agents.

Even if the process is detected and investigated by the security group, they face an uphill battle. If the techno-spy uses digital dead drops properly, the "control agent" from their team or customer contact will be unloading the contents soon after the agent loads them. This downloading operation will be done using another expendable account, probably a new web-mail or front company address for every transmission. This will be done from a safe location, probably outside the country. The contents will then be transferred to a safe location

---

[7] http://www.freediskspace.com

inside the sponsor's home corporation, probably outside the target's homeland. Using a number of foreign locations for the transfer and processing of the stolen contents will make recovery more complicated and reduce the ability of the security officials to gain search warrants and execute them on a timely basis against multiple foreign locations and operations.

14.5   Steganography

Hiding information by embedding a file inside another, seemingly innocent, file is a technique known as "steganography". It is most often used with graphics, sound, text, HTML and PDF files. Steganography with digital files works by replacing the unused bytes of data in a computer file with bytes that contain concealed information.

Steganography (which translated from Greek means *covered writing*) has been in use since ancient times. One technique was to carve secret messages into wooden objects and then cover the etched words with coloured wax to make them undetectable to an uninitiated observer. Another method was to tattoo a message onto the shaved messenger's head. Once the hair grew back they were sent on their mission. Upon arrival the head was shaved revealing the message. The microdot, which reduced a page of text to the size of a typewriter's full point so that it could be glued onto a postcard or letter and sent through the mail, is another example.[8]

Usually, two types of files are used when embedding data into an image. The innocent image that holds the hidden information is a "container". A "message" is the information to be hidden. A message may be plain text, cipher text, other images or anything that can be embedded in the least significant bits (LSB) of an image.[9]

Steganographic software has some unique advantages as a tool for Netspionage agents, and also for protecting and defending information:

- First, if an agent uses regular cryptographic software on their computer systems, the files may not be *accessible* to investigators. But they *will* be visible, and it will be obvious that the agent is hiding something. Steganographic software allows the agent to "hide in plain sight" any valuable digital assets they may have obtained until they can transmit or transfer the files to a safe location or to their customer.
- As a second advantage steganography may be used to conceal and transfer an encrypted document containing the acquired information to a digital dead drop. The agent could then provide the handler or customer with the password to unload the dead drop but not divulge the steganographic extraction phrase until payment is received or the agent is safely outside the target corporation.
- This technique can be used to transmit sensitive information and even incorporated into an encryption scheme before transmitting.

---

[8] http://webopedia.internet. com/TERM/s/steganography.html
[9] http://www.jjtc.com/stegdoc/

- It can also be used to hide sensitive information in databases, on desktop systems, etc.
- As a final note, even when a file is known or suspected to contain information protected with steganographic software, it has been almost impossible to extract the information unless the pass phrase has been obtained.

14.6   Summary

Operating systems and applications software must be used and integrated as part of an overall IA program. Therefore, their use must not violate IA protection and defence policies and procedures, e.g. do not use an application that does not provide some sort of audit trail records and access control integration. There are various models of secure systems, one of which is the Bell-La Padula model that formally describes the allowable paths of information flow. Secure methods of operating systems include physical separation, temporal separation, logical separation and cryptographic separation. Databases must have integrity at all times, control access to itself or in conjunction with other software and must be auditable. Malicious codes, such as BO and Netspionage activities using digital tradecraft, offer new and greater challenges to the IA professional now and even more in the future. Software companies, such as Microsoft, have taken up the challenge and are developing and deploying new technologies designed to secure the computer and the network over which it communicates with other computers.

15

Applying Cryptography to IA

Cryptography is one of the key ingredients in a successful information assurance (IA) program. In this chapter, cryptography as it relates to IA in the modern commercial age will be discussed. Besides, a discussion on the role of cryptography in e-commerce, algorithms; public and private key; key management; digital signatures and the world of public/private key infrastructure is also included.

15.1 Principles of Encryption

In 1949, Claude Shannon proposed the following principles describing the characteristics of a good cipher:

- *Principle 1*: The amount of secrecy needed should determine the amount of labor appropriate for encryption and decryption.
- *Principle 2*: The set of keys and the enciphering algorithm should be free from complexity.
- *Principle 3*: The implementation of the process should be as simple as possible.
- *Principle 4*: Errors in ciphering should not propagate and cause corruption of further information in the message.
- *Principle 5*: The size of the enciphered text should be no longer than the text of the original message.
  Cryptography is used to fulfill the following functions:
- *Confidentiality*: The information contained in a message is available only to the people authorised to access it.
- *Authentication*: It should be possible for the receiver of a message to ascertain its origins; an intruder should not be able to masquerade as someone else.
- *Integrity*: It should be possible for the receiver of a message to verify that it has not been modified in transit; an intruder should not be able to substitute a false message for a legitimate one.
- *Non-repudiation*: A sender should not be able to falsely deny later that he/she sent a message.

At its simplest, there are two types of encryption: symmetric and asymmetric. A symmetric algorithm is a cryptographic algorithm that uses the same key to decrypt as it uses to encrypt.

The whole point of cryptography is to keep the plain text secret from eavesdroppers. (see Figure 15.1) Eavesdroppers are assumed to have complete access to the communication between the sender and receiver. There are seven types of attacks that a cryptanalyst can make against a cipher and these are:

- *Cipher text-only attack*: The cryptanalyst has the cipher text of several messages, all of which have been encrypted using the same encryption algorithm.
- *Known-plain text attack*: The cryptanalyst has access not only to the cipher text of several messages, but also the plain text of those messages.
- *Chosen-plain text attack*: The cryptanalyst not only has access to the cipher text and associated plain text for several messages, but he/she also chooses the plain text that gets encrypted. This attack is more powerful than a known plain text attack as the cryptanalyst gets to choose the plain text that is encrypted.
- *Adaptive-chosen-plain text attack*: This is a special case of a chosen plain text attack. Not only can the cryptanalyst choose the plain text that is to be encrypted, but can also modify his/her choice based on the results of previous encryption.
- *Chosen-cipher text attack*: The cryptanalyst can choose different cipher texts to be decrypted and has access to the decrypted plain text. This is the type of attack that is primarily applicable to public–private key algorithms.
- *Chosen-key attack*: This attack means that the cryptanalyst has some knowledge about the relationship between different keys.
- *Rubber-hose cryptanalysis*: The cryptanalyst threatens, blackmails or tortures someone until the key is given. Bribery is sometimes referred to as a purchase-key attack. These are all very powerful attacks and are often the best way to break an algorithm with a minimum amount of time and effort.

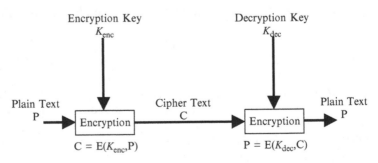

FIGURE 15.1. An Example of an Encryption process

15.2   Symmetric Ciphers

With a symmetric cipher the same key that is used to encrypt a message is used to decrypt it. These ciphers require both the sender and the receiver to have exchanged keys. Symmetric algorithms can be divided into two categories. Some operate on the plain text in a single bit at a time; these are called stream algorithms or stream ciphers. Others operate on the plain text in groups of bits. These groups are called blocks and the algorithms called block algorithms or block ciphers. The most commonly used block cipher is the data encryption standard (DES).

15.3   Asymmetric Ciphers

Public–Private key encryption is an asymmetric cryptographic method. It means that two keys are used: one to encrypt a message and the other to decrypt it. With a public key cipher each user has two keys: a public key and a private key. The user may publish their public key freely. The keys operate as inverses. Let K_{PRIV} be a user's private key, and let K_{PUB} be the corresponding public key. Then,

$$P = D (K_{PRIV}, E (K_{PUB}, P))$$

That is, a user can decode with a private key what someone else has encrypted with the corresponding public key.

$$P = D (K_{PUB}, E (K_{PRIV}, P))$$

That is, a user can decode with a public key what someone else has encrypted with the corresponding private key. This is used for digital signatures.

The simplest example of an asymmetric cryptographic algorithm is a 24-hour clock. The algorithm we use is that we add the key to the input to produce the output. So, if one wishes to encrypt the time 12:56 with a key of 3 hours 17 minutes (3:17), then the output is 16:13. However, one cannot use the same key to decrypt as was used to encrypt as adding 3:17 to 16:13 would give 19:30. So, a separate key is needed to decrypt. In this example, the key used to decrypt is 20:43. In effect, the 24-hour clock is implementing modulo arithmetic.

Within the world of e-commerce, it is the creation of asymmetric cryptographic algorithm that has facilitated the creation of an infrastructure that allows businesses to communicate with each other in a trusted manner, and to be able to depend on the systems to provide a commercially acceptable level of confidentiality and non-repudiation. Examples of products that are used in commerce to provide IA include:

Pretty good privacy (PGP) is a cryptophytic package that implements public–private keys and key management via various certification authorities.

The secure socket layer (SSL) is an add-on to the HTTP standard that makes use of both symmetric and asymmetric cryptographic algorithms to achieve secure communications across an insecure network.

15.4   Digital Signatures and Certificates

Signatures have for a long time been used as a method of authentication and proof of ownership. So the properties of a signature are:

- *The signature is authentic*: The signature convinces the recipient that the signer deliberately signed the document.
- *The signature is un-forgeable*: The signature is proof that the signer and no one else signed the document.
- *The signature is not reusable*: The signature is an integral part of the document and cannot be moved to another document without damaging the original document.
- *The signature is unalterable*: After the document has been signed, the signature cannot be altered.
- *The signature cannot be repudiated*: The signers of the document cannot deny at a later stage that they signed the document.

In reality, none of the above statements about a signature is completely true. A digital signature is a way of marking a document so that the above five principles hold. A digital signature should produce the same effect as a real signature: it is a mark that only the sender can make, which other people can easily recognise as belonging to the sender. Just like real signatures, a digital signature is used to confirm agreement to a message. Within open standards, such as IPSEC and Kerberos, digital signatures and a public/private key infrastructure (PKI) are used to implement and authenticate integrity and confidentiality on a network. Digital signatures must meet two primary conditions:

- *Unforgetable*: If person P signs a message M with a signature $S(P, M)$ it is impossible for anyone else to produce the pair $[M, S(P, M)]$.
- *Authentic*: If person R receives the pair $[M, S(P, M)]$ purportedly from P, R can check that the signature is really from P. Only P could have created this signature, and the signature is firmly attached to M.
  Two additional requirements are also desirable:
- *Not alterable*: After being transmitted, M cannot be changed by R or an interceptor.
- *Not reusable*: R will instantly detect a previous message presented.

While it is impossible to achieve perfection with regard to the five principles, digital signatures when combined with public–private key cryptography certainly make a very good start. In particular, a digital signature provides proof of ownership and an element of privacy:

For a given document M, Alice signs the message with her private key S_A.
$S_A[M]$
Alice encrypts the signed message with Bob's public key E_B and sends it to Bob.
$E_B[S_A[M]]$
Bob decrypts the message with his private key D_B.

$D_B[E_B[S_A[M]]] = S_A[M]$
Bob verifies with Alice's public key V_A, and recovers the message M.
$V_A[S_A[M]] = M$

The above example works as the whole document is encrypted with a private key and the act of encryption functions as the act of signing a document. There are many digital signature algorithms (DSAs) that have been developed, and they all make use of large prime numbers and modular arithmetic on the plain text to be signed.

- The DSA has been proposed by the US National Institute for Standards and Technology (NIST) for use in their digital signature standard (DSS). The standard was proposed in August 1991. The DSA was developed by the US National Security Agency (NSA).

The RSA is a general public-key/private-key encryption system.

Schnorr and ElGamal Algorithm is a specific DSA.

- *GOST DSA* is the Russian digital signature standard and officially called GOST R 43.10-94.

ENSIGN is a digital signature scheme from the NTT, Japan.

A public–private key certificate is someone's public key signed by a trustworthy person. Within the world of e-commerce, certificates are used to thwart attempts to substitute one key for another. Certificates will become the vehicle for e-commerce as laws are slowly introduced that give the same legal standing to digital signatures that is currently given to paper-based signatures. In some digital payment systems, such as SET, certificates and certification, authorities are already being used.

There are a number of advantages and disadvantages associated with the use of certificates and the protocols by which they are generated and used:

- What operational restrictions are there? For example, does the protocol for the use of certificates require a continuously available facility such as a key distribution centre?
- What trust requirements are there? Who and what entities must be trusted to act properly?
- What is the protection against failure? For example:

  - Can an outsider impersonate any of the entities in the protocol and subvert security?
  - Can any party of the key distribution cheat without detection?

- How efficient is the algorithm? An algorithm requiring several steps to establish an encryption key that will be used many times is one thing; it is quite another to go through several time-consuming steps for a one-time use.
- How easy is the algorithm to implement?

The person that is trusted and used to authenticate the key is called a certification authority (CA). The CAs can award certificates, and they can themselves have certificates. When using CAs, the central question becomes "what structure do the certification authorities have with each other?" Figure 15.2 depicts a tree structure for the CAs for a group of universities. The root of the tree functions to accredit all CAs under it. Each university accredits its own CAs. For example, the CA for the University of Glamorgan has three authorities underneath it called COMP, HASS and ISD, respectively. Each of them would function as a CA for a university department; so the COMP CA would function as the CA for the school of computing. A digital signature would be certified by the COMP CA, which in turn is certified by the Glamorgan CA.

There are four basic structures that CAs can adopt. They are:

- *A single root*: The single root model has a single agency functioning to acredit other CA. This root authority would have the power to revoke any other certificate or CA in the system. The problem with the single root model is that it introduces a single point of failure into the system and gives a single authority power over all other CAs.
- *Multiple roots*: In the multiple roots model, there are many root CAs. This model has the advantage over the single root model in that no one single root has absolute control over all of the other CAs. For example, with the multiple root model, you could have a single certification tree for all universities in the UK, and a single certification tree for all the banks in the UK. These two certification trees would then co-operate with each other and the root CA of each tree would trust the other root CA.
- *Peers*: In this model, each organisation has its own CA and each organisation defines the set of CA that their CA will trust and accept certificates from. Consequently, the effect of the peer models of CA is to create domains and for certificates to flow across domains via trusted relationships from one CA to another. The problem with this model is that one incorrect trusting relationship can allow an intruder to introduce a false signature into the system

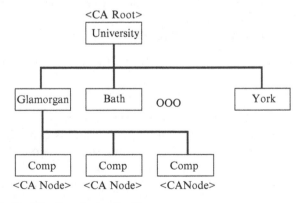

FIGURE 15.2. A Certification Authority Tree

and to get that signature certified by a valid authority. Having had a signature certified, an intruder can engage in fraudulent or other unauthorised acts.

- **Bridge**: This is where each organisation has many CAs. The CAs are used to bridge relationships between organisations. Thus, if an organisation has a commercial relationship with five other organisations, then it would require five CAs. The main problem with this model is its complexity.

15.5   Key Management and Key Distribution

The fundamental security requirement of every key management system is the control of keying material through the entire lifetime of the keys in order to prevent unauthorised disclosure, modification, substitution, replay and improper use. Technologies, such as Kerberos, make extensive use of key management and key distribution in order to achieve security.

- **Data confidentiality**: Secret keys and possibly other data are to be kept confidential while being transmitted or stored
- **Modification Detection**: Is to counter the active threat of unauthorised modification of data items.
- **Replay Detection/Timeliness**: Is to counter unauthorised duplication of data items. Timeliness is required that the response to a challenged message is prompt and does not allow for playback of some authentic response message by an impersonator.
- **Entity authentication**: Is to corroborate that an entity is the one claimed
- **Data origin authentication (proof/non-repudiation of origin)**: Is to corroborate that the source of a message is the one claimed.
- **Proof/non-repudiation of reception**: Is to show the sender that the message has been correctly received by its legitimate receiver
- **Notarisation**: Is the registration of messages to attest at a later stage their content origin.

Every management system must support and provide a set of management services, and these include:

- **Entity registration**: Any secure system ultimately requires a procedure by which an individual or device is authenticated to the system. A key management system has to provide some link between an entity and its uniquely defined keys. In any system, an entity is represented by some public data (called its public credentials), such as a user ID or an address, and some private credentials such as testimonials or passwords. When an entity is registered, a certificate based on its credentials is issued as a proof of registration.
- **Key generation**: This refers to the procedure by which keys or pairs of keys of good cryptographic quality are securely and unpredictably generated. This requires the use of a good method for generating random numbers.

- *Certification* (*online/offline*): Certificates are issued for authentication purposes. A credential containing identifying data together with other information (e.g. public keys) is rendered unforgeable by some certifying information (e.g. digital signatures provided by the key certification centre). Certification may be the following:

  - An online service where some CA provides interactive support and is actively involved in the key distribution processes
  - An offline service that issues certificates to each entity only at some initial stage

- *Authentication/verification*: The three main types of authentication are:(1) entity authentication, (2) message content authentication and (3) message origin authentication. The term verification refers to checking the appropriate claims, i.e. the correct identity of an entity. The validity of a certificate may then be verified using some public information (e.g. a public key) and can be carried out without the need for assistance from the certification authority.

- *Key distribution*: Key distribution refers to the procedures by which keys are securely provided to parties legitimately asking for them. The basic elements of a key distribution are:

- *Encipherment*: Enciphering the data item with an appropriate key can ensure the confidentiality of a data item.

- *Modification detection codes*: To detect the modification of a data item, one can add some redundancy that has to be calculated using a collision-free function (e.g. a CRC check).

- *Replay detection codes*: To detect the replay of a message and to check its timeliness, some explicit or implicit challenge and response mechanism has to be used, since the recipient should be able to decide on acceptance.

- *Proof of knowledge of a key*: Authentication can be implemented by showing knowledge of a secret (e.g. a secret key), or by responding to a challenge in a defined manner. This response will typically involve the use of the key to encrypt and decrypt messages.

- *Key maintenance*:

  Storage of keying material: Refers to a key storage facility that provides secure storage of keys for the future use, e.g. confidentiality and integrity for secret keying material or integrity for public keys. For all keying materials, unauthorised modification must be detectable by suitable authentication mechanisms.

  Key archival: Refers to procedures by which keys for notarisation or non-repudiation services can be securely archived. Archived keys may need to be retrieved at a much later date.

  Key replacement: Enables parties to securely update their keying material. A replaced key shall not be reused. A key shall be replaced when its compromise is known or suspected.

  Key recovery: Refers to cryptographic keys, which may be lost due to human error, software bugs or hardware malfunction.

  Key deletion: Refers to procedures by which parties are assured of the secure destruction of keys that are no longer needed.

15.6   Summary

Encryption is one of the best ways to protect information, whether it is being transmitted or stored in a database. It is used to fulfil the functions of confidentiality, authorisation, integrity and non-repudiation. There are at least seven types of attacks that can be made against a cipher. Ciphers are symmetric and asymmetric. Digital signatures and certificates are some of the latest techniques relating to practical applications of cryptography. Key management is one of the most crucial aspects of using cryptography to support IA. Within modern networks, encryption has become a key tool in the implement and achievement of secure communications.

16

IA Technology Security

This chapter addresses technology security, specifically the technical equipment available and in use to protect or attack the information assurance processes including biometrics, electromagnetic pulse weapons, high energy radio frequency guns, closed circuit television and transient electromagnetic pulse emanation standard.

16.1 Biometrics

16.1.1 The Role and Function of Biometrics

One of the most dangerous security threats that organisations face is the physical impersonation of a trusted employee. The security services that counter this threat are identification and authentication. Identification is the service in which an identity is assigned to a specific individual, and authentication is the service designed to verify a user's identity. The verifier can be identified and authenticated by what one knows (e.g. password), by what one owns (e.g. smart card) or by human characteristics (e.g. biometrics).

Specifically, identification is defined as a process whereby a real-world entity is recognised and its "identity" is established. Identity in the abstract world of information systems is a set of information about an entity that differentiates it from another. The set of information may be as small as a single code, specifically designed as an identifier, or may be a mixture of data such as a family name, date of birth and postcode. An organisation's identification process comprises the acquisition of the relevant identifying information. Therefore, there is a variety of means for identifying a person:

- Appearance (how the person looks, e.g. height, gender, weight, etc.)
- Social behaviour (how a person interacts with others, e.g. voice characteristics, style of speech, etc.)
- Name (what a person is called)
- Codes (what a person is called by an organisation)
- Knowledge (what the person knows)
- Possession (what the person owns)

- Biodynamics (what the person does, e.g. the manner in which one's signature is written, statistically analysed voice characteristics, keystroke dynamics, particularly in relation to login ID and password, etc.)
- Natural physiology (e.g. skull measurements, teeth and skeletal injuries, thumbprint, fingerprint sets and handprints, retinal scans, earlobe capillary patterns, hand geometry, DNA patterns, etc.)
- Imposed physical characteristics (what the person wears, e.g. tags, collars, bracelets, etc.)

On the other hand, authentication is defined as a process designed to verify a user's identity. The goal of authentication is to protect a system against unauthorised use. This element enables the authentication to be based on some basic approaches:

- In the first case, the verifier knows information regarding the claimed identity as this can only be known or produced by an assignor of that identity such as passport, password and personal identification number (PIN). This case is defined as proof by knowledge.
- In the second case, the claimant will be authorised by the possession of an object (e.g. magnetic card, smart card, etc.). This case is defined as proof by possession.
- In the third case, the claimant directly measures certain claimant properties using human characteristics (e.g. biometrics). This case is defined as proof by property.

Generally, members of big organisations use ID cards or passwords to identify themselves. This is a security risk because IDs can be stolen or passwords can be forgotten or cracked. Therefore, what is needed is a more secure approach to protect the information systems. This approach is the concept of biometrics.

Biometrics refers to the automatic identification of a person based on his/her physical or behavioural characteristics. Specifically, biometric systems verify a person's identity by analysing his physical features or behaviours (e.g. face, fingerprint, voice, signature, keystroke rhythms, etc.). The systems record data from the user and compare it each time the user is using it. Therefore, in this section we will:

- Define and analyse the basic models of biometrics in the security of information systems
- Compare biometrics with password techniques
- Discuss biometrics according to risks and threats
- Present the law implications when a biometric is hacked

16.1.2   Analysis of Basic Biometric Models

The biometric models can be separated into two main categories:

- The first category is *physiological-based techniques* that include facial analysis, fingerprint, hand geometry, retinal analysis and DNA and measure the physiological characteristics of a person.

- The second category is *behaviour-based techniques* that include signature, key-stroke, voice, smell analysis and measure behavioural characteristics.

Additionally, for biometric systems "templates" are required. By template, we mean the recorded biometric measurement of a user. A template is associated with an identifier (e.g. PIN, password, etc.) in order to be called up when it is requested. The templates can be stored in:

- *Memory of biometric device*: In this case, the templates can be stored in the memory of the biometric device. The memory capacity of the various biometric devices varies. Storing the templates in the memory of the device enhances security since the templates are not transmitted. It is also economic since no additional cost is required for issuing cards to the users. However, this is not the best choice if the application requires many users or the users need to be verified at different locations.
- *Central database*: The templates can be stored in a central database if the number of users required by the application is large or remote verification is needed. The security aspect of storing templates in a central database should be carefully considered.
- *Plastic cards or tokens*: This method of storage enables users to carry their templates in identification devices. This method is most appropriate when the number of enrolled users is too large to be stored in a central database.

16.1.3   Fingerprint Verification

The patterns and geometry of fingerprints are different for each individual, and they do not change when the body grows. The classification of fingerprints is based on certain characteristics (e.g. arch, loop, whorl, etc.). The fingerprint systems available for recognising these characteristics are complex. Some systems are not capable of differentiating a fingerprint from a live user or a copied fingerprint. Finger surgery, injury or condition of hands might affect the performance of the systems. The method has also the problem of public acceptance.

Fingerprint systems can be used in law enforcement and other applications. These two types of systems are different. In law enforcement, applications of fingerprints are compared (usually manually) with a large store of fingerprints, whereas in other applications, the fingerprint is stored once and it only checks that fingerprint. This technology is mostly used in welfare, immigration, law and banking applications.

Such networks have also been developed in USA with children's fingerprints in order to identify a child (whose identity might have been changed) by comparing the fingerprints against a national database of children's fingerprints.

Fingerprint verification is associated with criminality, and in many sections (e.g. medical) fingerprint technology would not be acceptable. In order to avoid the association with crime, fingerprints should be stored in a card rather than a large central database. It should also be emphasised that fingerprints cannot be reproduced in any law enforcement applications. So the fingerprint is preferred as very secure, fast, reliable and easy to use.

People with missing fingers cannot use fingerprint systems. People with injured or swollen fingers might have a problem being verified by these systems. In working environments where workers need to wear gloves (e.g. power plants, medical or chemistry laboratories, etc.), this method of identification will not be appropriate. Age, gender, occupation, race and environmental factors influence the validity of the fingerprint systems.

Fingerprints and palm prints are extremely accurate since they rely on physical attributes, but their use for access security requires special input devices. These devices are not always compatible with standard telecommunications and computing equipment. Thus, these are undesirable for remote access by travelling users. Some finger recognition systems concentrate only on the location and identification of small areas of details whether such areas are identical. Neural approaches allow automation of the fingerprint encoding process that allows higher matching performance. This is particularly useful in searching for a crime image in the files of prints of other convicts. A fingerprint verifier can work with card systems, such as smart cards and optical cards, to perform identity verification.

Some major credit card companies are testing fingerprint readers that are linked to the cash registers. The credit card holder gives the credit card to the store clerk who inserts it in the cash register while the customer inserts a finger into a reader. The cash register monitor displays the credit card information showing a digital photograph of the holder while comparing the fingerprint on the smart credit card with that of the alleged holder, as read by the reader.

One of the primary issues is cost as each machine is estimated to cost approximately $3–$500. So, to implement such a system on a national or global basis is not considered cost-effective by many of the merchants. This is especially true in such nations as USA where the cardholder is not liable for more than $50 of unauthorised purchases – usually they do not pay anything if the purchases in fact appear fraudulent. The cost of this process is picked up by cardholders who do not pay their credit card bills in full each month – note the monthly interest charges by credit card companies. Much of this cost is due to the fraudulent use of credit cards.

16.1.4   Iris Analysis

Ophthalmologists originally proposed that the iris of the eye might be used as a kind of optical fingerprint for personal identification. Their proposal was based on clinical results that every iris is unique and remains unchanged in clinical photographs.

The iris consists of trabecula meshwork of connective tissue, collagen stroma of fibres, ciliary processes, contraction furrows, rings and colourations. All these constitute a distinctive fingerprint that can be seen at a distance from the person. The iris trabecula meshwork ensures that statistical tests of independence in two different eyes always pass. This test becomes a rapid visual recognition method. The properties of the iris that enhance its suitability for use in automatic identification include:

- Protected from the external environment
- Impossibility of surgically modifying without the risk of loss of vision
- Physiological response to light, which provides a natural test
- Ease of registering its image at some distance from the subject without a physical contact

The retinal blood vessels highly characterise an individual, so accuracy is one of the advantages of this method of identification. Duplicate artificial eyes are useless since they do not respond to light. However, medical research has shown that retinal patterns are not as stable as it was once thought. They show critical variations when there is an organ dysfunction or disease.

16.1.5   Facial Analysis

The premise of this approach is that face characteristics (e.g. size of nose, shape of eyes, chin, eyebrows, mouth, etc.) are unique and makeup a portion of a person's physical identity. This highly developed method is expensive since it uses neural network methodologies. These use cameras to extract unique facial feature data that is stored on a chip card or a magnetic stripe card. The person swipes his card to a small camera to take an image. The software application on site compares the data with the person's stored data.

In the existing facial recognition systems, certain restrictions are imposed by the user such as he/she should be looking straight in the camera with a certain light in order for the system to analyse and identify the person. However, various new graph-matching techniques will enhance the quality of picture decreasing the constraints.

The system will not be able to analyse people with imposed physical characteristics such as beard, hairstyle or with certain facial expressions. Users find it very natural to be identified by their face since this is the most traditional way of identification. It is highly acceptable.

16.1.6   Hand Geometry

The biometric method is based on the distinct characteristics of the hands. These include external contour, internal lines, geometry of hand, length and size of fingers, palm and fingerprints, blood vessel pattern in the back of the hand, etc. They work by comparing the image of the hand with the previously enrolled sample. The user enters his identification number on a keypad and places his/her hand on a platter. A camera captures the image of the hand, and then the software analyses it.

Hand geometry systems are reasonably fast. They require little data storage space and the smallest template. They have short verification time. A technical problem that needs enhancement is caused by the rotation of the hand where it is placed on the plate.

The performance of these systems might be influenced if people wear big rings, have swollen fingers or no fingers. Dirt may also obscure the details of the hand. The reconstruction of the bone structure of an authorized user's hand may be a reason for circumvention. In those systems that are based on three-dimensional hand geometry in which the three dimensions, i.e. length, width and thickness, are measured, although they are more secure, there is still a chance of defeat. Additionally, bone structure models of the authorised users may deceive the hand systems. Paralysed people or people with Parkinson's disease will not be able to use this biometric method.

16.1.7   Speech Analysis

An individual can be identified by various characteristics of the sounds, pho-netics and vocals that they produce. Vocal characteristics, such as mouth, nasal cavities and vocal tract, make the production of speech different for each individual. Although humans can use these characteristics naturally for identifying someone, it is hard for a computer system to analyse the voice characteristics.

A person speaks over the telephone or into a microphone-attached system, then the system analyses the voice characteristics of that sample. Usually, these methods are applied to extract a set of biometric features associated with the voice. These are coded into a data set or a template. Finally, the system com-pares it to the voice characteristics of a pre-recorded sample.

Speech verification is not as accurate as biometric verification based on phys-ical characteristics such as fingerprint, palm print or retina scans. It is a suitable technology for environments where "hands free" is a requirement. System devel-opers combine speaker verification with other forms of security.

Computers find it hard to filter out background noise. Duplication of voice using a tape recorder is a major threat to these systems. Another danger is in anti-theft biometric systems. In these systems, physical damage (or removal) can occur to the devices if they are located. Additionally, women have more complex voice frequencies that make them harder to be identified. People with sore throats who are unable to speak will not be able to use such systems. People affected by alcohol, dental anaesthesia or oral obstruction might face a diffi-culty in being verified by speech verification systems.

16.1.8   Hand-Written Signature Verification

This biometric method is based on the fact that signing is a reflex action, not influ-enced by deliberate muscular control, with certain characteristics (rhythms, succes-sive touches of the writing surface, number of contacts, velocity, acceleration, etc.). The systems developed, based on this biometric method, fall into two categories:

• Pen-based systems use special pens to capture the information
• Tablet-based systems use special surfaces to collect the data

In the first category, the pen is the measuring device, which captures the information, whereas in the second class, the tablet contains the measuring device. Some of the above systems use statistics in verifying a signature, and some use event sequential methods. The items used in a statistical analysis include:

- Total time of writing a signature
- Measurements of spacing number of horizontal turning points
- Number of times
- Duration the pen touches the tablet

In the sequential methods, the system divides the signature into independent events and examines each piece separately. A number of signatures (depending on the system) are required for the enrolment process. At the time of verification, the user is asked to sign. The system compares various aspects of his/her signature in a hierarchical manner. If a good match is not found between the signature characteristics (shape, sequence of events, local characteristics, etc.) and the template, then the template is rejected.

16.1.9   Threats and Risks to Biometrics

Threats and risks can be seen as potential violations of security with expected or unexpected harmful results, and they exist because of vulnerabilities in a system. If an unauthorised user invades a system, he/she can destroy information, operating systems and programs. They can disclose information or cause disruptions or interruptions (damage to systems, networks, organisations or institutions).

In biometric technologies in which communication networks might be used for transferring templates, when a LAN can be used in identifying users in an organisation where the storage and transmission of templates from a database is essential or when the biometric devices are installed in insecure organisations, then the system might be abused by abusing its components (e.g. networks, computers, algorithms/protocols, database, organisations, etc.). Thus, threats and risks arising in these areas (telecommunication systems, networks, computers and organisations) become the threats that the biometric technologies face as well. How biometric technologies face these threats and risks is critical in evaluating their effectiveness. The following are some of the threats and risks:

- *Physical*: This includes natural disasters (fire, storm, water damage, etc.) and environmental conditions (dust, moisture, humidity, etc.).
- *Technical*: This is the equipment of a system (or software) that might fail to carry out its functions (failure) or might carry them out in an inappropriate way (malfunction).
- *Human*: This is the main source of communication breaches. It includes unauthorised users, who wish to damage a biometric system, and authorised users, who misuse the system either deliberately or accidentally. The human threats can be further categorised into internal and external. Internal human threats are disgruntled employees, hackers, former employees, system administrators, LAN, database administrators and the like. External human

threats arise from commercial espionage, government-sanctioned espionage, vendors, manufacturers, kids looking for kicks, nosy reporters, etc.

- **Theoretical**: This includes the vulnerability of the algorithms, protocols and mathematical tools used in the methods that are implemented in the systems.
- **Accidental**: This consists of risk and threats, including accident or injury to the user.

16.2   EMP Weapons and HERF Guns

Electromagnetic pulse (EMP) weapons are devices that when detonated create an EMP. The goal of the EMP is to induce an electrical current in the target device capable of destroying that device. This EMP device produces a pulse that radiates in all directions and is indiscriminate in the computers that it destroys. The EMP weapons may only produce a pulse once, as the act of producing the pulse destroys the device. The act of producing the pulse also has the side effect of producing a physical explosion. These physical explosions can have the effect of causing more damage than the EMP itself. Currently, EMP weapons (or e-bombs as they are known to the military) do exist and form an integrated part of a form of warfare called electronic warfare. For example, in the Gulf War e-bombs were used to neutralise Iraqi radar systems.

A high energy radio frequency (HERF) gun is a device that produces a directed radio frequency that is capable of being targeted at an area/object. The objective of the radio frequency is to induce an electrical current in the target device, which is capable of destroying that device. One of the differences between HERF and EMP weapons is that a HERF gun can be used multiple times. It has been alleged that HERF guns have been used to extort millions of dollars from various organisations. Currently there are no documented cases in the public domain of organisations being attacked via HERF weapons. The major problem with HERF guns at the moment is the amount of power that they require in order to operate. While the gun itself may be hand held and operated by a single user, the power pack required is large; however, as with other technologies, miniaturisation may soon make this a mute point.

However, there can be little doubt that as technology develops so the level of threat posed by the EMP and HERF weapons to computer based systems will only increase. The best defence that currently exists against the EMP and HERF weapons is the use of transient electromagnetic pulse emanation standard (TEMPEST).

16.3   TEMPEST

The previous sections have demonstrated that there is much in common between the national security and private sector information assurance (IA) needs and information environment. However, there is one topic that is little understood or even discussed and that is TEMPEST. The word TEMPEST is an acronym for transient electromagnetic pulse emanation standard, transient electromagnetic pulse surveillance technology, or both. Some also consider it a short "name" when referring to the topic of compromising emanations from information processing equipment. Compromising emanations can be defined as those emanations that are emitted by systems that are unintentional and which disclose information being transmitted, received and processed.

Years ago, TEMPEST was a major factor to consider in the use of computers and telecommunications equipment in the classified environment. Several years ago in USA, the National Security Agency decided that there was little risk of systems' emanations compromising National Security in USA. Thus, with a few exceptions, TEMPEST considerations were made less stringent or eliminated from government contracts saving sometimes millions of US dollars in the process. That aside, a little information on TEMPEST may be of value to the IA professionals.

When an adversary wanted to take advantage of TEMPEST vulnerabilities, they were usually a government agency as the equipment to pick up system emanations was somewhat unique and also very expensive. In addition, picking up specific emanations was often made difficult just by the sheer number of emanations from the hundreds or thousands of systems in the facility being targeted. Another reason that it is not often talked about is that no spy agency of any country wants anyone to know that they have the capability to sit out in a van and pick up every piece of information being processed by targeted information systems.

With the cheaper, smaller and more sophisticated equipment available, the use of such equipment and methods to spy on one's competitors is more likely than ever. Besides, because global economic warfare seems to be replacing or supplementing military warfare, nation-states' spy agencies are more and more targeting foreign corporations in order to support their nation's corporations in gaining the competitive advantage in the global marketplace. What is the easier way to do massive collections of information than to take it from information systems of the adversaries without even being within physical reach of their systems? Also, by now, the chances are pretty good that the emanations may even be available from satellites targeting specific government agencies, government contractors and commercial enterprises.

All systems emanate; however, not all at the same distance. So, such things as a physical "zone of control" can be considered as a possible defence. This method is just what the name implies. If one can physically control an area to such an extent that neither a person nor any equipment can be used within that zone without being subject to security review, evaluation and control, then much of the TEMPEST risk can be eliminated or at least mitigated to a great extent. Thus, if one knows how far a system emanates and can control the physical area to at least that length, then one can be pretty well assured that the emanating signals would not be compromised – at least by that "broadcast" method.

It is possible to take more elaborate and expensive measures. These include special shielding walls that would not allow the emanations out of the walled area. There are filters used on telecommunications lines to protect telephone communications. There are also specific distances a networked, unclassified system must be separated from systems processing classified information. Beside these, there is the use of "red-black" engineering specifications for separating telecommunications lines transmitting at least some classified information from those transmitting absolutely no classified information. Then, all classified information leaving a classified area is encrypted using the latest government-supplied encryption equipment.

From a corporate viewpoint, an IA professional would do well to look into these phenomena and when conducting a risk assessment, determine if the threat agents' capabilities are such that TEMPEST should be in some way considered for implementation when processing and transmitting the corporate "crown jewels". If "TEMPESTING" certain portions of your facility or systems is deemed appropriate, one will find that it may be quite expensive; however, there are companies that may assist by making TEMPEST-shielded systems that will meet your needs.

We hope that the information security professional in the corporate world will not be too quick to discount the requirements, policies, procedures and processes now being used in the national security environment. One can learn from them and adapt them to the business world where today there are serious threats from global competitors and their nation-states who have the means to collect sensitive corporate information – and are doing it right now.

16.4   Closed Circuit Television

Closed circuit television (CCTV) is used as a tool for the implementation of physical security. A CCTV system uses a hand-held or stand-mounted video camera to project a magnified image onto a video monitor or a television (TV) screen. There is considerable versatility in the types of CCTV systems available today. Cameras with zoom lenses provide variable magnification and are used in the more expensive CCTVs. In most of these systems, magnification level and focus are set after choosing a comfortable and functional working distance between the camera and the material to be viewed. Lower cost CCTV systems often use cameras that have a fixed focus and cannot vary magnification or camera-to-target distance. Most cameras also need their own light source.

Cameras that are mounted on a fixed stand require the reading material to be placed under the camera and moved across and down the page. Stand-mounted cameras are particularly effective for handwriting because a hand can fit under the camera. To make the process of viewing easier, a table that is movable from the top of the page to the bottom and side-to-side is used with most stand-mounted cameras.

In contrast to stand-mounted cameras, hand-held cameras are portable systems designed for bringing the camera to the material to be viewed. They can magnify almost anything within reach, including labels on packages of food and medicine. Hand-held cameras are often on rollers that make them easier to move across a flat working surface. When used in conjunction with a small (5-inch screen) video monitor or TV, hand-held cameras can be highly portable. Some manufacturers of CCTV systems that use hand-held cameras offer a writing stand as an accessory.

There are many specially designed CCTV systems that incorporate cutting edge technology. There is a portable system that combines the camera and the display screen in a hand-held housing. A vacuum-fluorescent display provides a magnified image as the camera is moved across the reading material. A radical departure in design from conventional CCTV systems is the use of head-mounted displays (HMD). They offer portability and new ways of viewing the display. All monochrome CCTV systems offer the option of viewing black letters on a white background or white letters on a black background. Controls for contrast and brightness are also standard. Video monitors provide a sharper image than do TVs, and many CCTVs that use video monitors also provide other special features such as underlining/overlining text, masking, etc. Some systems offer the option of simultaneous viewing of the computer screen and the CCTV using either a video monitor or a computer monitor. Colour CCTVs are useful for reading materials in which colour is crucial such as maps and colour photographs.

In some areas, CCTV cameras have been linked into Websites to provide pictures of a given area that are updated at regular intervals. A typical example of this is CCTV cameras that are mounted over roads, and an example of a site that provides access to such images in the UK is the Nottingham Travel Wise Website (http://utc.nottscc.gov.uk/roadeye.htm). This site provides comprehensive traffic and travel information for the Nottinghamshire area, catering for car users, public transport users, pedestrians, cyclists and disabled travellers.

Within Europe, Human Rights legislation is brought into force. These laws give individuals the right to privacy within their private lives. Within the UK, the *Human Rights Act 1998* was enacted, and this act under Article 8 gives the following rights:

- Everyone has the right to respect for his/her private and family life, home and correspondence.
- There shall be no interference by a public authority with the exercise of this right except such as is in accordance with the law and is necessary in a democratic society in the interests of national security, public safety or the economic well-being of the country, for the prevention of disorder or crime, for the protection of health or morals or for the protection of the rights and freedoms of others.

Thus, the *Human Rights Act 1998* has implications for how and why organisations use CCTV. For example, it can be argued that a commercial organisation does not have the right to use CCTV to capture pictures of individuals in a public place, such as a road, without the express consent of an individual. The accepted practice currently within the UK is for signs to be placed informing the public that they are being monitored. Then by proceeding it can be argued that the person is giving consent to the monitoring.

16.5   Microsoft and Network Security

Over the past 10 years, the development and application technologies in the area of network security have accelerated. In particular, three technologies stand out: Firewalls, IPSEC and Kerberos. Within the Microsoft 2000 and XP operating systems, there are a number of technologies that are designed to improve security. The first is that Microsoft has introduced a firewall that from XP service pack 2 is turned on by default. This firewall is designed to block access to certain ports over the network. The following is the configuration dialog box that is used on the Windows XP operating system to define the TCP/IP ports that the computer is making available to the outside world (Figure 16.1). In this figure, for example, we can see that TCP port 80 (WWW) is open on the computer system.

The second is that with version NTFS version 5.0, we can encrypt a section of the file-system via strong encryption algorithms. The application of such technology on a section of the file-system can dramatically improve security – but it is also an element of risk. The risk is that if a user forgets the pass-phrases that are used to unlock the file-system (and no recover agent is defined), then he/she will be unable to recover the encrypted data. The encrypted file systems (EFS) make use of both symmetric and asymmetric encryption algorithms to secure that data stored on the file-system.

The third is the use of open standards, such as IPSEC and Kerberos, to secure network traffic and provide secure authentication. The IPSEC is designed to provide security through the encryption of, and/or digital signing of, the data segment inside the IP datagram. Via the application of this technology, for example, we can implement virtual private networks (VPNs). This is achieved via the use of IPSEC to establish a secure tunnel between two routers/nodes on the Internet. This secure tunnel is implemented via the application of asymmetric ciphers for key exchange and digital certificates and symmetric ciphers for the encryption of bulk data. The IPSEC achieved this via the application of

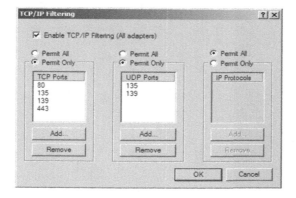

theses ciphers to the creation of: (a) an encapsulating security payload for confidentiality and integrity and (b) the authenticated header for integrity and authenticity.

Kerberos is an open standard that is used to authenticate a user and a computer on a network. First developed for UNIX networks, it is now one of the key technologies used by Microsoft to secure Windows 2000/2003/XP networks. It functions via the exchange of public/private keys to allow for the sharing of tokens. These tokens allow users to prove that they are who they claim to be and to access resources on the Network. Once users have authenticated themselves, then Kerberos will grant them a token that can be used by the user to authenticate themselves while accessing other resources such as network file shares on a corporate network.

16.6   Summary

Biometrics is becoming a more accepted and reliable form of controlling access to physical areas and logical access to information systems and information. Such biometric systems as facial, fingerprints, iris, hand geometry and speech analyses are just some of the methods being used or under development. However, such devices have some risks: Physical, technical, human, theoretical and accidental.

Weapons, such as the EMP-based and HERF guns, are developed to attack information systems, while TEMPEST-based activities are available to steal sensitive information from adversaries and competitors.

17

Security Standards

Over the past 10 years security standards have come a long way from the original Rainbow Book series that was created by the US Department of Defense and used to define an information security. Today we have security standards that allow us to define information assurance at both the technical and organisational level.

17.1   BS7799 and ISO17799

ISO17799:2005 establishes guidelines and general principles for initiating, implementing, maintaining and improving information security management systems (ISMS) in an organisation and based on the British Standard BS7799. The objectives outlined provide general guidance on the commonly accepted goals of information security management (ISM). BS7799 defines a six-stage process model as shown in figure 17.1.

BS7799 makes some assumptions. It assumes that you have already defined all of your key information assets that exist within an organisation. When performing a risk assessment, it assumes that you have also conducted a threat/vulnerability and impact study on your organisation and its key information assets. The most important part of BS7799 is that it requires senior management buy-in to the whole security standard process. It also does not mandate any security solution, but it does require that some person in the organisation has thought about each of the Best Practice sections. BS7799 also requires that the security policy is placed under constant review and becomes a living document that will evolve over time.

BS7799-2:2002 instructs you how to apply ISO17799 and how to build, operate, maintain and improve an ISMS. The 1999 edition only instructed you to apply ISO17799 and build an ISMS.

ISO17799:2005 contains best practices of control objectives and controls in the following areas of ISM: security policy, organisation of information security, asset management, human resources security, physical and environmental security, communications and operations management, access control, information systems acquisition, development and maintenance, information security incident management, business continuity management and compliance.

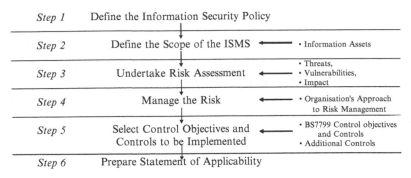

FIGURE 17.1. The BS7799 Process Model

The control objectives and controls in ISO17799:2005 are intended to be implemented to meet the requirements identified by a risk assessment. ISO/IEC 17799:2005 is intended as a common basis and practical guideline for developing organisational security standards and effective security management practices and to help build confidence in inter-organisational activities. The ISO17799 standard consists of recommended information security practices. These recommended practices are found in Sections 3–12 of the standard.

3. Security Policy
    3.1 Establish an information security policy.

4. Organisational Security
    4.1 Establish a security infrastructure.
    4.2 Control third party access to facilities.
    4.3 Control outsourced information processing.

5. Asset Classification and Control
    5.1 Make information asset owners accountable.
    5.2 Use an information classification system.

6. Personnel Security Management
    6.1 Control your personnel recruitment process.
    6.2 Provide information security training.
    6.3 Respond to information security incidents.

7. Physical and Environmental Security
    7.1 Use secure areas to protect facilities.
    7.2 Protect equipment from hazards.
    7.3 Control access to information and property.

8. Communications and Operations Management
    8.1 Establish operational procedures.
    8.2 Develop plans to provide future capacity.

8.3 Protect against malicious software.
8.4 Establish housekeeping procedures.
8.5 Safeguard your computer networks.
8.6 Protect and control computer media.
8.7 Control inter-organisational exchanges.

9. Information Access Management Control
9.1 Control access to information.
9.2 Manage the allocation of access rights.
9.3 Encourage responsible access practices.
9.4 Control access to computer networks.
9.5 Restrict access at operating system level.
9.6 Manage access to application systems.
9.7 Monitor system access and use.
9.8 Protect mobile and teleworking assets.

10. Systems Development and Maintenance
10.1 Identify system security requirements.
10.2 Build security into your application systems.
10.3 Use cryptography to protect information.
10.4 Protect your organisation's system files.
10.5 Control development and support.

11. Business Continuity Management
11.1 Design a continuity management process.

12. Compliance Management
12.1 Comply with legal requirements.
12.2 Perform security compliance reviews.
12.3 Carry out operational system audits.

17.2 ISO13335

The aim of ISO13335 is to describe and recommend techniques for the successful management of information technology (IT) security. These techniques can be used to assess security requirements and risks and help to establish and maintain the appropriate security safeguards, i.e. the correct IT security level. The results achieved in this way may need to be enhanced by additional safeguards dictated by the actual organisation and environment. ISO13335 provides guidelines for the Management of IT Security, and these are:

1. Concepts and Models
2. Management and Planning
3. Techniques for IT Security Management
4. Selection of Safeguards
5. External Connections

17.3   Common Criteria

The Common Criteria (CC) defines standards to be used as the basis for evaluation of security properties of IT Products and Systems. The aim of the CC is to allow for people to have confidence in the evaluation of a product and what that level of evaluation means. So for example when we perform a security assessment and arrive at the conclusion that we require an EAL4 firewall, what we are really saying is that we require a firewall that has been methodologically designed, tested and reviewed.

The CC permits comparability between the results of independent security evaluations. The CC does so by providing a common set of requirements for the security functionality of (collections of) IT products and for assurance measures applied to these IT products during a security evaluation. The evaluation process establishes a level of confidence that the security functionality of these products and the assurance measures applied to these IT products meet these requirements.

Evaluation should lead to objective and repeatable results that can be cited as evidence, even if there is no totally objective scale for representing the results of a security evaluation. The existence of a set of evaluation criteria is a necessary pre-condition for evaluation to lead to a meaningful result and provides a technical basis for mutual recognition of evaluation results between evaluation authorities. As the application of criteria contains both objective and subjective elements, precise and universal ratings for IT security are infeasible.

The evaluation results may help consumers to determine whether these IT products fulfil their security needs. The standard addresses protection of information from unauthorised disclosure, modification or loss of use, in particular:

- *User view*: A way to define IT security requirements for some IT products: hardware, software and combinations of hardware and software
- *Developer view*: A way to describe security capabilities of their specific product
- *Evaluator/scheme view*: A tool to measure the confidence we may place in the security of a product

What the CC is a Common *structure* and *language* for expressing product/system IT security requirements and a set of *Catalogs* of standardised IT security requirement components and packages. The CC Version 3 consists of three parts:

1. Introduction and general model
2. Security fundamental components
3. Security assurance components

The CC is used to: (a) *develop* protection profiles (PP) and security targets (ST) – specific IT security requirements for products and systems – *consumers then use them for decisions* and (b) *evaluate* products and systems against known and understood requirements. A typical CC evaluation will only look at a single configuration of the *product*. This is called the Target of Evaluation (TOE). The CC defines two types of requirements: functional and assurance. The role and function of a functional requirements (FR) is to define what the product does, while the role and function of an assurance requirement is to define the build quality of the product and whether it is fit for purpose.

A PP is a template for an ST. An ST always describes a specific TOE, whereas a PP is intended to describe a TOE type (e.g. firewalls). In general, an ST describes requirements for a TOE and is written by the developer of that TOE, while a PP describes the general requirement for a TOE type. Figure 17.2 gives the structure of a PP or an ST.

A PP is therefore typically written by the following:

1. A user community seeking to come to a consensus on the requirements for a given TOE type
2. A group of developers of similar TOEs wishing to establish a minimum baseline for that type of TOE
3. A government or large corporation specifying its requirements as part of its acquisition process

The PPs can be evaluated (by applying the APE criteria to them). The goal of such an evaluation is to demonstrate that the PP is complete, consistent and technically sound and suitable for use as a template to build an ST on.

Security functional components, as defined in the CC, are the basis for the security functional requirements (SFRs) expressed in a PP or an ST. These SFRs describe the desired security behaviour of a TOE and are intended to meet the security objectives for the TOE as stated in a PP or an ST.

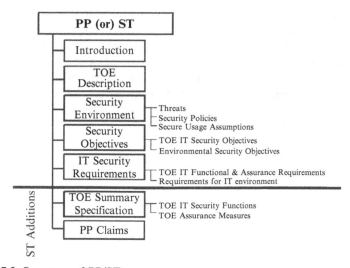

FIGURE 17.2. Structure of PP/ST

While the FRs are composed of the following classes:

FDP: data protection and privacy
FIA: identification, authentication and binding
FAU: audit
FPT: protection of TSF
FMI: miscellaneous

The assurance requirements are composed of the following classes:

APE: PP evaluation
ASE: ST evaluation
ADV: development
AGD: guidance documents
ALC: life cycle support
ATE: tests
AVA: vulnerability assessment
ACO: composition

The evaluated assurance levels specify levels of detail associated with the development of the TOE are given below:

EAL1:   functionally tested
EAL2:   structurally tested
EAL3:   methodologically tested and checked
EAL4:   methodologically designed, tested and reviewed
EAL5:   semi-formally designed and tested
EAL6:   semi-formally verified design and tested
EAL7:   formally verified designed and tested

17.4   Summary

The infromation assurance professionals' world standards have a vital role to play. They allow the security professional to speak with a common language. They also facilitate in the specification and development of security solutions to problems by providing a common set of components and processes that allow for reproducibility and function to increase confidence. BS7799 and ISO17799 approach security from an organisational perspective, while the CC approach security from a technical perspective. Together they attempt to provide an integrated solution to the security problem.

Section 4

The Future and Final Comments

This section summarises the main points of the book in Chapter 18, draws some conclusions and looks into the future and its impact on information assurance as we enter the 21st century.

18

The Future, Conclusions and Comments

This is the concluding chapter of this book and as such, it is only fitting that we provide a combination summary, some history and a look at the future and its impact on information assurance. This chapter provides that perspective as well as some concluding comments.

18.1   Information Assurance: Getting There

This book was originally written over 4 years ago. Since that time, much has changed in the world, but very little in the information assurance (IA) arena. Sad but true. In the First Edition we said:

So, now we come to the end of this book on IA. In doing so, we reflect back on writing this book and want to draw the readers to also reflect back on what they read and form their own conclusions on the entire topic of information protection, assurance and defences.

The IA is a step in the process of how we manage the protection of information and information systems. When we look back from where we came, we see that we began by first protecting, not so much information, as stand-alone computers and their associated programs. This was accomplished through some personnel security, e.g. background checks on personnel using the computers and physical security.

We gradually moved to the field of computer security and expanded some of its functions, such as logical access controls and audit trail recording. Yet, the protection of information was not a major factor in computer security since we always had hardcopy backup. If the computers went down, as they often did, people reverted back to the old paper forms and typewriters.

Then we began to rely more on computers and the information that they stored, processed and sometimes transmitted. Networks developed, and we began to think of these computers as more than some physical, electrical calculating machines. These were information systems and the information that they processed, stored and almost always transmitted somewhere – the "*crown jewels*" of modern, information-based and information-dependent corporations. The professions of computer security, information systems security and now IA, were (and are) being developed as systems develop. Hardcopy forms are hard to find and by the way, no more carbon paper although we continue to use "cc" on e-mails and the like to indicate "carbon copy".

The IA is the next step in the ongoing process and encompasses much more than computer security. However, this is not the end, but a step in the process and development of both the protection and defence processes of information and systems. As systems become more sophisticated, so do the attacks on them and our tools and techniques for protecting and defending these vital assets. We have so much to go further and so much to learn. However, even corporate executive management, who once did not recognise the need for information protection, is now allocating resources we only dreamed of as little as 10 years ago. So, although we have a very long way to go to get one-step ahead of the attackers, we are slowly making progress.

So, although the abovementioned was written over 4 years ago, we are still stuck in the rut when it comes to major IA improvements. Well, it seems that not much has changed since then but possibly the increased terrorists' activities around the world and, of course, some additional progress due to high technology – that is the microprocessor-based technology.

18.1.1   The New Threat of Terrorism

The "war on terrorism" has been heated up, while the "war" to protect our valuable information assets has not. One just has to look at USA and its desire to protect its critical information infrastructure (II). The US information assurance, as part of that effort, has waned as the politics of the time have moved this effort into the Homeland Security Department. Not only that, but the agency responsible for that protection has apparently been moved down on the bureaucratic ladder, with three of its leaders in succession leaving the organisation.

Yes, the war on terror is important. So is the war against these terrorists, hackers and other miscreants who want to modify, illegally use or destroy our systems and the information that they display, store, process and transmit. So, it is the old "two-steps forward, one-step backward routine"; however, in this case it seems "one-step forward and two-steps backward".

It is a fact that terrorists use the Internet to communicate. It is a fact that terrorists use identity theft as a means of obtaining funds as other sources of finance are drying up. It is a fact that information gleaned form the Internet and other networks assist them in collecting information for future attacks.

The terrorist hit the US World Trade Center building because bin Laden and company wanted to hurt the US economy and they succeeded. Right now, these terrorists have an idea that hurting the US economy will help their cause. However, for whatever reason, they have not as yet gone after the US critical II. One wonders why not? Keep in mind that the II is owned and operated by corporations and not the US government. Therefore, those corporations that are part of that infrastructure must now more than ever apply aggressive and proactive defensive IA measures. Will they? Probably not. Sad, but true!

One must also keep in mind that each information-dependent nation-state is pretty much in the same category. We have seen that by the terrorists' strikes against other nations. So, far they have been content to blow-up buildings, cars, people and themselves. Some of us believe though that it is just a matter of time before they will decide to hit our economic centres with not only physical bombs but logic bombs and other malicious devices.

On a somewhat encouraging note, it seems that the terrorist,[1] Abu Musab al-Zarqawi, was almost captured in Iraq in early 2005; however, he escaped and left behind his computer full of valuable information. "...They also took a computer from the truck containing what the officials said was "a treasure trove of information". The officials said the find was significant..." At first, it was thought that it contained mis-information but the information turned out to be factual leading to some arrests and other vital intelligence information. So, luckily the terrorists are just as bad as many corporate and government officials in protecting valuable information and notebooks computers. In this case, luckily the terrorists are not familiar with the IA techniques!

18.2   Welcome to the World of Constant Change

Professional IA specialists must find time to get out of the reactive mode and into a proactive one. The trends that impact the protection of information and information systems must be studied and plans, techniques, processes, tools and the like must be developed now. If not, they will not be ready 5 years from now when adverse changes occur that will affect the protection and defence of information and information systems.

The trends that impact IA are based on many, and often subtle, changes. They can be categorised in many ways that include the following.

- *Societies*, those of nation-states and the global society
- *Economic*, global competition
- Threat agents and their techniques; and of course
- Technology

18.2.1   Changes in Societies

We are now in the 21st century. We entered the new century with new hope and, of course, were again disappointed as the world seems to have got more violent, chaotic and just plain nutty!

We continue to be faced with many challenges brought on not only by technology, but also other changes – human changes. As we said 4 years ago, and it is still true: nations will be torn apart with ever-increasing chaos and rapid disintegration into factions. These factions will use the Internet to communicate their grievances,

---

[1] http://www.cnn.com/2005/WORLD/meast/04/26/iraq.zarqawi/index.html

desires and try to build a "world consensus" in their favour to force governments to allow more freedom to these factions, as well as dissolving portions of these nations into smaller nations. The nations will use the Internet to justify their controls, government policies, etc. The break-up of the Soviet Union and the old Yugoslavia are just two examples of what other nations may have to look forward to in the 21st century. Such break-ups have made some nations, such as China, left in a quandary. How can they compete in the global economic market with technology and the information it brings; and yet, control the information that their citizens can access? Make no mistake about it; more than ever before, information is power. Power in the hands of the citizens, and knowledge of the real world they live in, is not what a communist or dictator wants to happen. They must maintain control of information or perish. Is it any wonder that many nations are doing what they can to control access to information through Internet, radio, faxes, cellular phones and the like in the societies who lack even the basic freedoms?

The people of all the nations who have Internet, global radio and satellite communications connections will become more sophisticated in the use of the these information devices. They will have ever-increasing, massive amounts of information at their disposal; thus, allowing them to become more knowledgeable on global matters. They also will become more aware of those throughout the world who have similar and different views.

With the Internet as the base for a massive, personal communications pipeline, technology will provide the means for people to communicate globally as never before. Such massive one-on-one communications will be the driving force that will affect governments, businesses and societies to such an extent that the governments and businesses will develop extremely sophisticated techniques to influence these Internet communicators on a global scale.

- For the IA professionals, one may have to decide on what side of the "*freedom of information*" line they will stand. Will they help assure that information is accurate and available to members of society and the world? Will they instead be involved in supporting nation-states in controlling information – not from competitors or other nation-states, but their fellow citizens? Will they help a nation-state perpetuate propaganda as factual information? There are some interesting choices that some IA professionals will have to make – and maybe are even making as you read this book.

The Internet and other global networks will also become some of the primary education vehicles replacing many of today's Industrial Age school systems. Already, colleges and universities are offering courses and degrees through the Internet accesses. This will allow individuals to obtain degrees from universities and colleges located in different nations of the world. Thus, external forces will influence the societies of nation-states as never before.

Our "Global Society" continues to evolve while individual societies and groups continue their quest for power and "ethnic cleansing" – which always seems to be too nice a phrase for the slaughter of innocent men, women and children. We should not use such "nice words" to describe these slaughters. It is societies' way of putting a less emotional face on it. Corporations do the same as they do not fire people and "throw them out in the streets" but instead "downsize". Today's societies do not want to face the harshness of the world we create but put a neutral face on it.

As IA and general security professionals, we tend to always look at the glass as half-empty. On the half-full side, we see more societies in the world embracing personal and economic freedoms and communicating on a global basis. Hopefully, that will lead to better understanding of each other over time. Better understanding hopefully will lead to fewer conflicts, which in turn mean IA threat agents will play a lesser role from a society and nation-state viewpoint.

18.2.2   Economic, Global Competition

We are still in the beginning stages of global economic warfare, not only among corporations but among nation-states. The Cold War is over and there is no great global military power in the world. Yes, some nations, such as Russia and USA, can still pretty much destroy civilisation, as we know it. However, each is also controlled by world influence on when and how they can use that power. The United States cannot act alone as its military has been "downsized" as has been the case with other nations. A good example of that is the US actions in the Middle East. The recent need to obtain allied support in Afghanistan, Iran, Iraq and Serbia are some examples. So, the power once got out of the barrel of a gun is now second to the power of world economics – world trade.

The influence one nation has over another is now often measured in terms of imports and exports – balance of trade concepts. Trade wars can devastate the global and regional power of a nation today just as surely as any nuclear bombs, excluding physical damage of course.

Nation-states derive their economic power from their government businesses, e.g. Chinese People's Liberation Army's (PLA) global businesses, as well as private corporate businesses. The PLA has been directed to divest themselves of these businesses, but they will undoubtedly continue their present course but maybe in a less visible way. Large, international corporations now have more money, influence and power within some nations than the government of that nation.

Many of the changes in the world environment are the basis for the rapid changes in how we do business, both nationally and internationally. Businesses can, and do, adapt to these changes quite rapidly. However, in government agencies, these changes come more slowly, and sometimes threaten the very existence of some government agencies.

If we look at current trends in technology, Internet crime, attackers and security, we can project with some degree of certainty what the Internet electronic business environment will be like as we enter the 21st century. The following is a look into that future.

- Internet will continue to rapidly expand.
- The number of attacks on Internet that impact electronic business will increase.

- The attackers will increasingly be the techno-criminals (not hackers without malicious intent), a nation's adversary and terrorists who see electronic business as a means to damage a country and bring down its government.
- Economic and industrial espionage on the Internet (Netspionage) will increase.
- Security products will continue to improve and thwart the less sophisticated attackers.
- Attacks will be more sophisticated, harder to detect and more difficult to identify the criminals, and once identified, prosecution of theses international criminals will continue to be inhibited by the lack of treaties and agreements between nations relative to international co-operation and subsequent prosecution.
- Businesses and government agencies will continue to be slow to react and continue to treat security as a lower priority.
- Attackers will continue to network internationally and share attacking techniques and systems' vulnerabilities.
- As electronic contracts are relied on for business deals, there will be more challenges to the legality of the contracts: agreed to as written by all parties involved, proving provisions changed or not changed after "signing", proving contracts are "originals" and "electronic signatures" will be tested in court.

It would seem that what we said more than 4 years ago are as true today as they were then. However, these trends were easy to predict based on the past trends and human nature. We see no reason to change our view for the next 4+ years – with one exception. It seems the electronic contracts have not greatly increased and will probably continue to be slowed by corporations' fear of their legality and judicial systems, which have a difficult time accepting such documents as original, legal documents, while the supporting software does not provide 100% assurances against unauthorised contract changes.

18.2.3   Technology

The saying, *"the world wants to talk to the world"* is closer to reality than ever before. These global communications phenomenon with all its hopes, promises and problems is based primarily on the Internet and its associated and connected nation-states and businesses' networks. However, it is not all Internet connected as yet. This massive global communications networks include cellular phones, private branch exchanges, fax machines and various other communications tools. These non-Internet networks are quickly being integrated and becoming part of one massive, global communications system. This massive system is developing into the global II (GII) that is made up of the II of nation-states. It is very important for the IA professionals to understand this new and growing, global information age environment because it is the environment in which the IA professional will work.

The current trend in technological advancements will continue and probably increase in speed. The power of the computer will continue to increase as its price as well as its size decline. It is expected that communication devices, such as televisions, computers, cellular phones and even watches, will combine to provide miniaturised, wireless, global communication tools for information-dependent users. Advancements in robotics will allow for them to accomplish more human tasks, as well as tasks that are beyond our comprehension today. The use of nano-bots may be used not only in the medical field, but also as techno-spies who steal, compromise or corrupt information and information systems. The day may come when it will be impossible to protect sensitive information except by going full-circle. That is, store, process but not transmit the most sensitive information on a stand-alone information system in a secure room with alarms, robotic guards and closed circuit television monitors.

The development of more sophisticated systems that are able to understand and react to normal human speech will become commonplace. This technology will be a major breakthrough that will allow previously computer illiterate individuals to use the power of the computers, networks and the Internet to work, play and communicate. This will allow poor people and minorities who could neither afford a computer, nor learn how to use one, to become better educated and valuable members of societies with less effort.

The future will also bring us biological computers. For example, it is rumoured that some are even looking at using electrically charged amoebas or other methods that can allow a direct interface with the human brain! Such incredibly advanced computers could perhaps store the entire history of the human race on a single chip. Who will determine what is contained in that history? What are the social ramifications of such dramatic extensions to personal information access? What happens if a criminal or a terrorist embeds a virus, logic bomb or other malicious software in a computer extension attached to your brain? The IA professionals may require a degree in some field of medicine in order to successfully perform their duties vis-à-vis tele-medicine IA.

The *"wireless age"* is already upon us and with it the increased use of technology allowing mobile electronic communications from any place on earth to anywhere. As the growth of networks continues worldwide, it will bring with it more threats from sophisticated, international criminals. Such threats will include an increased use of jamming techniques as a -of-service (DoS) to commit electronic extortion or adversely impact a competitor's ability to perform e-commerce on the Internet. As more forms of public communication come to rely on the Internet, we expect more sophisticated eavesdropping techniques will rise, which will allow Internet robbers, businesses and government agencies to invade personal privacy to their respective ends. The increasing use of the many Internet telephone and video teleconference systems, which are vulnerable to eavesdropping will make this more common.

Software robots have already bombarded us and soon nano-bots will be used everywhere for a multitude of purposes: from spies to "artery cleaners". Software robots or "bots" are already, constantly being sent out to roam the Internet. Some belong to corporations while some are personal. However, they can cause accidental DoS attacks, destroy information, violate copyright laws and test the limits of information systems resources. As pointed out in a CNN.com article,[2] "...Early bots crawled the Net for information. Archie looked for software available through the Net's file-transfer protocol. The World Wide Web Wanderer and its successors scoured the Web or site to list search engines.... Bots have already been developed for corporate information-gathering and espionage...bots raise privacy issues...". As the Internet and other global networks are integrated and the use of today's bots and future, more sophisticated bots are developed and let loose on the networks, the IA professionals will have a more difficult time in protecting and defending their information systems and sensitive information.

The high technology is making our lives in many ways better, especially in the world of medicine. So, all is not gloom and doom. However, as IA professionals, we must always look at worst-case scenarios. If they come, we will be prepared. If not, then hey, nice surprise!

Some interesting notes are that progress is made as some take the high-technology leap into the unknown.

- *Interactive TV poised for rollout... Dozen markets will see form of IPTV later this year...NEW YORK (AP) – Internet Protocol, the language of most online communications, was supposed to have revolutionised the way we watch television by now, enabling a wide range of multimedia bells and whistles: from multiple camera angles to on-screen Web searches while viewing Gilligan's Island to see which actors are still living.[3]*
- *2005 'year of mobile broadband'...STOCKHOLM, Sweden (AP) – LM Ericsson said Tuesday that 2005 is set to be the year of mobile broadband, painting a portrait of fast downloads for cell phone users who want information quickly.[4]*
- *In England, there is one scientist who has gone so far as attached a computer to his body to conduct some interface experiments.*
- *... Is the human body a fit place for a microchip? The debate is no longer hypothetical. The same computing power that once required an entire building to harness now can be inserted in your left arm...*
- *Professor Kevin Warwick, director of cybernetics at the University of Reading in the UK, is that somebody else...Warwick became the first human to host a microchip. During a 20-minute medical procedure described as "a routine silicon-chip implant" by Dr George Boulos, who led the operation, doctors inserted into Warwick's arm a glass capsule not much bigger than a pearl. The capsule holds several microprocessors. The British Broadcasting Corporation was on hand to document the historic event – and to trouble the professor's already frayed nerves. "In theory, I was able to see what was going on," Warwick says in a phone interview several days after the operation (which he described as slightly*

---

[2] CNN.com/Sci-tech, 10 February 2001, Software robots roam the net, for better and worse. (http:// www,cnn.com/2001/TECH/02/10/robots.net.ap/index.html)

[3] http:// www.cnn.com/2005/TECH/02/14/interactive.tv.ap/index.html

[4] http:// www.cnn.com/2005/TECH/02/16/3gsm.ericsson.ap/index.html

more pleasant than a trip to the dentist), "but I was looking in the opposite direction most of the time."...[5]

Oh by the way, let's not forget the continued strides in robotics. This is a high-technology area that offers some interesting potential for good and bad. They may be used to drive us around and clean up after us while they may also be turned into soldiers possibly making wars easier; after all, they are robots and not real human soldiers. So what if they get killed? "I Robot" may not be that far off. What can they do to help provide IA? Of course, they can be used as a security guard force replacing humans. However, they may one day take the place of some IA professionals also.

18.2.4   The IA Professional

The IA professional who does not look ahead at the trends in society, technology, business, global competition and any associated rapid changes will have a stagnant IA program that does not meet the needs of the corporation or government agency. After all, an IA program must be a service and support organisation. Therefore, it must be responsive to the needs of its customers.

Remember the saying, "time is money"? Well, in our world of international, global competition and global communication, that saying is truer now than ever before. The IA professional must understand this better than ever before. The IA process cannot be a roadblock to business. Yet, they must provide the protective and defensive framework required by the corporation or government agency.

Another area for the IA professional to consider is that the people in other countries are becoming more educated and they have a better understanding of the world and technology. There are more world travellers. People in the Information Age seem to demand more from their government and society while demanding less of themselves. They expect and demand professionalism at all times. This too will have a major impact on the IA programs. More computer-literate people in the world, with increased global communications, mean more access through worldwide networks and also more potential threat agents, taking advantage of the global communications to attack the IA defences of a corporation or government agency. The protection and defence of information systems and the information that they process, store and/or transmit is of vital concern in this information world.

Many people look at the use of technology as an excellent tool that can be used now and into the new century. It is ushering in a new beginning, the beginning of an age when, with the help of technology, we can make life better for all of us. However, our journey of leaving the old century and starting into the new one will not be without hardships and with some chaos. This too will have an impact on how successful the IA program will be.

---

[5] IDG, January 14, 1999, Web posted at: 3:21 p.m. EST (2021 GMT) on CNN.com article by Sam Witt.

It is important for the IA professional to think about trends and changes and reflect on its meaning for the IA program and its relationship and responsibilities in the global communications environment of the 21st century. As society changes, so must many of the old processes that include how the IA functions are performed.

Have we made great strides as information warfare professionals? Are we making any progress? Let's be optimistic and say that we are at least making progress. In truth, we still tend to think "inside the box and not outside the box". This must change if we are ever to get into a position where IA is, well, assured! After all, where is the fun, the adventure of doing the same things the same way and also by the way, getting the same poor results?

18.3   Summary

The IA professionals' world of the 21st century will continue to rapidly change. IA will play a major role in how nations, societies, business and technology; will change. By looking at current trends, one can see many indications of the changes yet to come; while at the same time, the IA professionals can only be sure of one thing: they and their profession must also rapidly change. However, one should be cautious. It is great to be on the cutting edge, but not on the bleeding edge. Good luck and be sure to carry a few bandages with you, just in case!

Biography

Dr Andrew J. C. Blyth, Ph.D.

Dr Andrew Blyth received his Ph.D. from the Computing Laboratory at the University of Newcastle Upon Tyne, UK in 1995. In 1996, he took up an appointment as a senior lecturer at the School of Computing University of Glamorgan, UK.

He is currently the scheme leader of the M.Sc. Information Security and Computer Crime. Dr Blyth has published several papers in the area of information security and intrusion detection systems. His main research area is: *How do you specify, design, build, deploy, manage and defend trusted information systems within an organisation so as to achieve and maintain a competitive advantage?*

Dr Blyth also works as a consultant in the area of information security and computer crime and functioned as an expert witness for the police. He also performs IT security health checks and penetration tests in his spare time.

Dr Gerald L. Kovacich, CFE, CPP, CISSP

Dr Kovacich graduated from the University of Maryland with a bachelor's degree in history and politics; the University of Northern Colorado with a master's degree in social science; Golden Gate University with a master's degree in telecommunications management; the US Department of Defense (US DoD) Language Institute (Chinese Mandarin); and August Vollmer University with a doctorate degree in criminology. He is also a Certified Fraud Examiner, Certified Protection Professional and a Certified Information Systems Security Professional.

Dr Kovacich has over 40 years of corporate security, investigations, information systems security and information warfare experience in the US government as a special agent; in international corporations as a technologist and manager and as a consultant to USA and foreign government agencies and corporations.

Dr Kovacich has taught both graduate and undergraduate courses in criminal justice, technology crimes investigations and information systems security for Los Angeles City College, DeAnza College, Golden Gate University and August Vollmer University. He has also lectured internationally and presented workshops on these topics for national and international conferences, as well as written numerous, internationally published articles on high-technology crime, information systems security and information warfare.

Dr Kovacich currently resides on Whidbey Island, Washington, where he continues to conduct research, writes and often lectures nationally and internationally on such topics as: global, nation-state and corporate aspects of information systems security, fraud, corporate security, high-technology crime, information assurance, proprietary information protection; as well as netspionage, economic and industrial espionage, and information warfare. He is also the founder of *ShockwaveWriters.Com*, an informal association of writers, researchers and lecturers who concentrate on the above mentioned topics. (See http://www.shockwavewriters.com)

Index